A MODERN METHOD FOR GUITAR

william leavitt

volume 3

Editorial Consultants: Larry Baione and Charles Chapman

Berklee Media
Vice President: Dave Kusek
Dean of Continuing Education: Debbie Cavalier
Director of Business Affairs: Robert Green
Associate Director of Technology: Mike Serio
Marketing Manager, Berkleemusic: Barry Kelly

Berklee Press
Senior Writer/Editor: Jonathan Feist
Production Manager: Shawn Girsberger
Marketing Manager, Berklee Press: Jennifer Rassler

ISBN 978-0-87639-017-7

1140 Boylston Street
Boston, MA 02215-3693 USA
(617) 747-2146

Visit Berklee Press Online at
www.berkleepress.com

DISTRIBUTED BY

HAL•LEONARD®
CORPORATION
7777 W. BLUEMOUND RD. P.O. BOX 13819
MILWAUKEE, WISCONSIN 53213

Visit Hal Leonard Online at
www.halleonard.com

Printed in the United States of America.

Introduction

This book is a continuation of *A Modern Method for Guitar, Volumes I and II.* Most of the terms and techniques are directly evolved from material presented in those books. Fingerings for two-octave scales and arpeggios are developed to the ultimate, in that any other patterns that you may discover will consist of nothing more than combinations of two or more of those presented here. Three-octave patterns will be shown in later volumes, but many can be worked out with the aid of the position-to-position fingerings on pp. 76 and 77.

With regard to chords and harmony, diagrams are totally dispensed of, and everything is worked out from a knowledge of chord spelling and the construction of voicings. There will be further development later in this area of study.

Mastery of the "Right-Hand Rhythms" pages should enable you to perform any rhythmic combinations that may confront you at any time, assuming, of course, that you have the ability to swing. (If this property is lacking, then perhaps you had better throw the pick away!)

Should you be fortunate enough to possess a creative soul, I'm sure that the pages devoted to chord and scale relationships will be a rather large help. In any event this knowledge can certainly keep you out of trouble when you have some on-the-spot filling to do.

As in the preceding volumes, all music is original and has been created especially for the presentation and perfection of the lesson material.

Once again, all the best and good luck.

William G. Leavitt

It is important that you cover the following material in consecutive order. The index on pg. 158 is for reference purposes only and will prove valuable for review or concentration on specific techniques.

Outline

Evolution of Major Scale Fingering Patterns

Type I fingerings evolve through cycle 5 (down a 5th). Using the second position as a sample, we start with C major, fingering Type 1, then proceed to F major (Type 1A), B♭ major (Type 1B), E♭ major (Type 1C), and A♭ major (Type 1D). Observe that each new key requires additional first-finger stretches. Also note the optional fourth-finger stretch shown on the 2nd string of Type 1D. This will occasionally be necessary for certain melodic patterns, such as 3rds.

Type I

TYPE 1

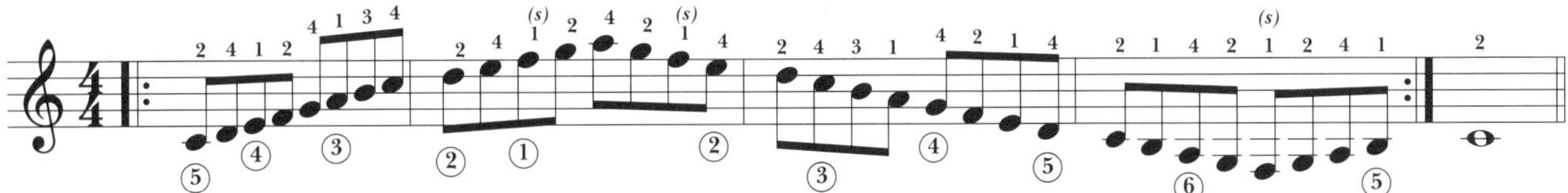

TYPE 1A

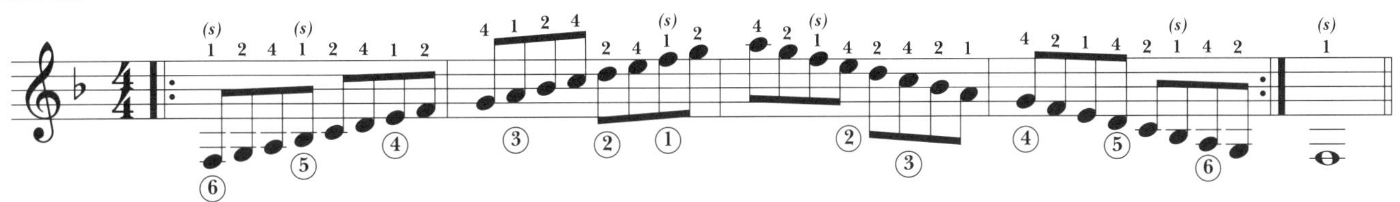

TYPE 1B

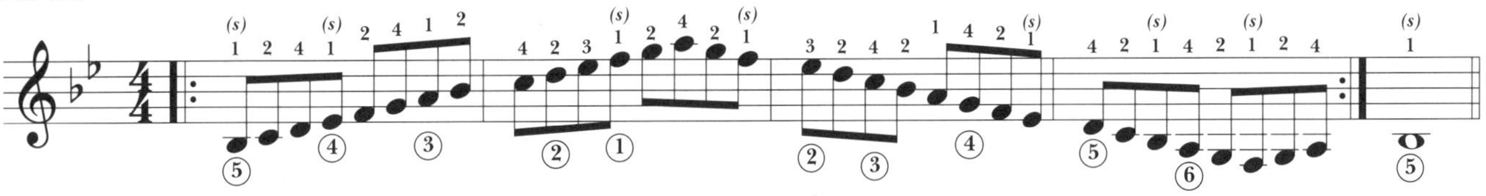

TYPE 1C

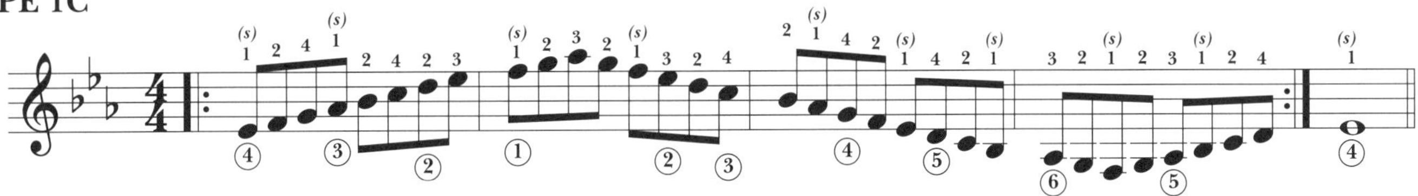

TYPE 1D

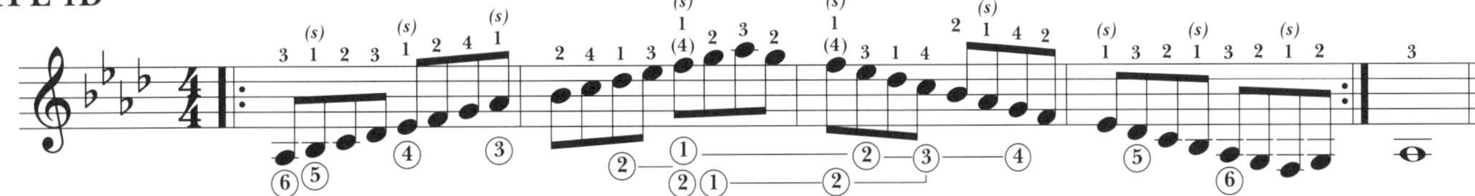

Type II

TYPE 2

- No derivative fingerings

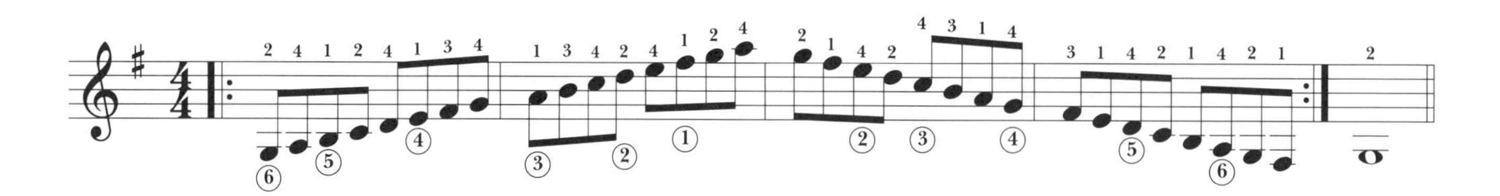

Type III

TYPE 3

- No derivative fingerings

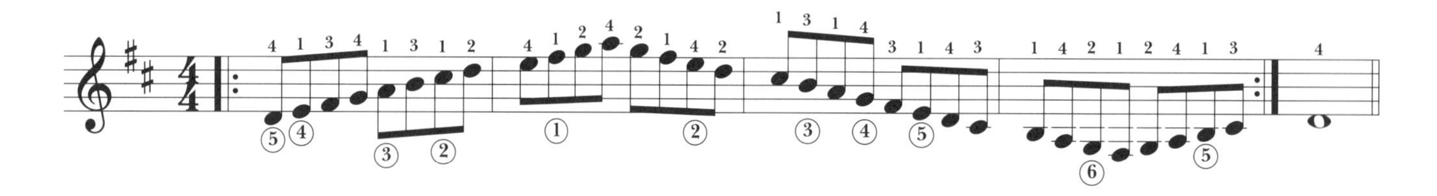

Type IV

TYPE 4

Type 4 fingerings evolve through negative cycle 5 (up a 5th). Using the second position as a sample, we start with A major, fingering Type 4, then proceed to E major (Type 4A), B or C♭ major (Type 4B), F♯ or G♭ major (Type 4C), and C♯ or D♭ major (Type 4D). Observe that each new key requires additional fourth-finger stretches.

Also note that fingering Type 4D is shown with optional first-finger stretches, which actually represent a combination of Types 1 and 4. The combined pattern is usually best.

TYPE 4

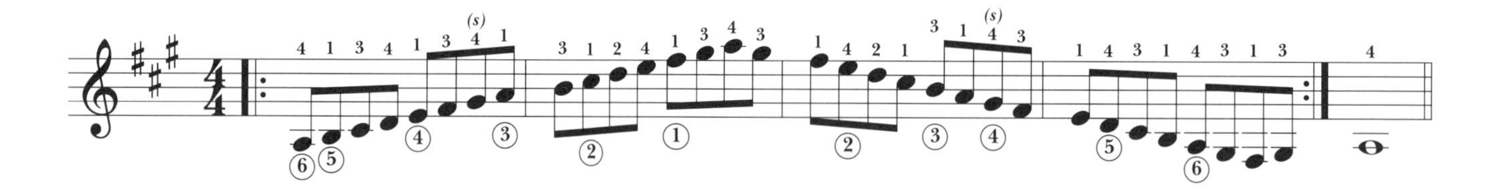

TYPE 4A

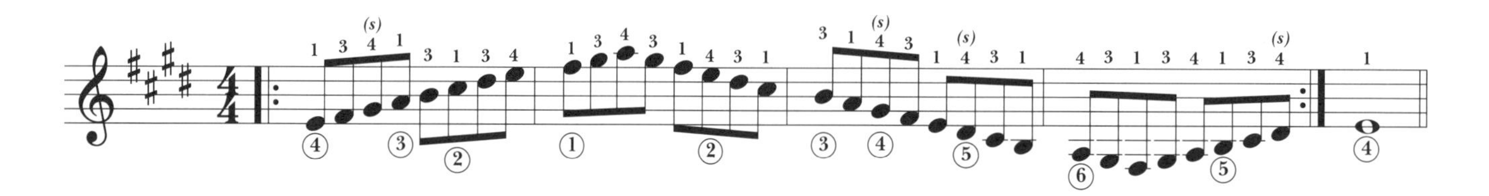

TYPE 4B

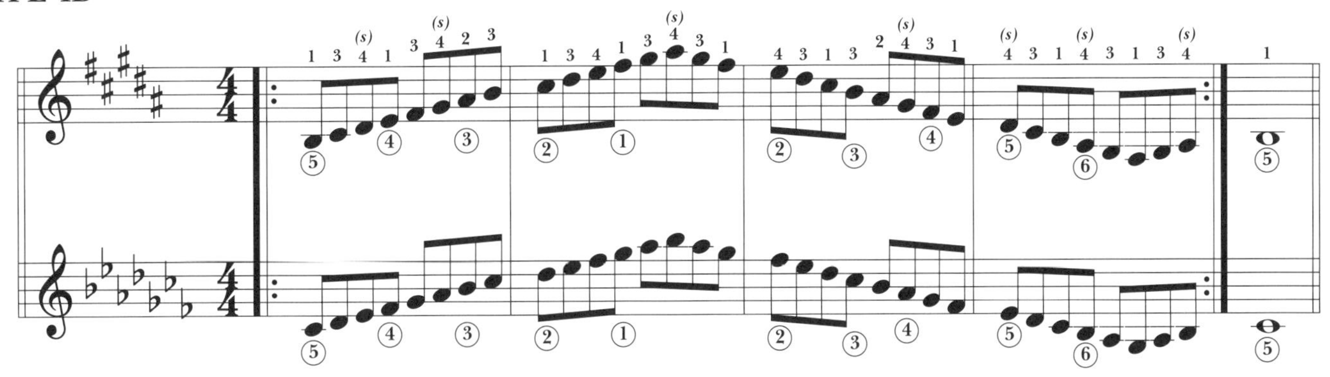

TYPE 4C

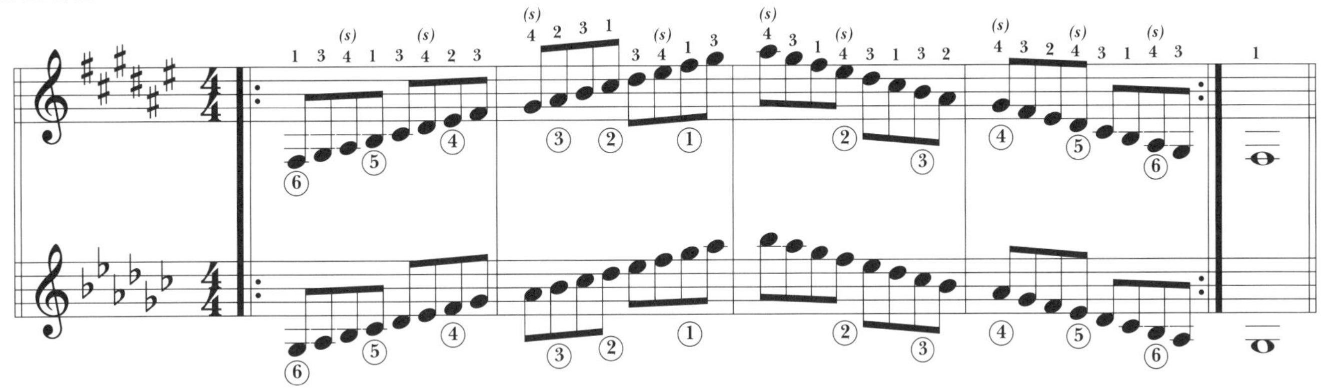

TYPE 4D*

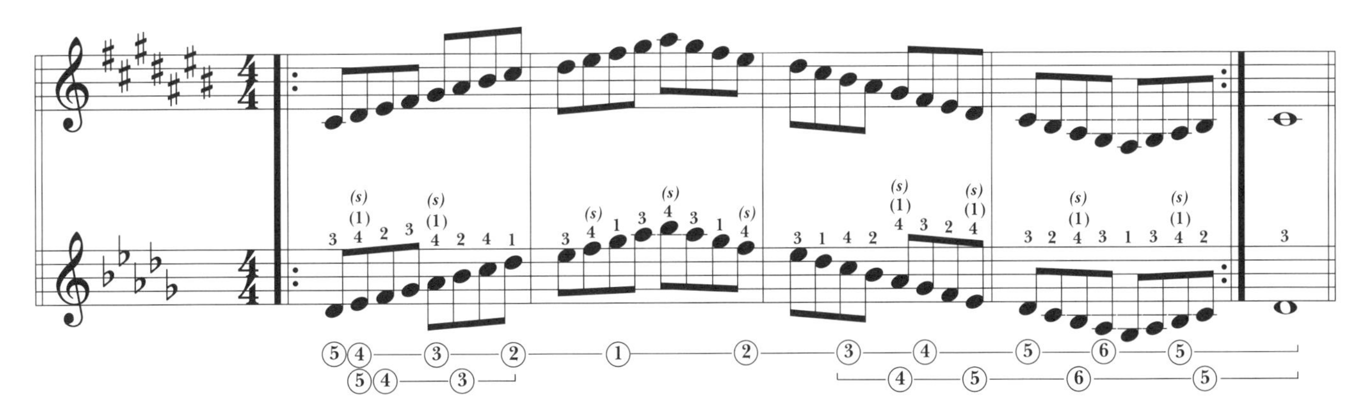

* Although this fingering has evolved from Type 4, it is best played in combination with Type 1. On the following pages only this mixed fingering will be shown. (It will be referred to as 1D/4D.)

Familiarity with all twelve major scale fingerings is valuable, especially when reading something for the first time. All forms do not, however, convert to really practical minor scale fingerings. On the following pages, only the nine best minor forms resulting from the conversion of the preceding major patterns will be emphasized. Eventually, all possibilities will be shown.

A Refined Definition of Position

Now that we have encountered many finger stretches with all the fingering possibilities, let's refine the definition of position. Let's now say: *one fret below the placement of the second finger determines the position.*

Speed Study

Tempo must be constant throughout.

Change the signature and practice in other keys in this position. Possible keys include C through all sharps and up to four flats. Later, convert to minor keys.

Solo in B♭

In the following arrangement, strings are indicated by numbers in circles to aid in positioning the chord voicings.

Rhythm Guitar—The Right Hand

Rhumba: Basic and Orchestral

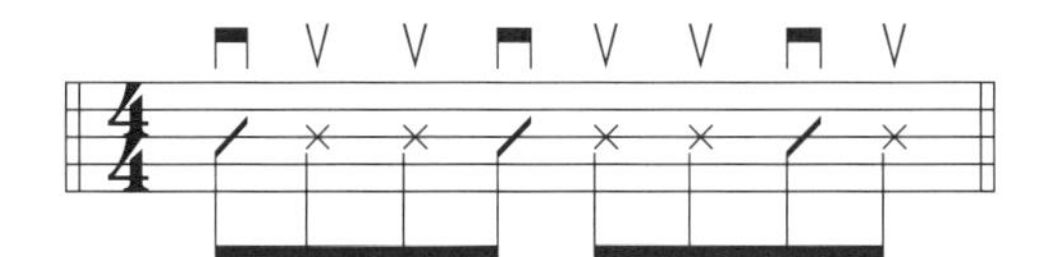

This is difficult but very good for the right hand. It may help to count the eighth notes: 1, 2, 3–1, 2, 3–1, 2 while learning.

■ **EXERCISE**

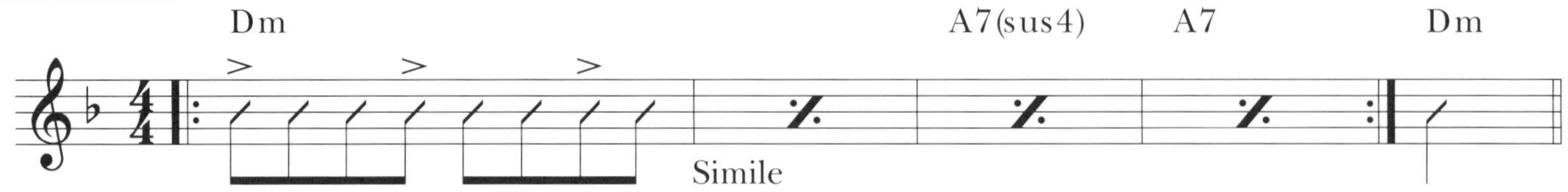

Variations

Practice with above exercise.

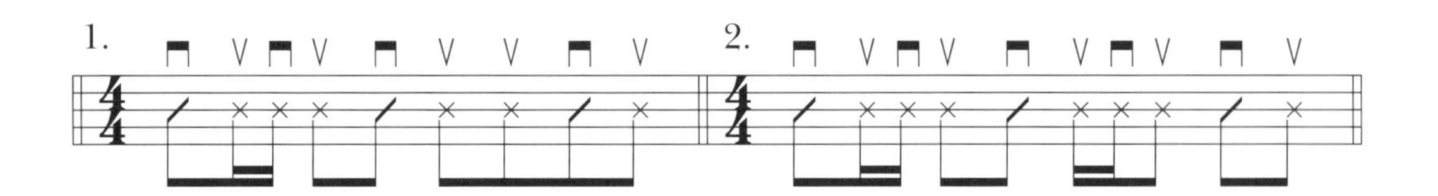

Optional Orchestral

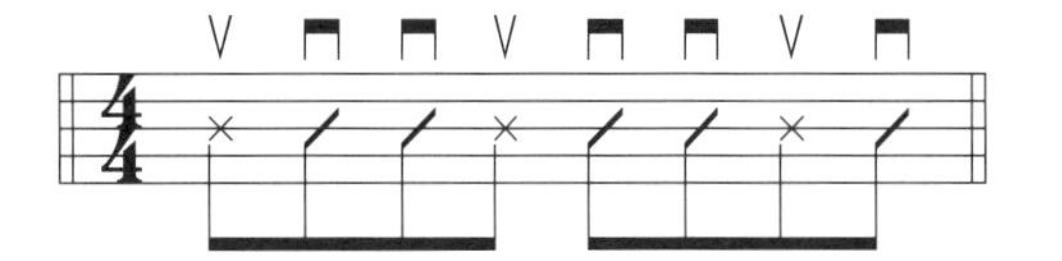

This is the exact opposite of the preceding basic stroke, and it produces complementary accents.

■ **EXERCISE**

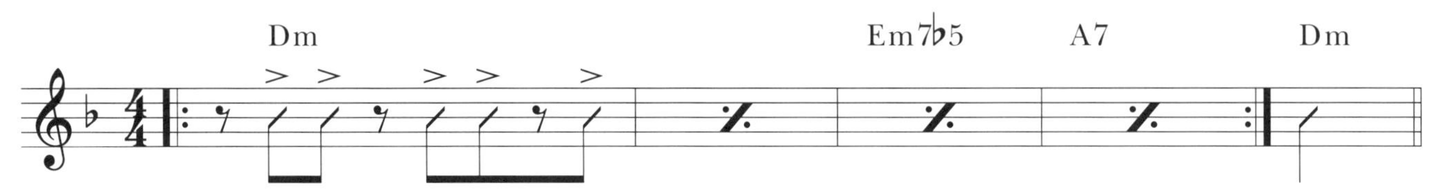

Variations

Practice with above exercise.

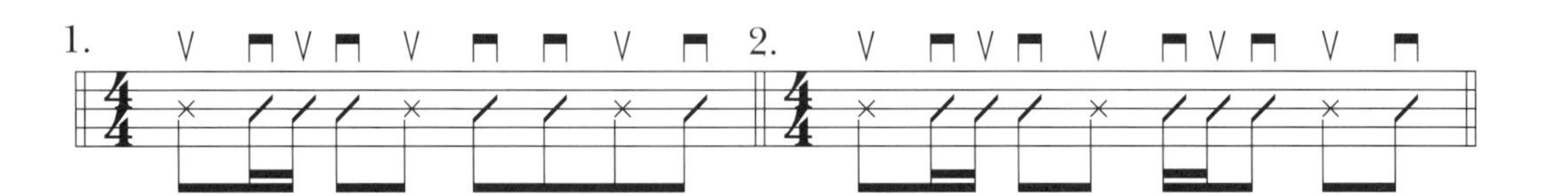

(Also see "Orchestral Beguine," *Vol. II,* pg. 93.)

Each note in a chord is called a "voice." These voices are numbered from the top down. The top note is always called the first voice. The note immediately below it is the second voice. The next note down is the third voice, and so on, depending on the number of notes in the chord. This is always the same, regardless of whether the chord appears in close or open harmony.

Triad Studies: Chords in C Major

The following triad studies are primarily to train the fingers to move from chord to chord, with emphasis on related (or economical) finger movement. *Pay strict attention to fingerings.*

CLOSE VOICINGS

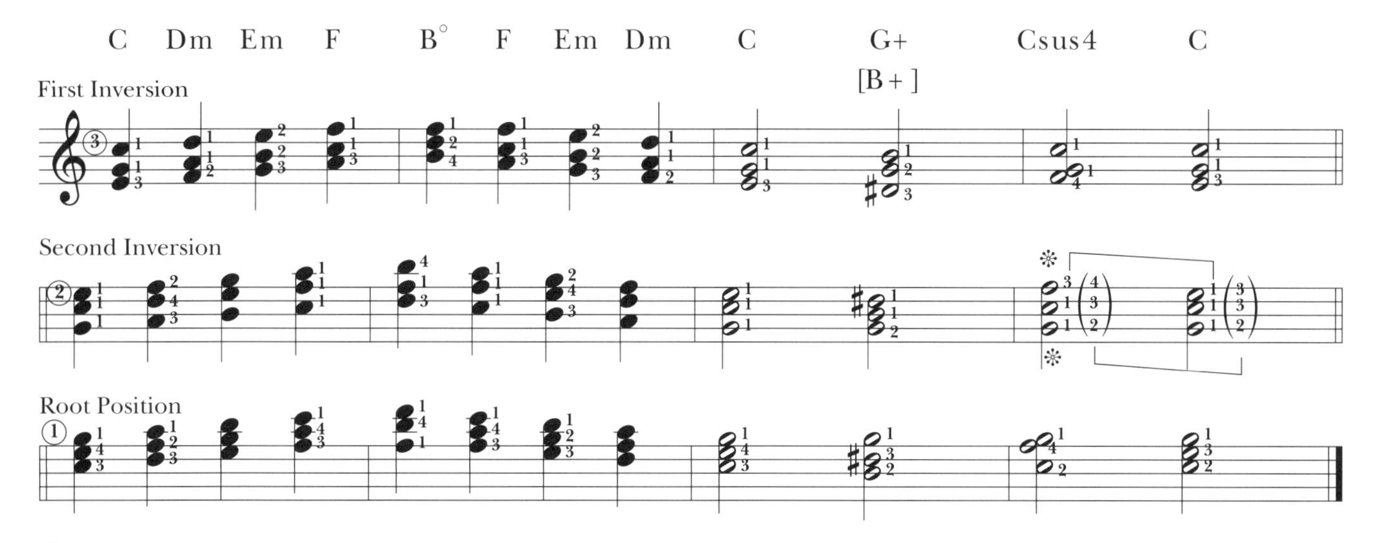

✱ These brackets represent related fingerings. Do not mix them.

OPEN VOICINGS

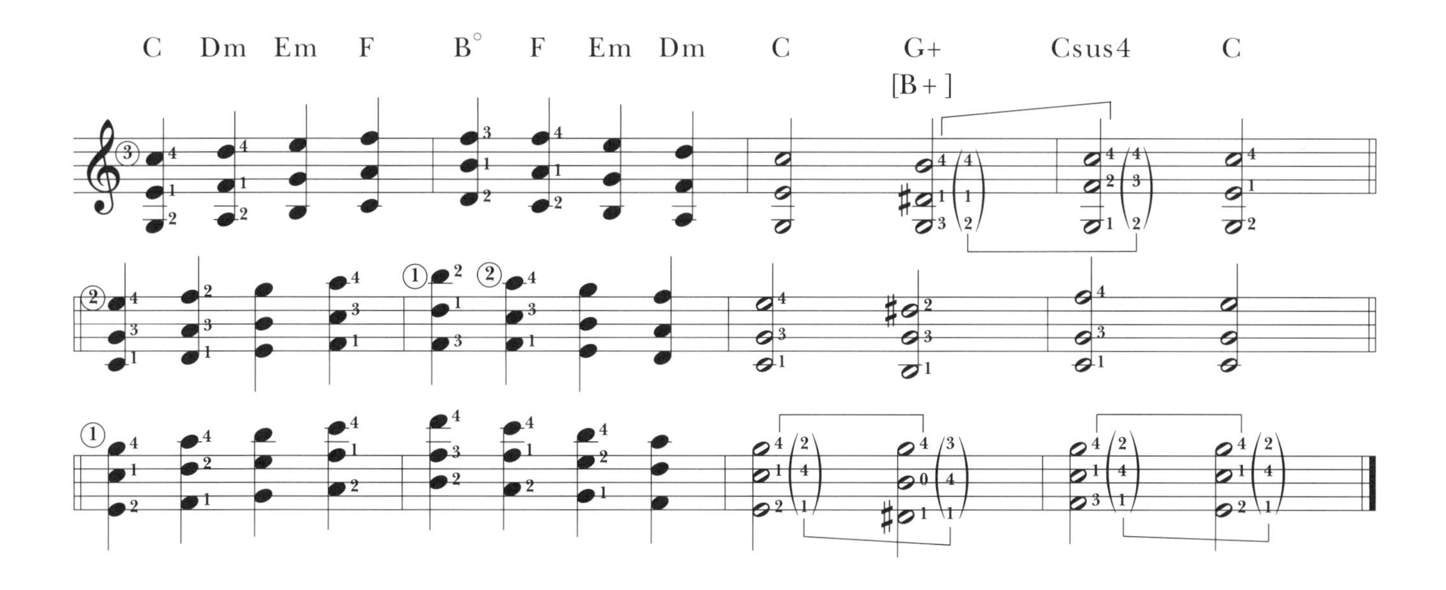

In the preceding open-voiced triads, the chords on the first stave have the 5th degree on the bottom. Chords on the second stave have the root on the bottom. These are strongest chord degrees and therefore are the best "bass" notes. The open voicings on the third stave have the 3rd degree on the bottom, but because they do not (and cannot) sound in the "real bass" range, special handling is not necessary. (See *Vol. II*, pg. 84.)

Adjacent Strings—Common Finger Exercises

"Roll" the fingertip from string to string so the notes flow from one to the next without running into each other.

In the following exercise, roll the finger from the tip to the first joint. Do not let the notes ring together as a chord.

Major Scales—Position II

Twelve keys—ascending chromatically.

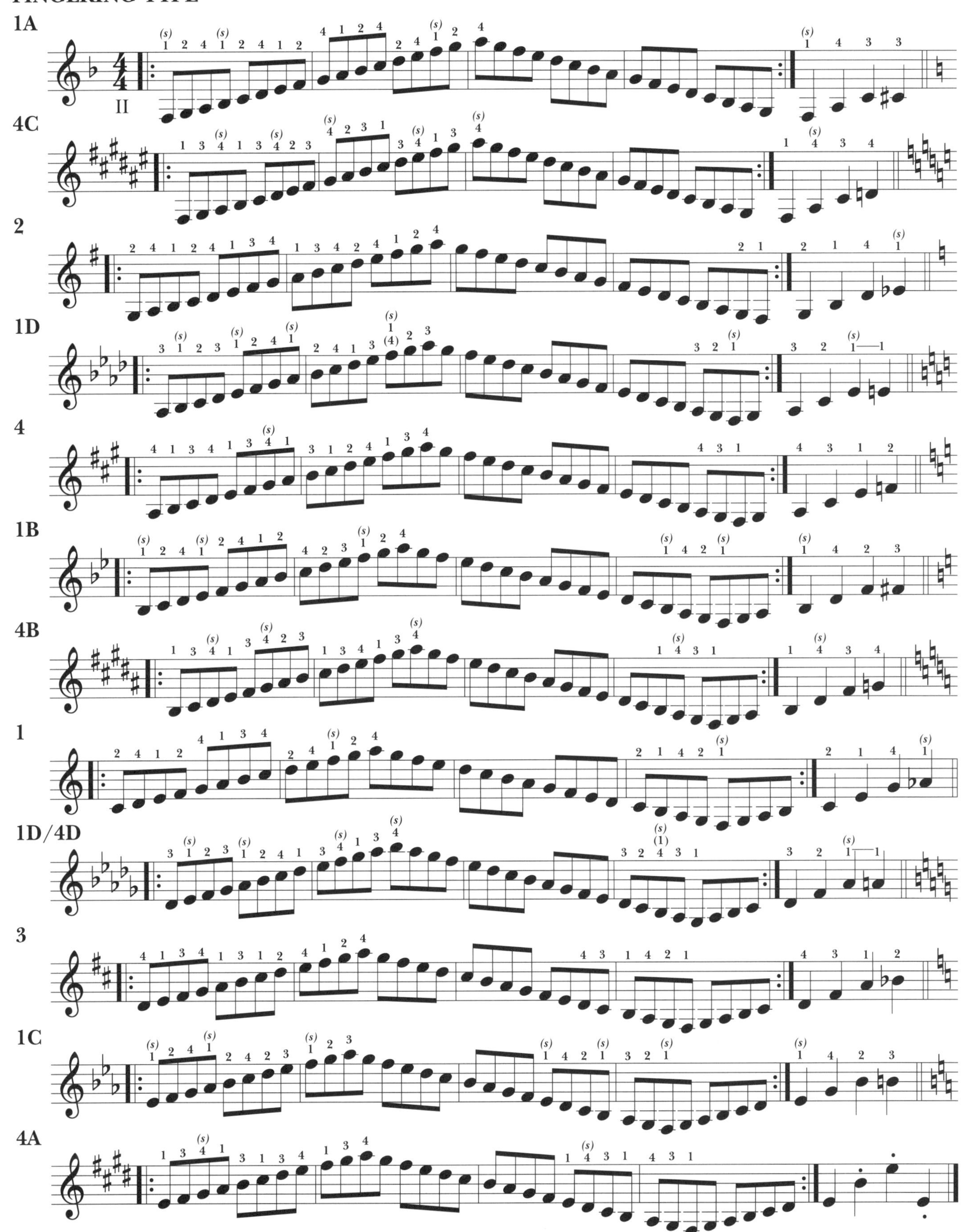

Principal Real Melodic Minor Scales—Position II*

Nine Practical Fingerings

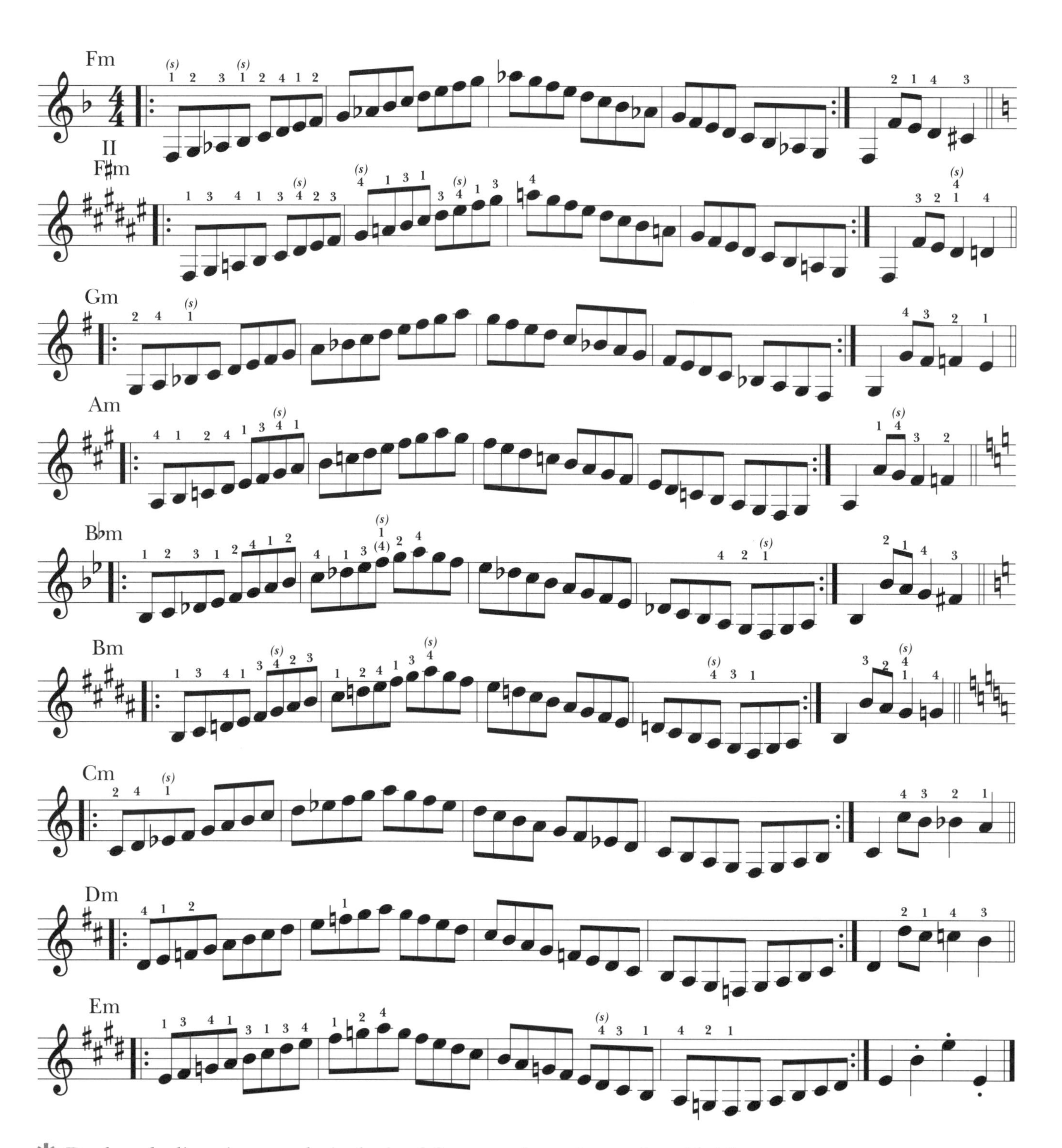

✱ Real melodic minor scale is derived from tonic major scale with ♭3.

Triad Studies—Chords in G Major

Pay strict attention to fingerings.

CLOSE VOICINGS

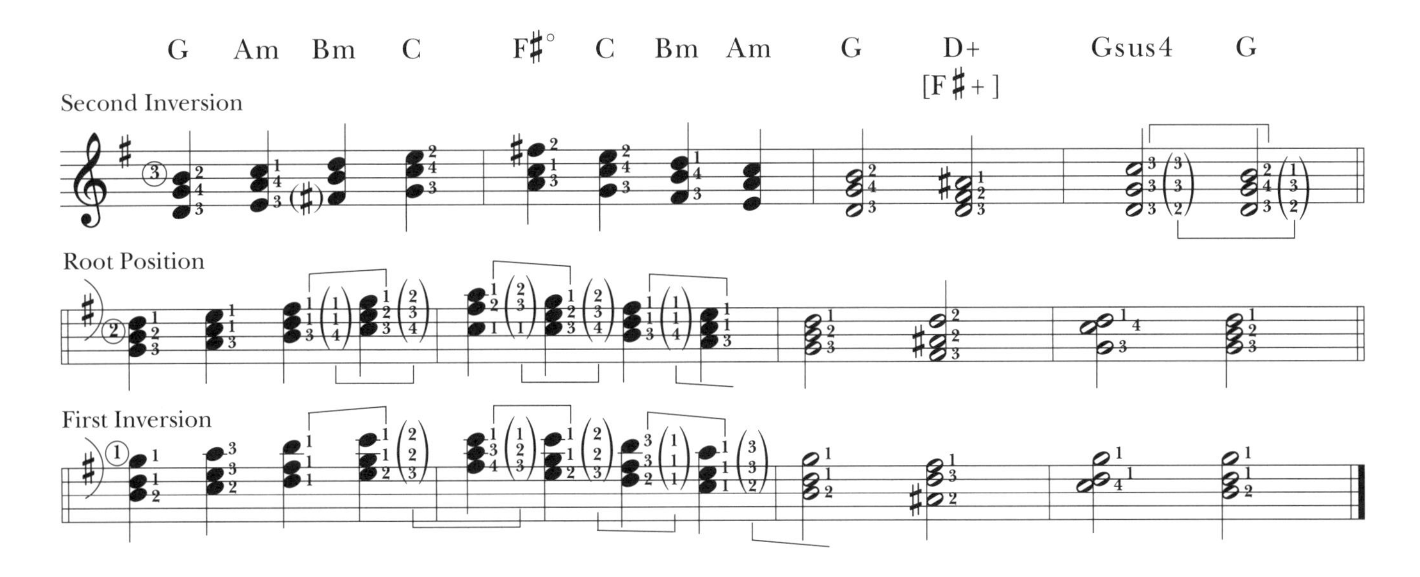

OPEN VOICINGS

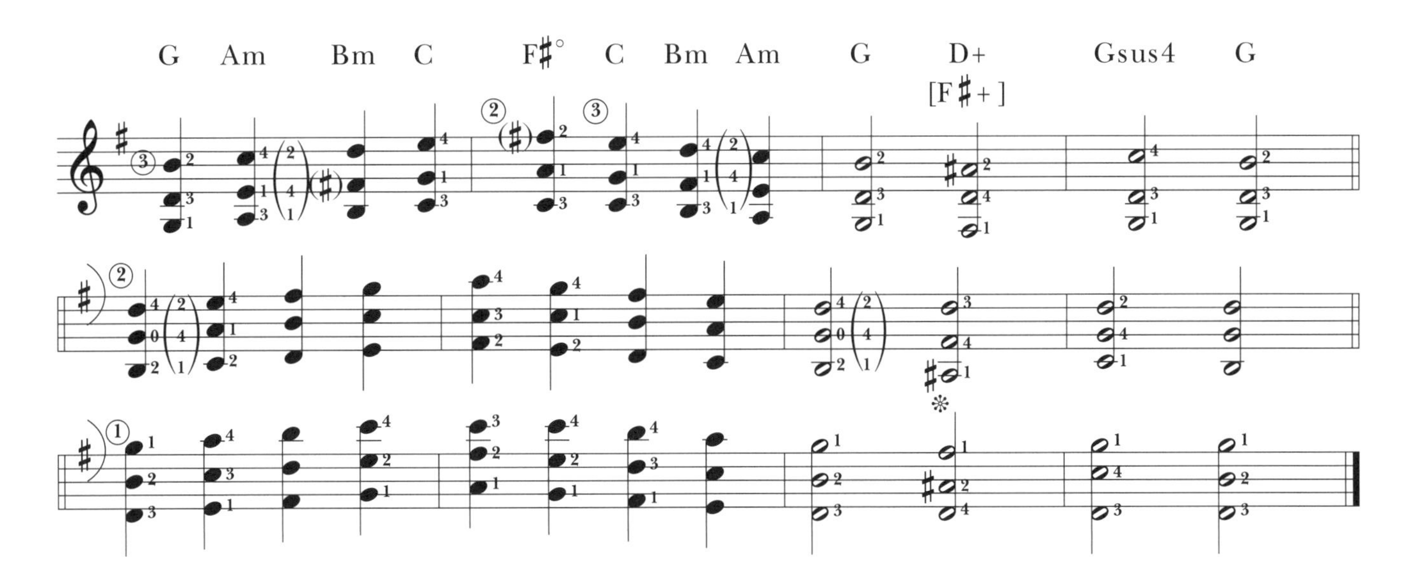

✱ The augmented 5th is a weak bass note unless used in passing. Treat ♯5 the same as the 3rd in the bass. (See *Vol. II*, pg. 84.)

Arpeggios—Three-Note Chords

All major triads (Position V) presented chromatically.

A♭ G G♭ F E E♭
D D♭ C B B♭ A
A♭ G G♭ F E
Second Inversion
D♭ D E♭ E F
F♯ G A♭ A B♭ B
C D♭ D E♭ E F
F E E♭ D D♭ C
B B♭ A A♭ G G♭
F E E♭ D D♭

Arpeggios—Three-Note Chords

All minor triads (Position V) presented chromatically.

Am Ab m Gm F# m Fm Em
Eb m Dm C# m Cm Bm Bb m
Am Ab m Gm F# m Fm
Second Inversion
C# m Dm Eb m Em Fm
F# m Gm Ab m Am Bb m Bm
Cm C# m Dm Eb m Em Fm
Fm Em Eb m Dm C# m Cm
Bm Bb m Am Ab m Gm F# m
Fm Em Eb m Dm C# m

About Chord Symbols

Chord symbols are a form of musical shorthand to indicate chord structures. They can sometimes be so explicit as to indicate both the harmonic content as well as the voicing and melodic potential. The following facts may help clear up some of the discrepancies that exist in their interpretation.

Any chord symbol involving the number 7 or higher (9, 11, 13) and containing no descriptive term or special mark (maj, min, —, dim, °, etc.) always represents a dominant 7 structure.

The abbreviation "alt" (for altered) means to play the indicated chord degree chromatically altered up and/or down. This term is used exclusively with the 5th degree of major chords and minor 7 chords, and with the 5th and 9th degrees of dominant 7 chords. When the term alt appears with no specific chord degree indicated—and this only happens with dominant 7 chords—then chromatically alter both the 5th and 9th degrees (in either or both directions) in the same structure.

REFERENCE CHART FOR MAJOR SCALE FINGERING TYPES

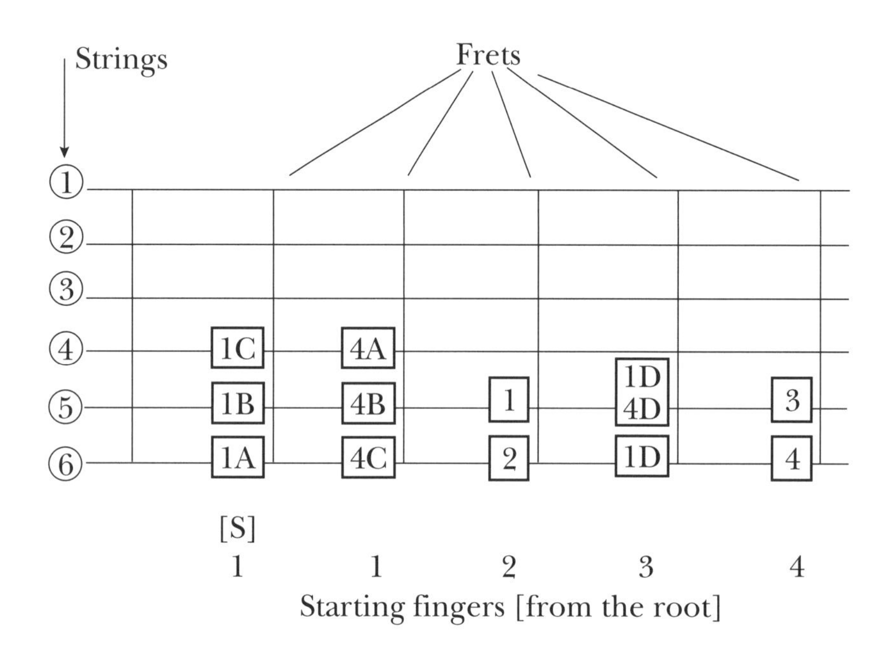

EXAMPLE: Notated in Position V (All notes are roots.)

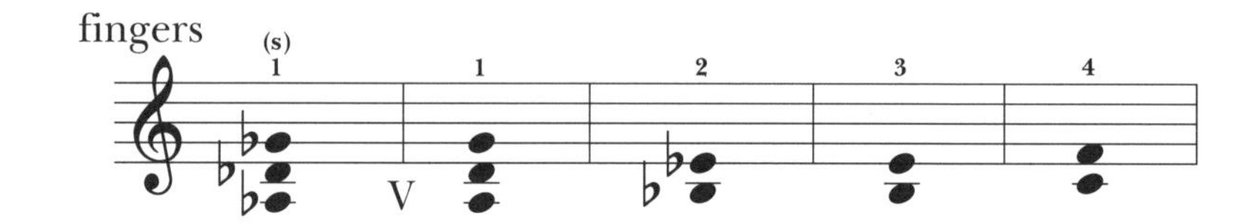

Major Scales—Position III

Twelve keys—descending chromatically.

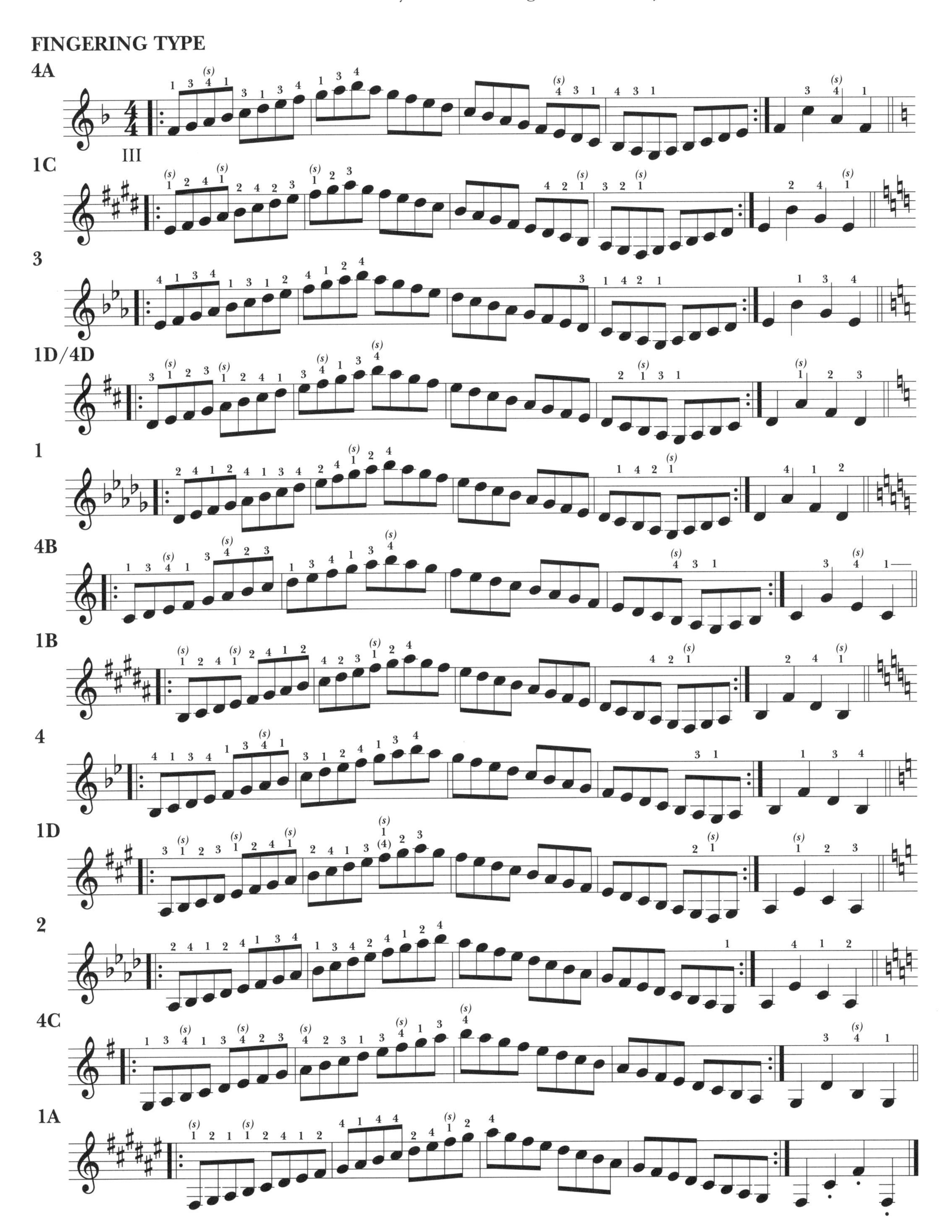

Melodic Rhythm Study No. 8 (duet)

About Practicing

Because the guitar is a percussive instrument, it is easy and natural to play staccato phrasing. Therefore emphasis should be placed on legato practice of all studies—a smooth performance of connected notes (with absolutely minimal silences between attacks). This type of phrasing is considerably more difficult and consequently more beneficial. A slow, strict tempo is best for legato practice, as the slightest inaccuracy is far more apparent.

The amount of time involved in practice varies with the individual, as concentration spans vary from person to person. For most students, I suggest that instead of one long session, the maximum benefit is derived from two or three shorter periods of daily practice.

Triad Studies—Chords in F Major

Pay strict attention to fingerings.

CLOSE VOICINGS

OPEN VOICINGS

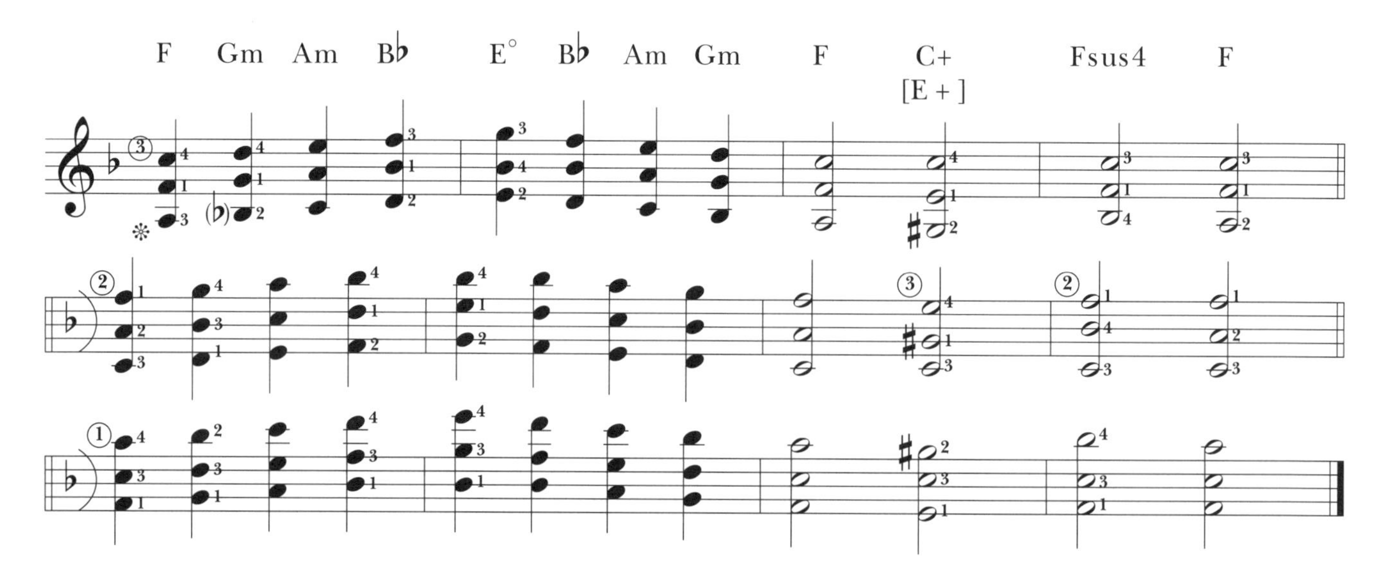

* All voicings in this sequence have the 3rd in the bass. (See *Vol. II*, pg. 84.)

Technical Study

Practice with all possible fingerings, picking each note and also picking on the first note of each triplet group and slurring the rest.

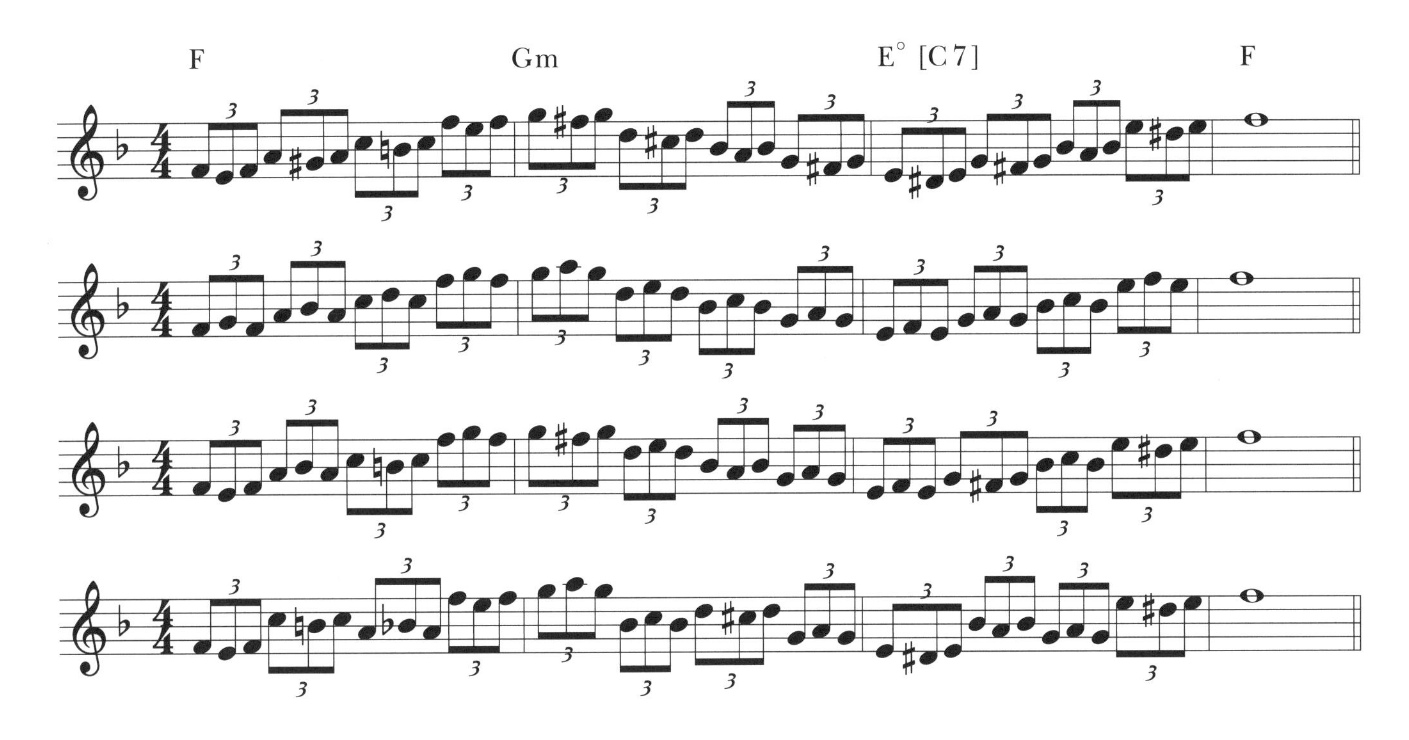

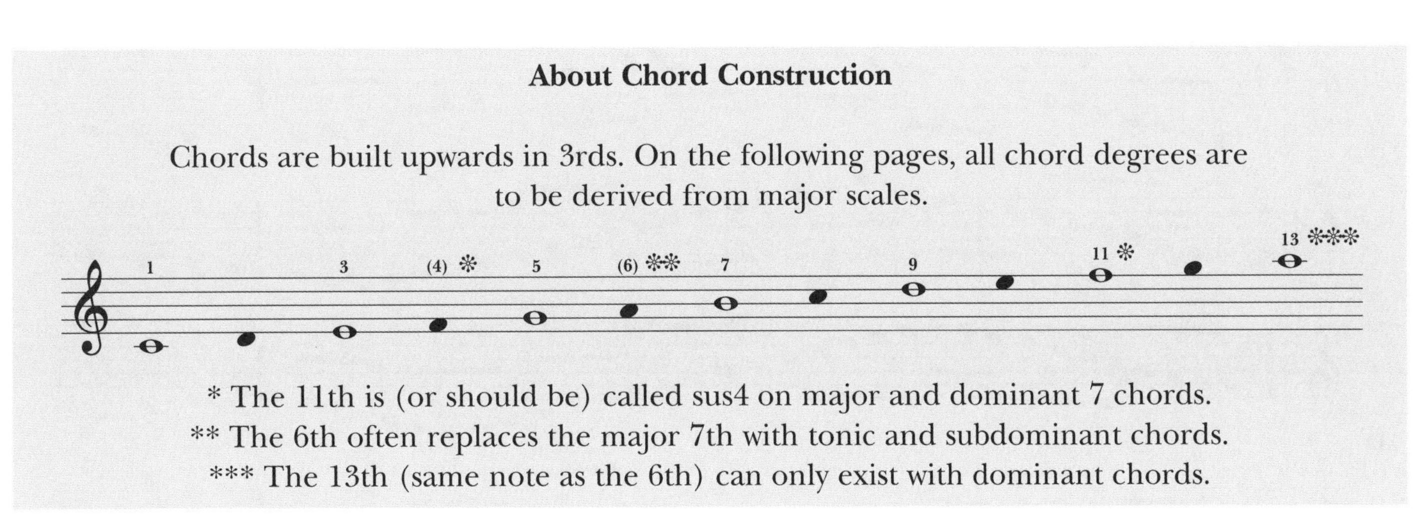

About Chord Construction

Chords are built upwards in 3rds. On the following pages, all chord degrees are to be derived from major scales.

* The 11th is (or should be) called sus4 on major and dominant 7 chords.

** The 6th often replaces the major 7th with tonic and subdominant chords.

*** The 13th (same note as the 6th) can only exist with dominant chords.

Major Scales—Position IV

Twelve keys—through cycle 5.

FINGERING TYPE

4A

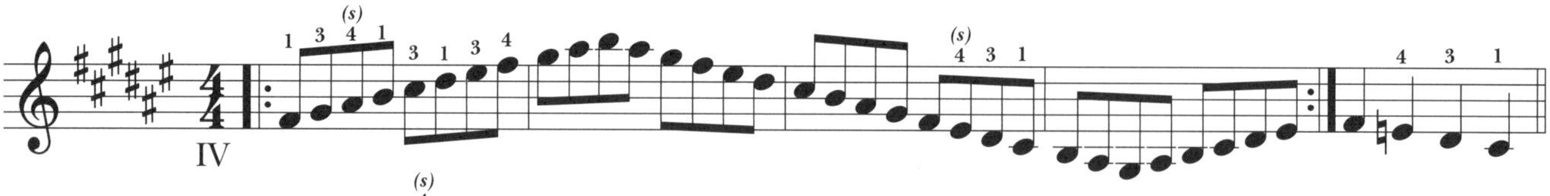

4

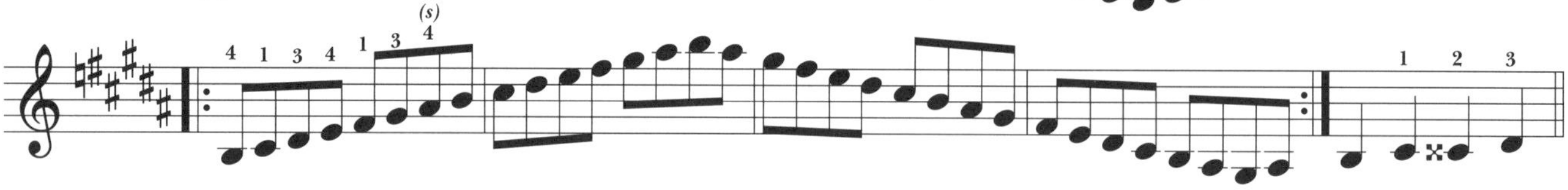

3

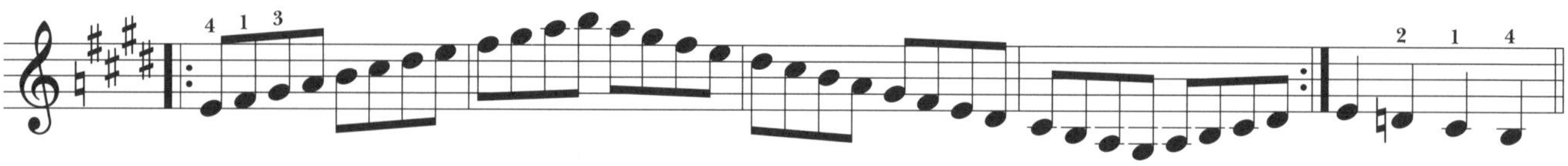

2

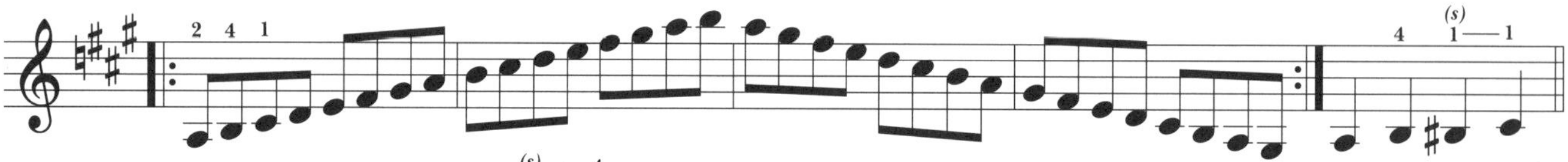

1

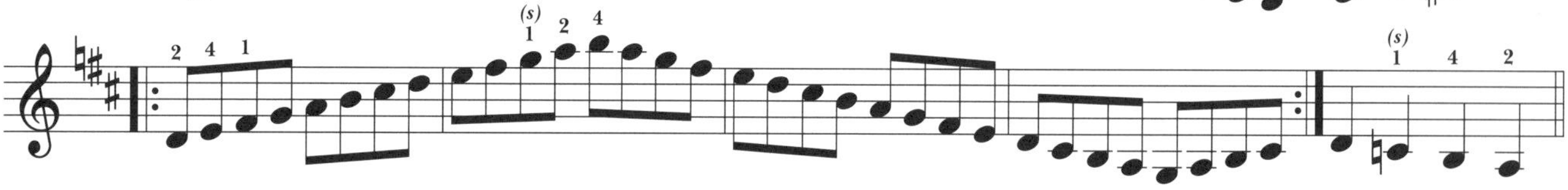

1A

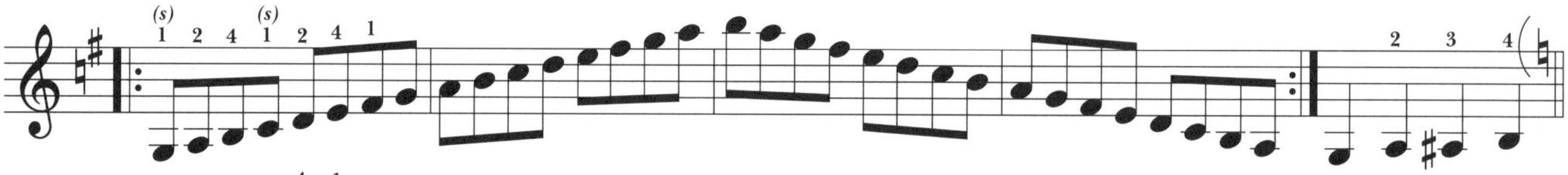

1B

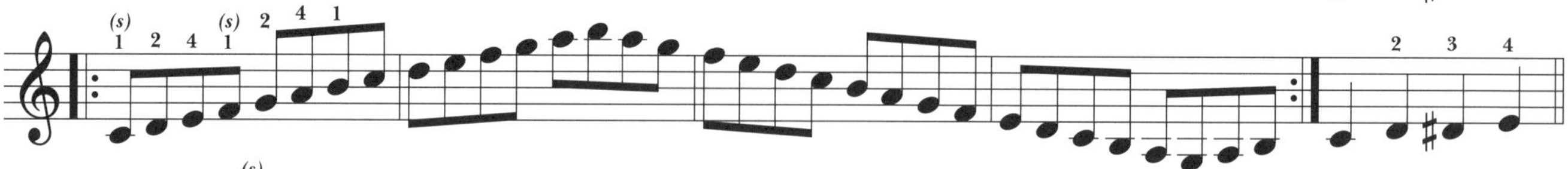

1C

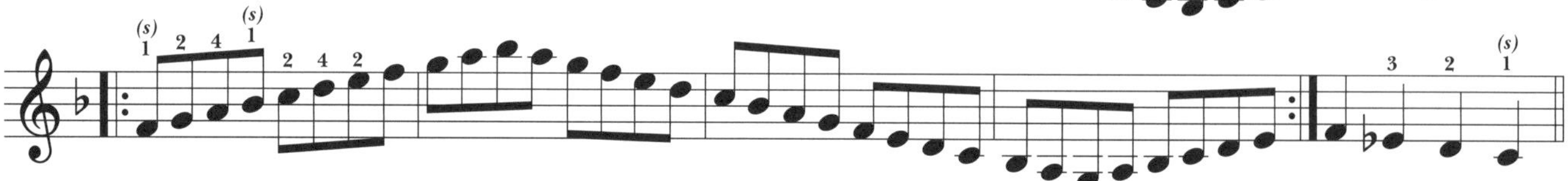

1D

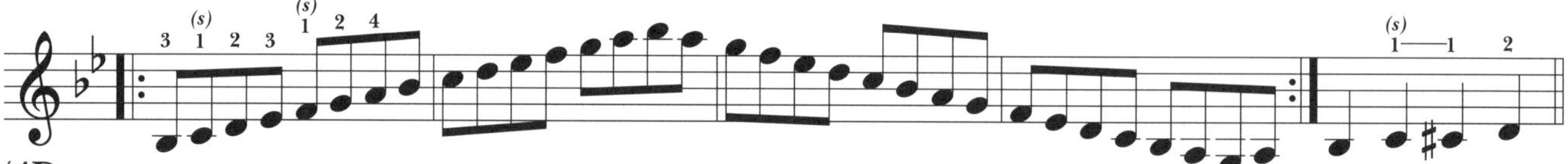

1D/4D

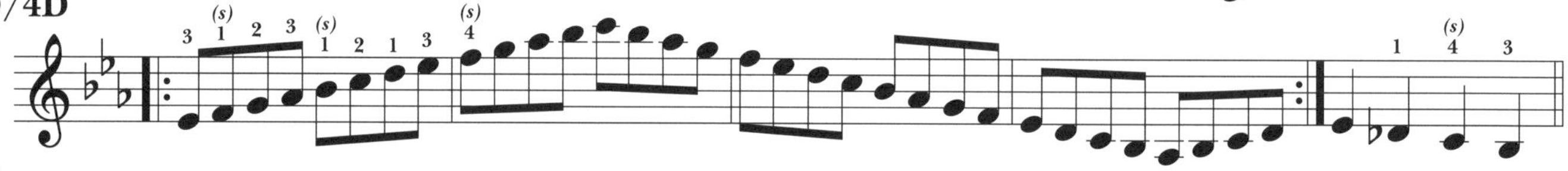

4C

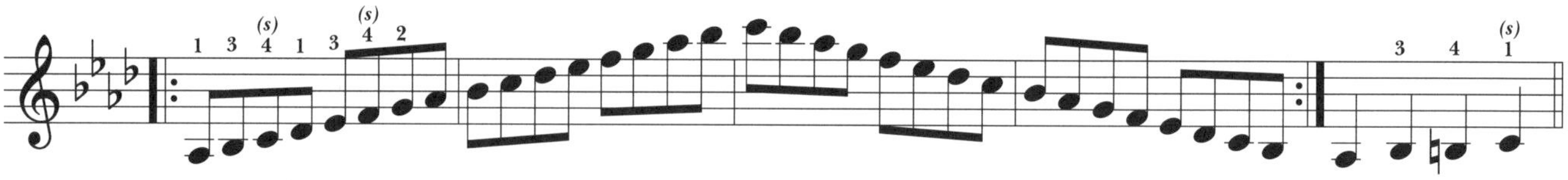

4B

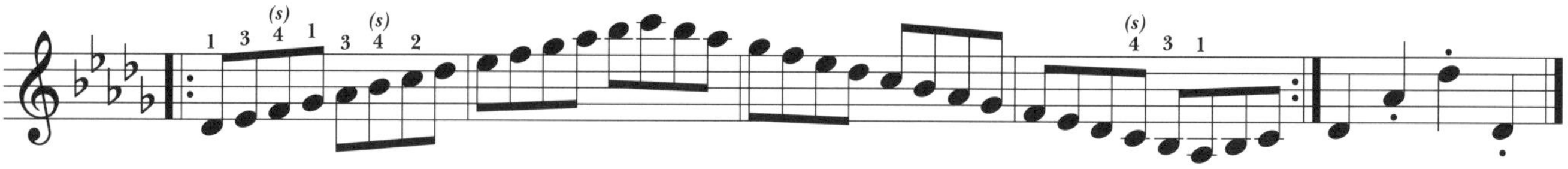

Principal Real Melodic Minor Scales—Position IV

Nine Practical Fingerings

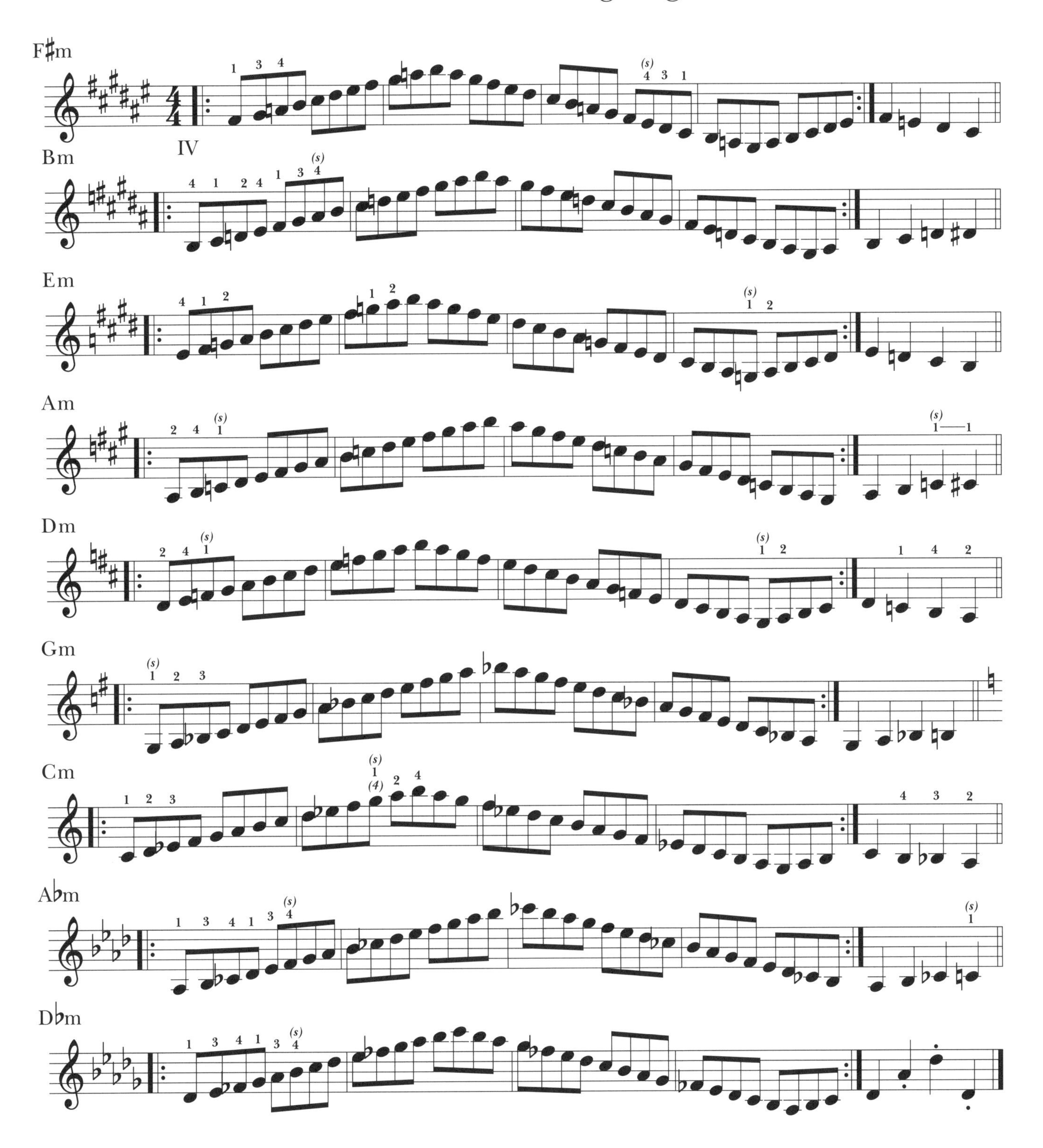

Chord Construction—Four-Part Harmony

All chords are constructed from major scale degrees.

▌ Major scale degrees appear below each staff.

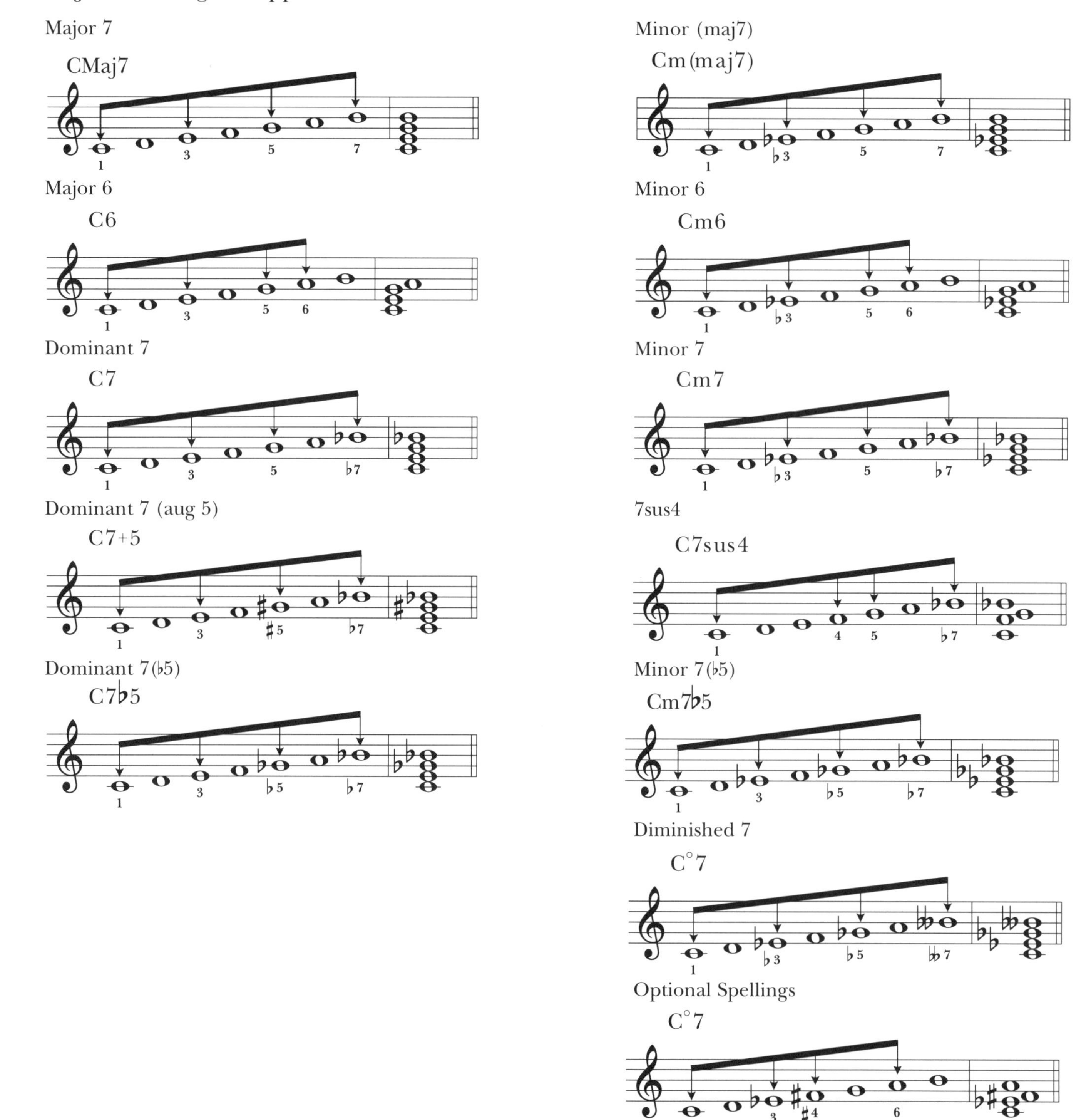

As it is impossible to play most close-voiced structures as chords, we must learn their spelling by practicing them as arpeggios. This must be done so thoroughly that chord spelling becomes automatic. Fingerings are derived from the twelve major scales. Practice them until they require very little, if any, conscious effort.

✱ See special pp. 96 and 97 for information on diminished 7 and dominant 7(♭5) chords.

Arpeggios—Four-Note C Chords

Chord Spelling

Fingering for all four-note chords is shown in the fifth position, with temporary changes to adjacent positions when necessary. After learning the spelling and fingering for each group of arpeggios as written, you must learn to spell and play all structures from all letter names existing from position II through position X. (I suggest doing this transposition on the guitar without writing it out.)

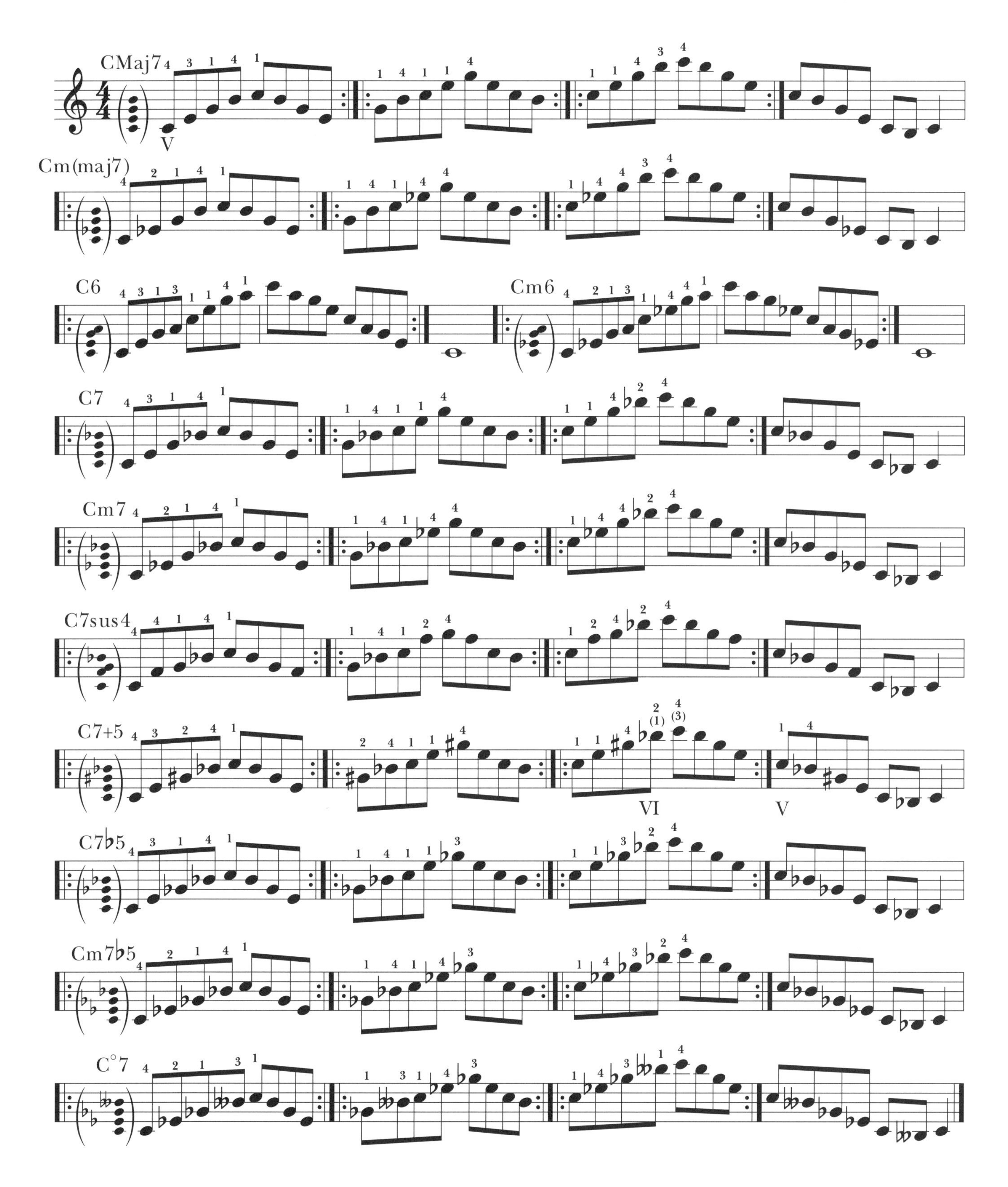

Rhythm Guitar—The Right Hand

Tango 1
Moderately slow
to slow

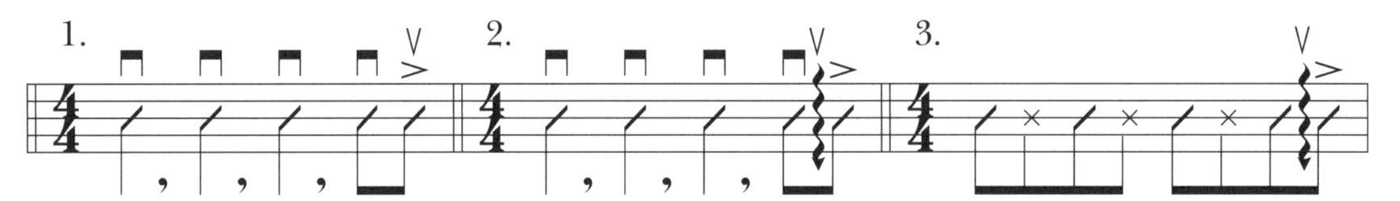

- Practice with each preceding tango beat.

■ EXERCISE

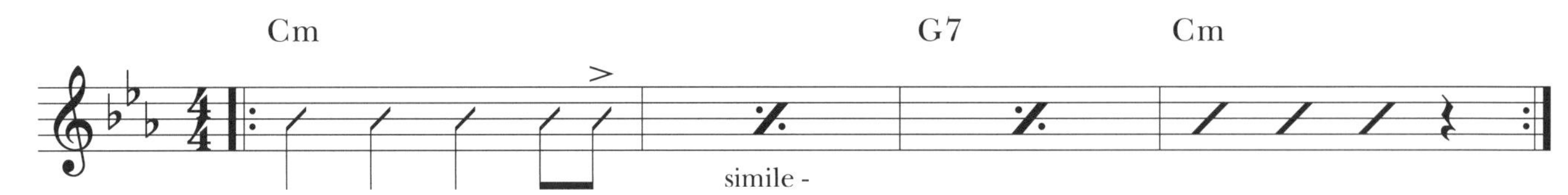

Tango 2

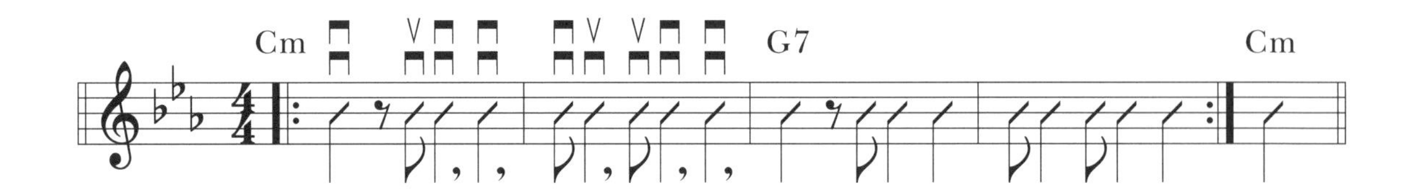

Tango 3

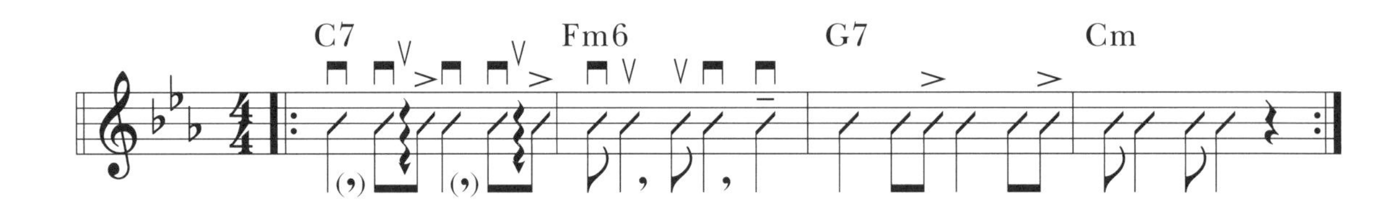

Merengue 1
Fast in 2

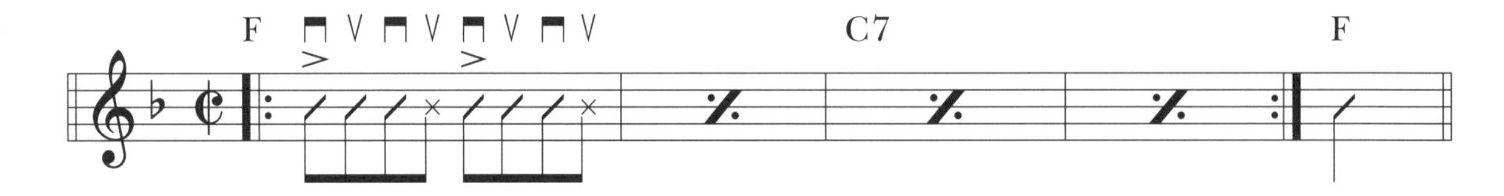

Merengue 2

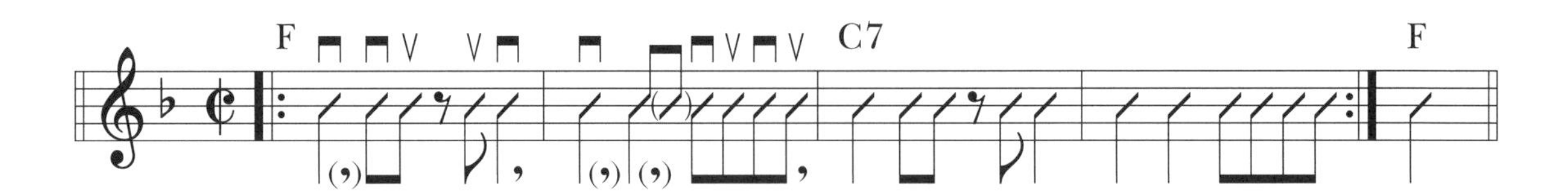

Merengue 3

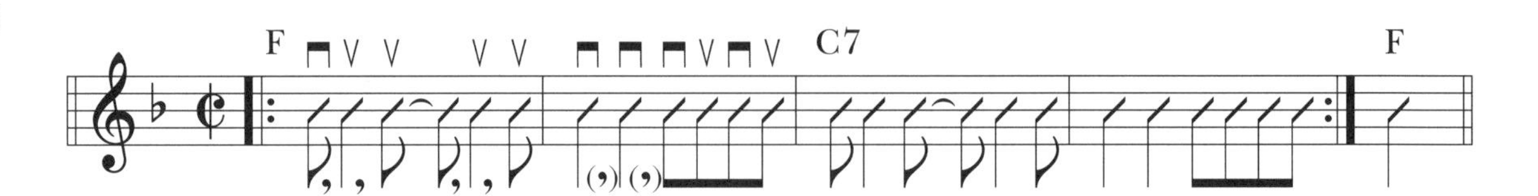

C Major Scale (Twelve Positions)

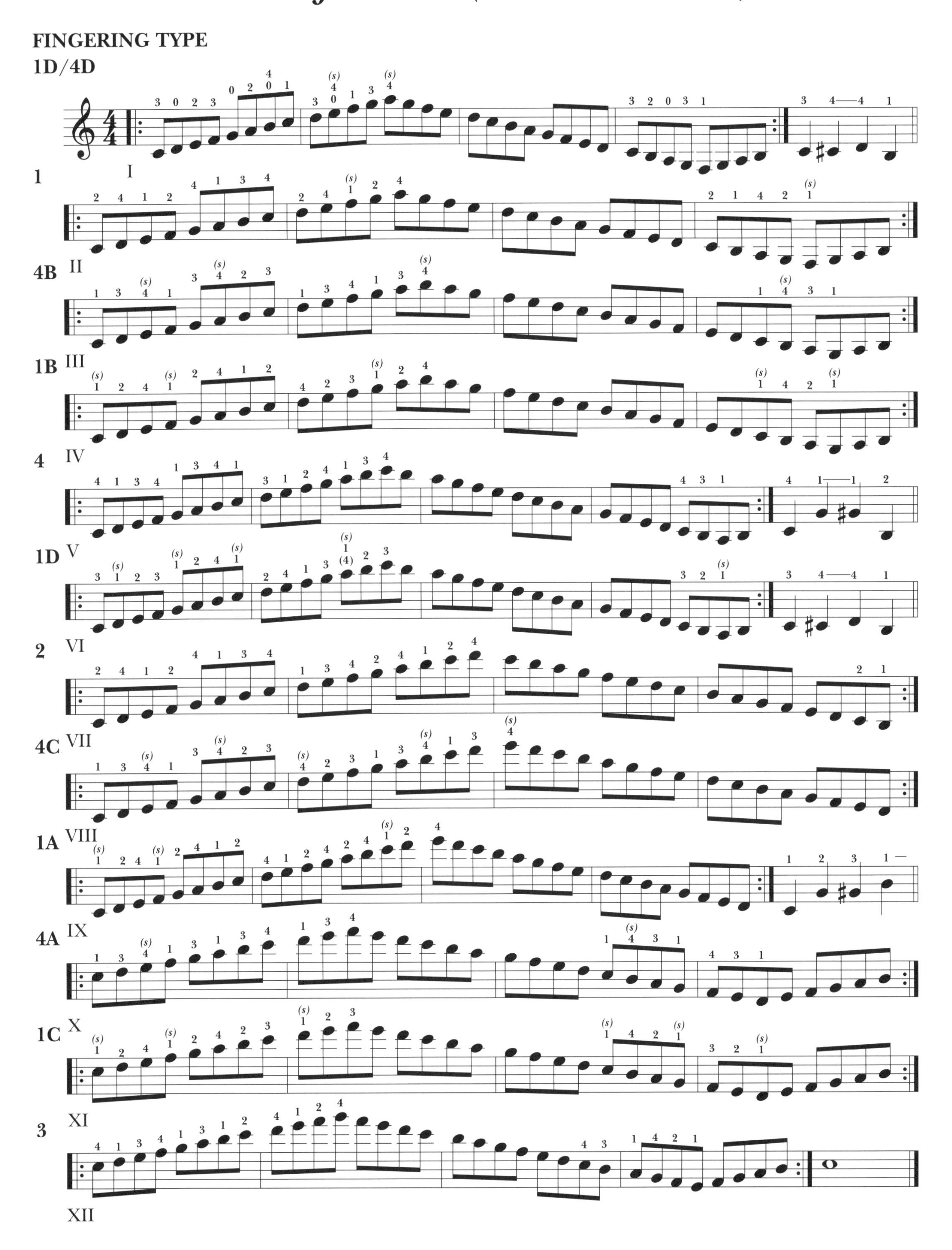

Natural Minor Scales

The natural minor scale has the same key signature and exactly the same notes as its relative major scale. Start on the 6th degree of any major scale. Consider this note as the tonic (1st degree) of the natural minor scale. Renumber the notes (1 through 7 upwards) from this new tonic for the degrees of the relative natural minor scale.

C Major Scale Degrees

A Natural Minor Scale Degrees

Another way to construct the relative natural minor scale is to take the notes a *diatonic 3rd below those of the major scale. (Take the note one line below a note on a line, or one space below a note on a space; do not change the key signature.)

 Diatonic: Confined to the notes of the key signature, with no alterations.

F Major

D Natural Minor

TABLE OF RELATIVE MAJOR-MINOR KEYS

C major A minor	D major B minor	E♭ major C minor	F major D minor	G major E minor	A major F♯ minor	B♭ major G minor

When you play a major scale from its 6th degree, this is called the natural minor or Aeolian mode.

No exercises in natural minor scales are given here, as the fingerings are exactly the same as the relative major scales shown before. (For reading practice, see modal transposition in the next section.)

Modes: A Brief Discussion

There are names to indicate the playing of a scale from each of the seven notes. These are called modes. They are as follows:

Ionian	From the tonic (or 1)
Dorian	From the 2nd
Phrygian	From the 3rd
Lydian	From the 4th
Mixolydian	From the 5th
Aeolian	From the 6th
Locrian	From the 7th

There are two ways in which these modal terms are expressed:

- **Dorian mode, key of C**, means the C scale starting on the second note (D).
- **C Dorian**, means to start on the note C and play the scale of which C is the 2nd degree, i.e., the B♭ scale, starting from C.

Automatic Modal Transpositions: Playing the notes as written on the staff, but with a different key signature from the original.

Addition of 2 flats to a key signature produces the Dorian mode.
Addition of 4 flats to a key signature produces the Phrygian mode.
Addition of 1 sharp to a key signature produces the Lydian mode.
Addition of 1 flat to a key signature produces the Mixolydian mode.
Addition of 3 flats to a key signature produces the Aeolian mode.
Addition of 5 flats to a key signature produces the Locrian mode.

Note: When you add flats to a signature containing sharps, each flat cancels out one sharp. Example: Adding two flats to the key of D major = C major; adding two flats to G major = F major.

To familiarize your ear with the sounds of these modes (and for extra reading practice from music you already own), refer to reading studies, speed studies, or any completely diatonic music in *Volumes I* and *II.* Transpose first into the Aeolian mode (add of three flats to the signature), as it has the most natural sound to our ears. Then later (in this order), transpose to Phrygian, Dorian, Lydian, Mixolydian, and Locrian modes.

Harmonic Minor Scales

The harmonic minor scale has the same key signature as its relative major scale and all notes but one are the same. Follow the same procedure as with natural minor, except raise the 7th degree one half step. This raised 7th degree becomes the leading tone of the harmonic minor scale.

EXAMPLE:

								1	2	3	4	5	6
Degrees	1	2	3	4	5	6	7	(8)	(9)	(10)	(11)	(12)	(13)
Major Scale ⟶	C	D	E	F	G	A	B	C	D	E	F	G	A
Minor Scale ⟶						a	b	c	d	e	f	g♯	a
				Degrees		1	2	3	4	5	6	7	(8)

The fingerings of a harmonic minor scale are easily mastered when you realize that it is nothing more than the relative major scale with one note raised. Therefore, all playing positions and fingering types coincide. Learn harmonic minor by converting from relative major to minor. Use any major scale fingering pattern. Sharp the 5th scale degree of the major, and you are playing the relative harmonic minor scale. Or, use the natural minor scale and give it a **leading tone** by raising its 7th degree.

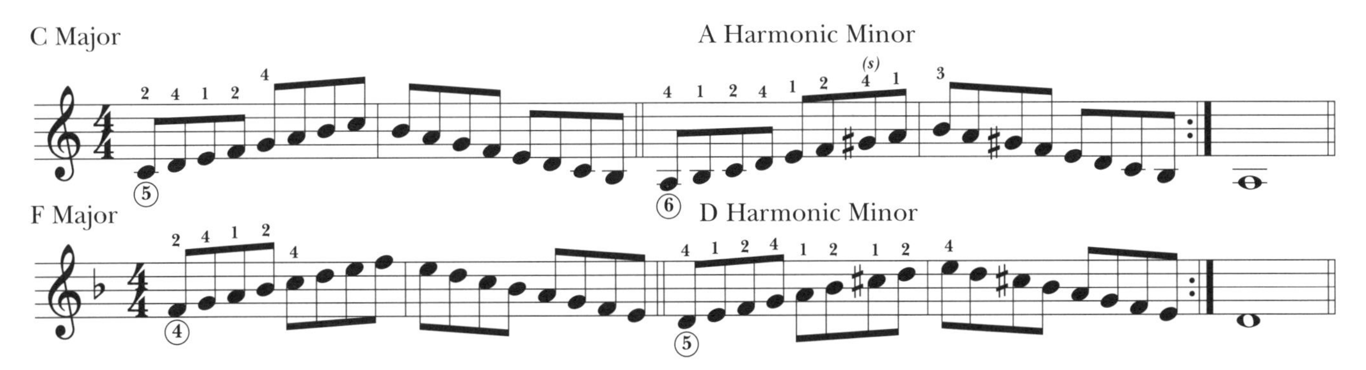

Note: Harmonic minor is the only scale that contains an interval of an augmented 2nd. It occurs between the 6th and 7th scale degrees.

A Harmonic Minor (Nine Positions)

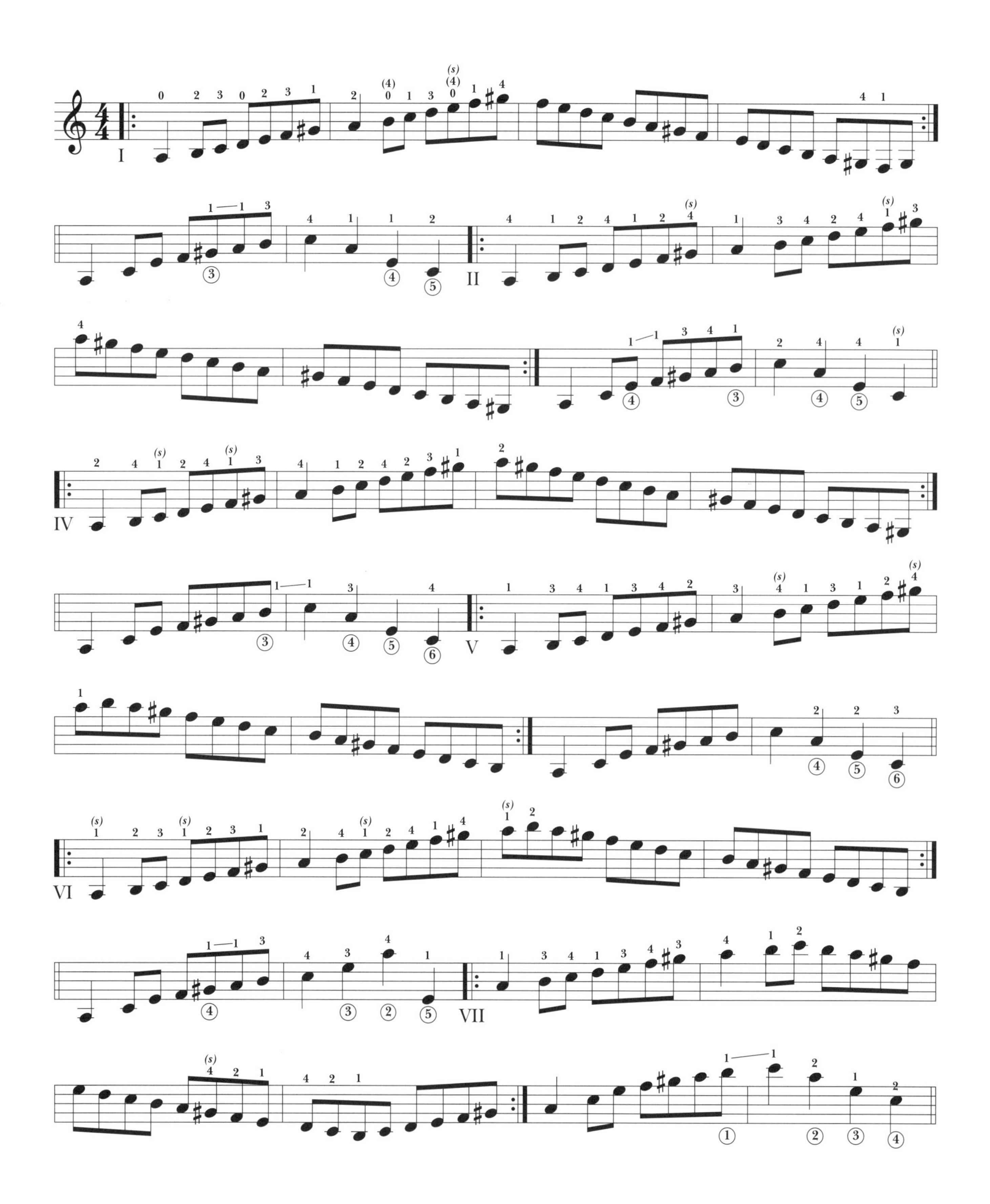

A Minor Etude (solo)

The guitar is a very difficult instrument on which to see exactly what you are playing. There are multiple choices for playing single notes and many chord voicings in the same octave. The strings are not tuned with constant intervals between them (like the violin, viola, or cello), so the relative location and fingering for the same group of notes varies from one set of strings to another.

The fact that the guitar is not a very visual instrument can prove to be quite a problem at times, especially when dealing with the study of harmony. Position marks are a great help, but they don't begin to clarify the layout of sounds like the physical appearance of the other harmonic instruments: the black and white keys of the piano, harpsichord, and accordion, the staggered bars of the xylophone and vibes, even the colored strings of the harp.

With regard to all this, and because I feel it is very important to be able to apply directly to the guitar (without any intermediate steps), in the following studies involving chord construction, melodic analysis, etc., we shall concentrate on three-note chord voicings.

Melodization of Triads

Melodization of triads is accomplished by replacing the top note of a triad (the root, 3rd, or 5th, depending on the inversion) with a higher degree of the scale from which the chord is formed. These notes (other than 1, 3, or 5) are referred to as tension notes, tensions, or high degrees.

MELODIC TENSIONS POSSIBLE FOR TONIC MAJOR CHORDS

Root Position			First Inversion		Second Inversion	
5	6	maj7	1	9	3	sus4*
3	3	3	5	5	1	1
1	1	1	3	3	5	5

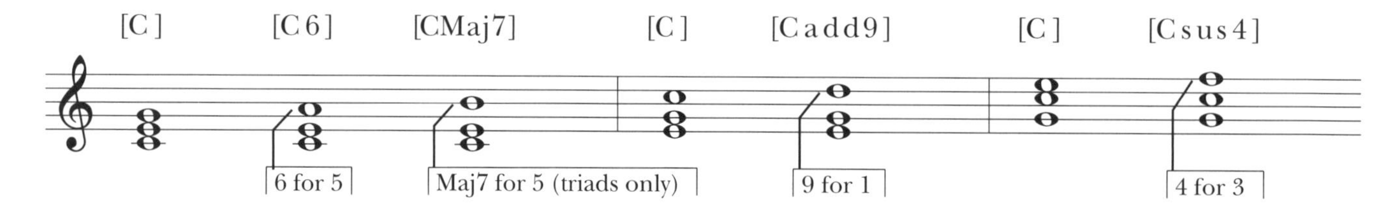

General Rule: A melodic tension replaces the first triadic tone directly below it in pitch (usually found on the same string).

Note that the 3rd is present in all voicings (except sus4*). The 3rd is the most important chord degree, as it alone indicates whether the chord structure is major or minor.

Tensions are also used as inside voices of chords, but because these are more difficult to "see," we shall not emphasize them until later.

*The symbol sus is an abbreviation for "suspension." It is a dissonant note that eventually resolves into the same chord. It usually moves downward to a lower chordal degree, or into a different chord that contains the same note.

Recognition of Melodic Degrees

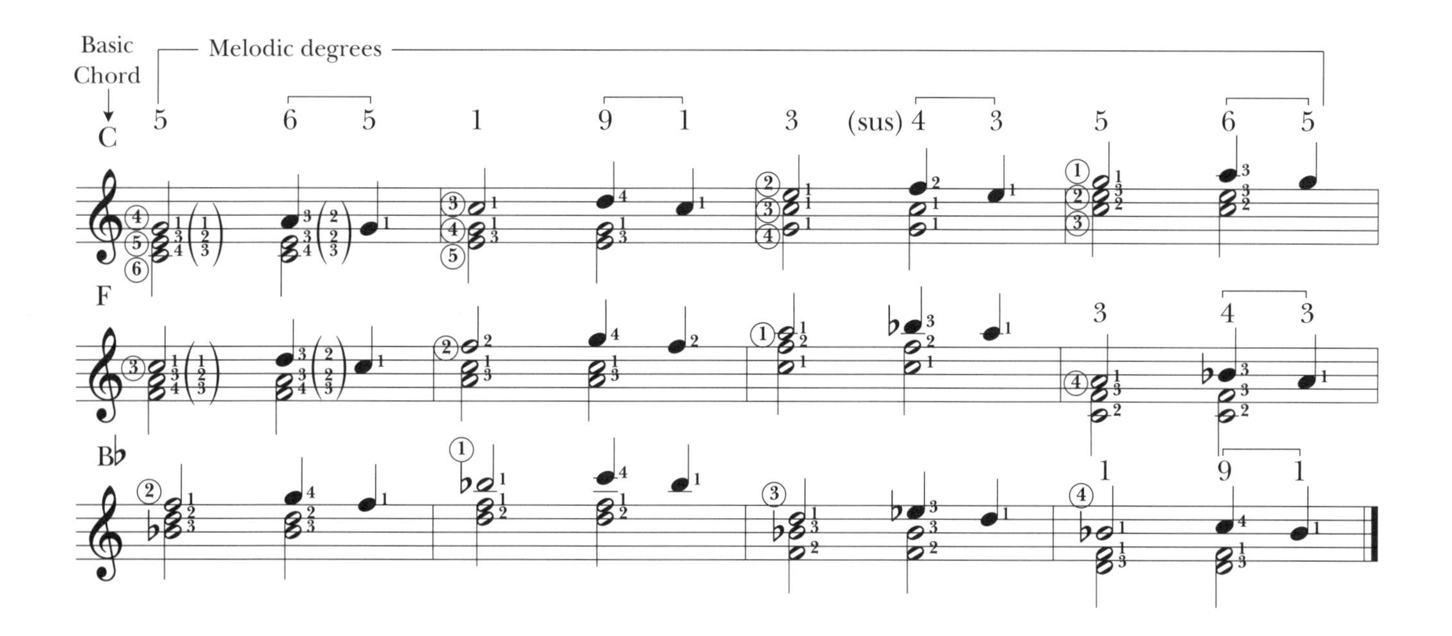

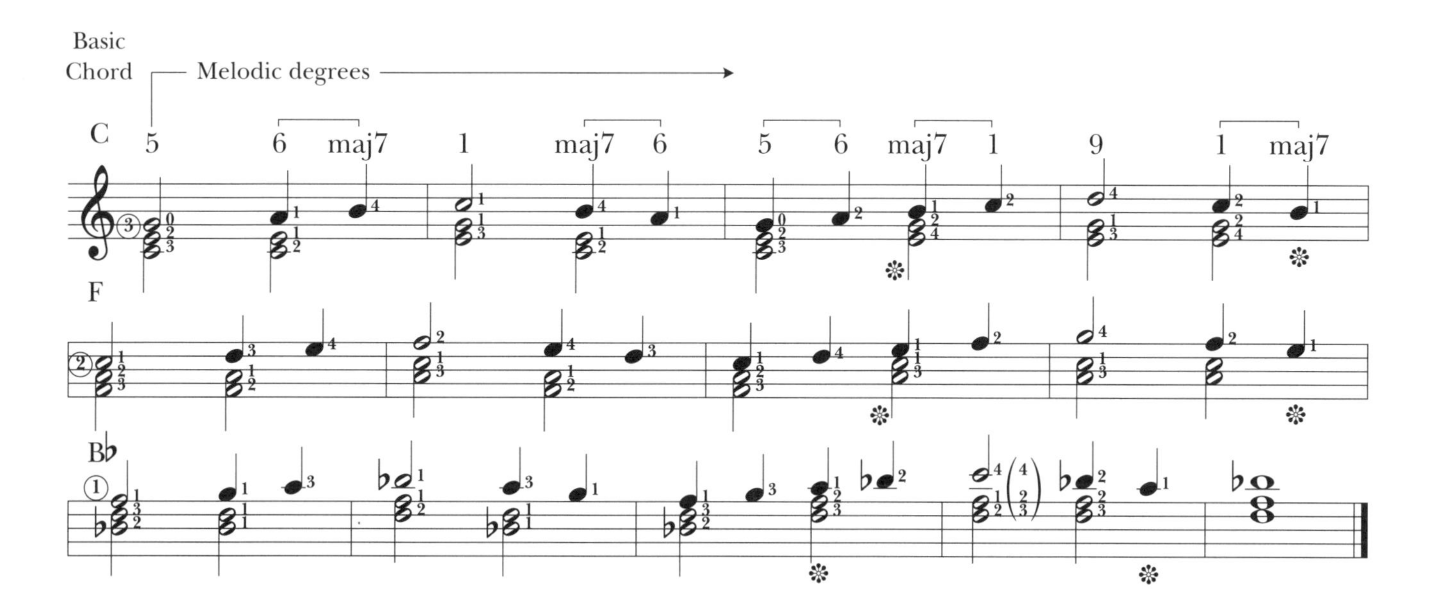

✱ The 7th degree offers an exception to the general rule for tensions on three-part voicings, in that it may replace the 1st triadic tone above it, i.e., maj7 for 1 (usually located on the same string).

The abbreviation alt (for altered), when used with chord symbols, means to chromatically raise and/or lower the indicated degree.

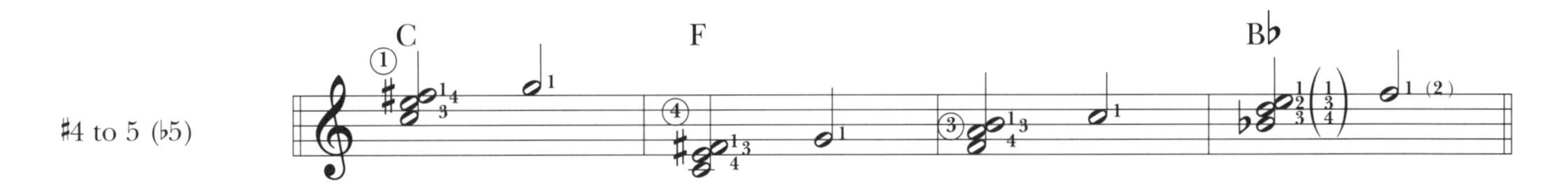

✱ ♯4 (like 7) may replace the first triadic tone above it, i.e. ♯4 for 5. This is because the ♯4 is the enharmonic equivalent of ♭5. (Enharmonic = two different letter or number designations for the same tone.)

Note: ♯4 is a diatonic tension on subdominant (IV) chords.

About Chord Voicings

On the guitar, it is usually impossible to play all notes in chords containing tensions or double alterations. The lack of mobility of five (or more) note structures and the sounding range involved in voicings with double alterations prohibits their use even when they are physically possible—which is seldom. However, any and all chord degrees that are present in a voicing must conform to the instructions contained in the chord symbol. Remember: Additions to chord structures are dangerous (major 7ths, 6ths, etc.), at least until after you have heard what is sounding around you. Alterations not indicated are madness; deletions are the norm, smart, sensible, and usually the most musical.

Because of all this, it is important to remember that the root and 5th are the most dispensable degrees of almost all types of chord structures. The 3rd is the most necessary. Like the frosting on a cake, more than one tension is nice if physically available, but it is certainly not a requisite.

Arpeggios—Four-Note F Chords

Chord Spelling

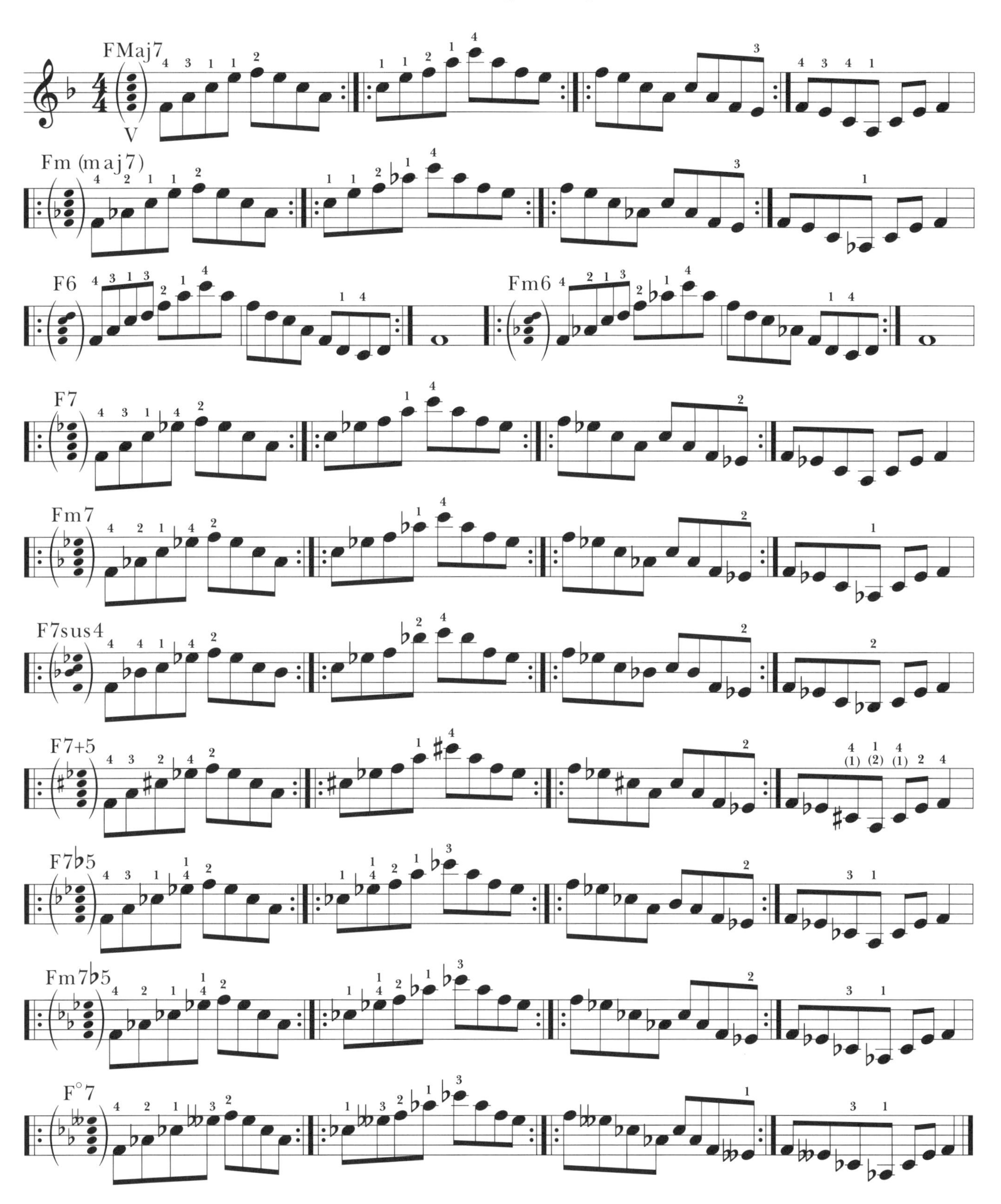

Arpeggios—Four-Note G Chords

Chord Spelling

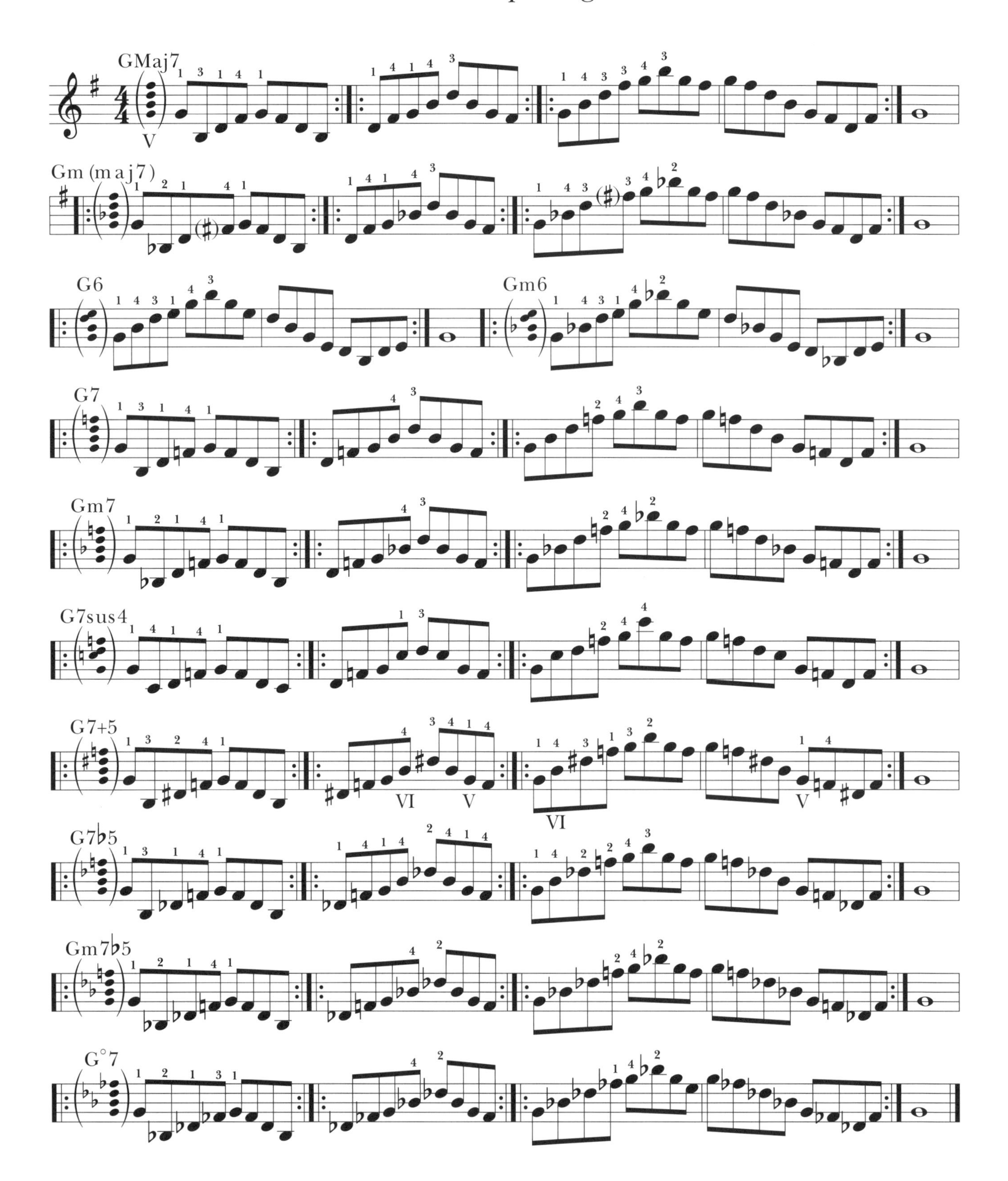

Chord-Scale Relationships—Dominant 7 Chords

For improvisation.

The Basic Idea: Chord-scale relationships are the result of alterations forced on the preceding scale sound by the actual construction of the chord itself.

An E7 chord occurring in the key of C major forces the G♮ to become G♯. Therefore until the occurrence of the next chord, you are functioning in the scale of A harmonic minor. An E7 chord occurring in F major alters the existing G♮ to G♯ and forces the B♭ to become B♮. Therefore, once again the scale for the duration of the E7 chord is A harmonic minor. An E7 chord occurring in the key of G raises the G to G♯, as in the previous examples, but when this G♯ is added to the F♯ that already exists in the scale, the sound that results is A real melodic minor.

EXAMPLES: Scales are named below each sequence of chords.

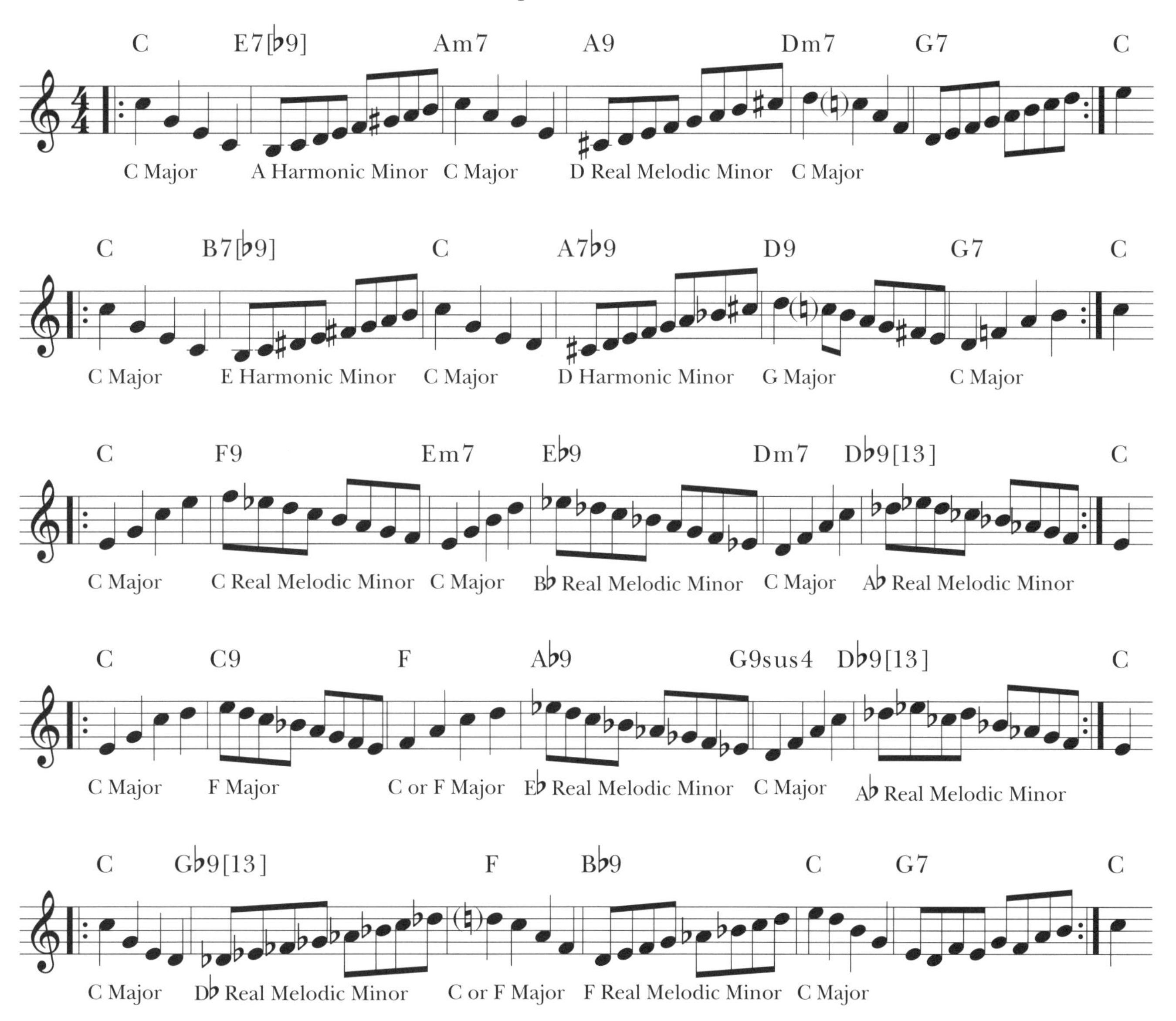

A more in-depth look at dominant 7 chord-scale relationships follows later.

Major Scales—Position V

Twelve keys—descending chromatically.

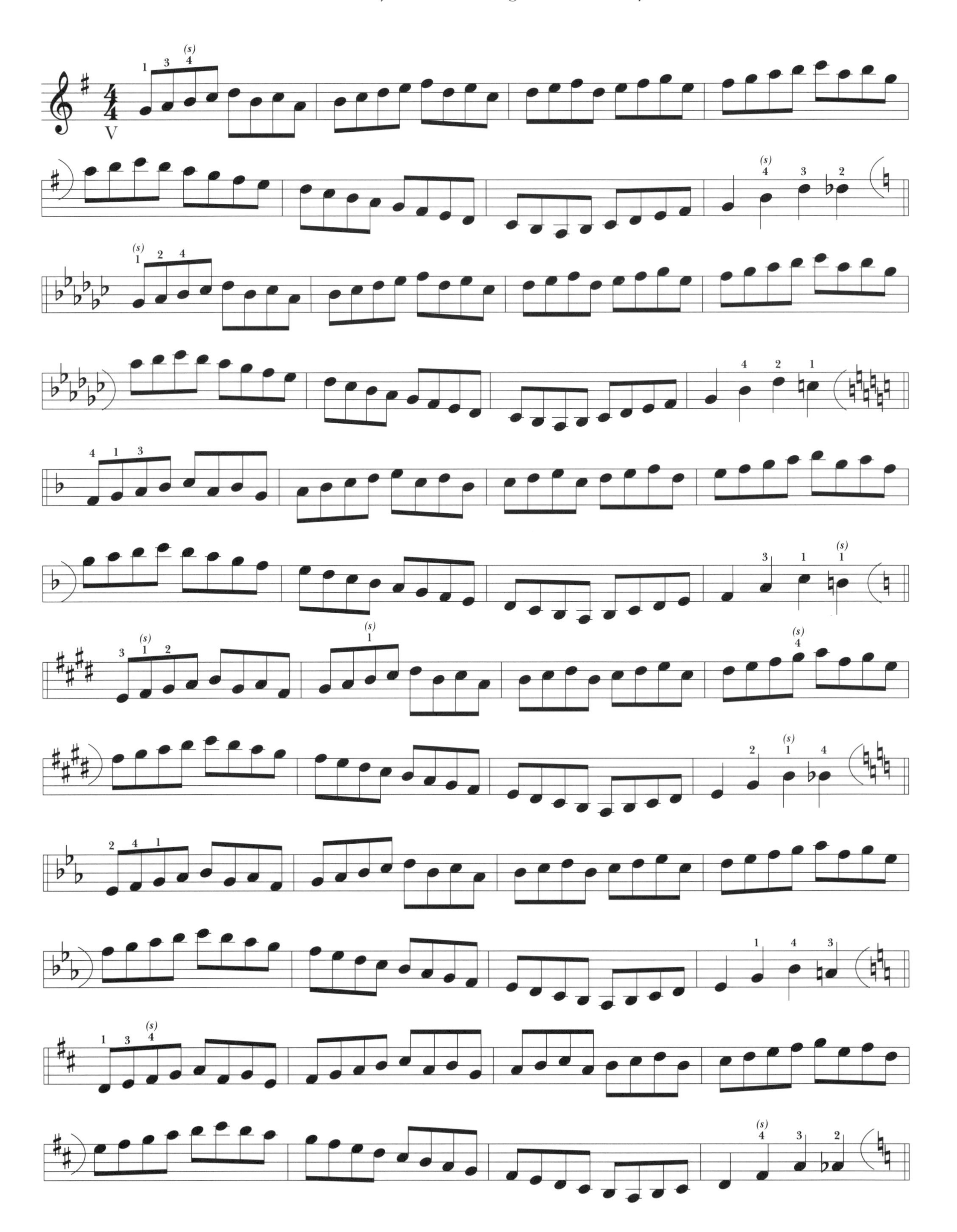

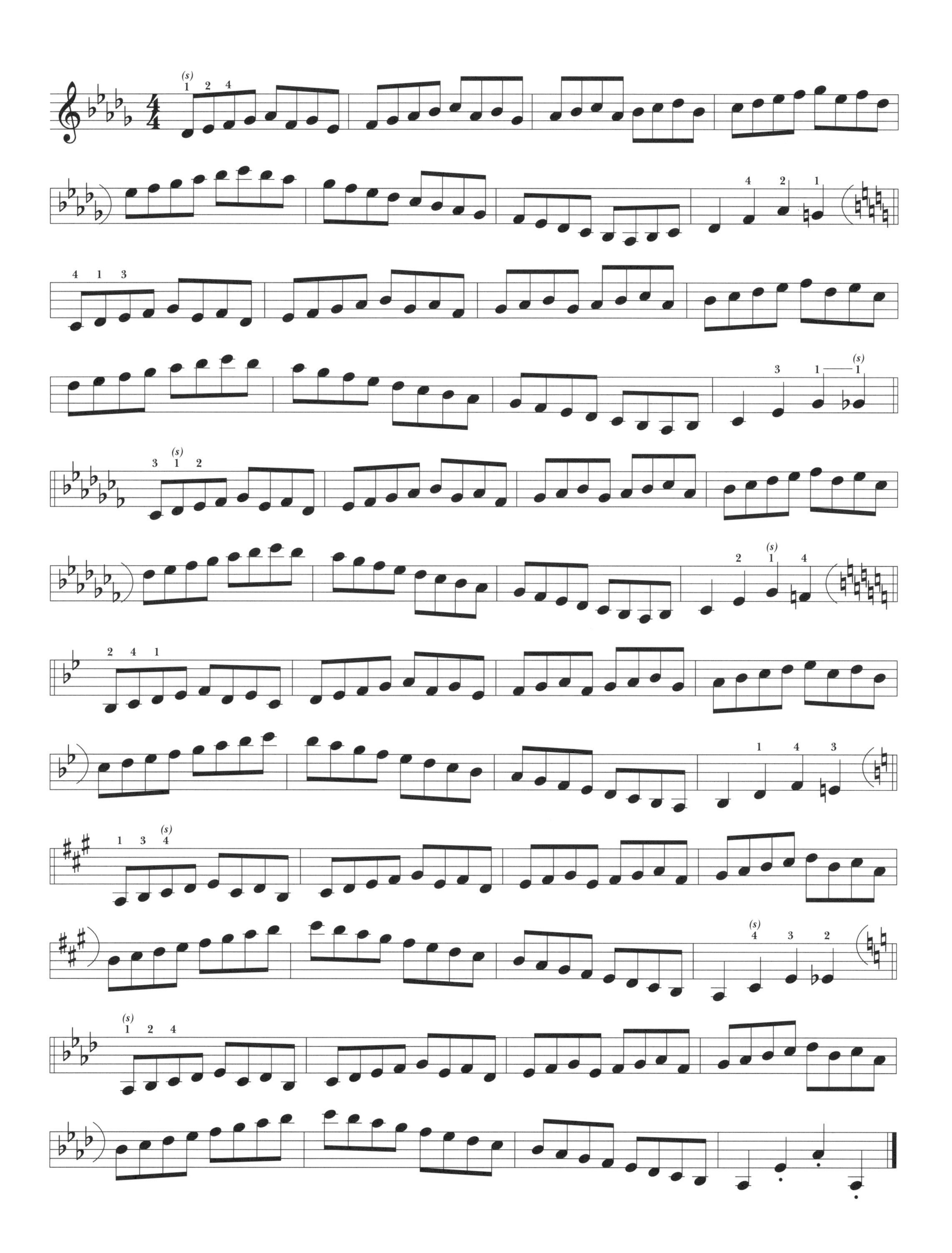
(s)
1 2 4
4 2 1
4 1 3
3 1 1
3 1 2
2 1 4
2 4 1
1 4 3
1 3 4
4 3 2
1 2 4

Principal Real Melodic Minor Scales—Position V

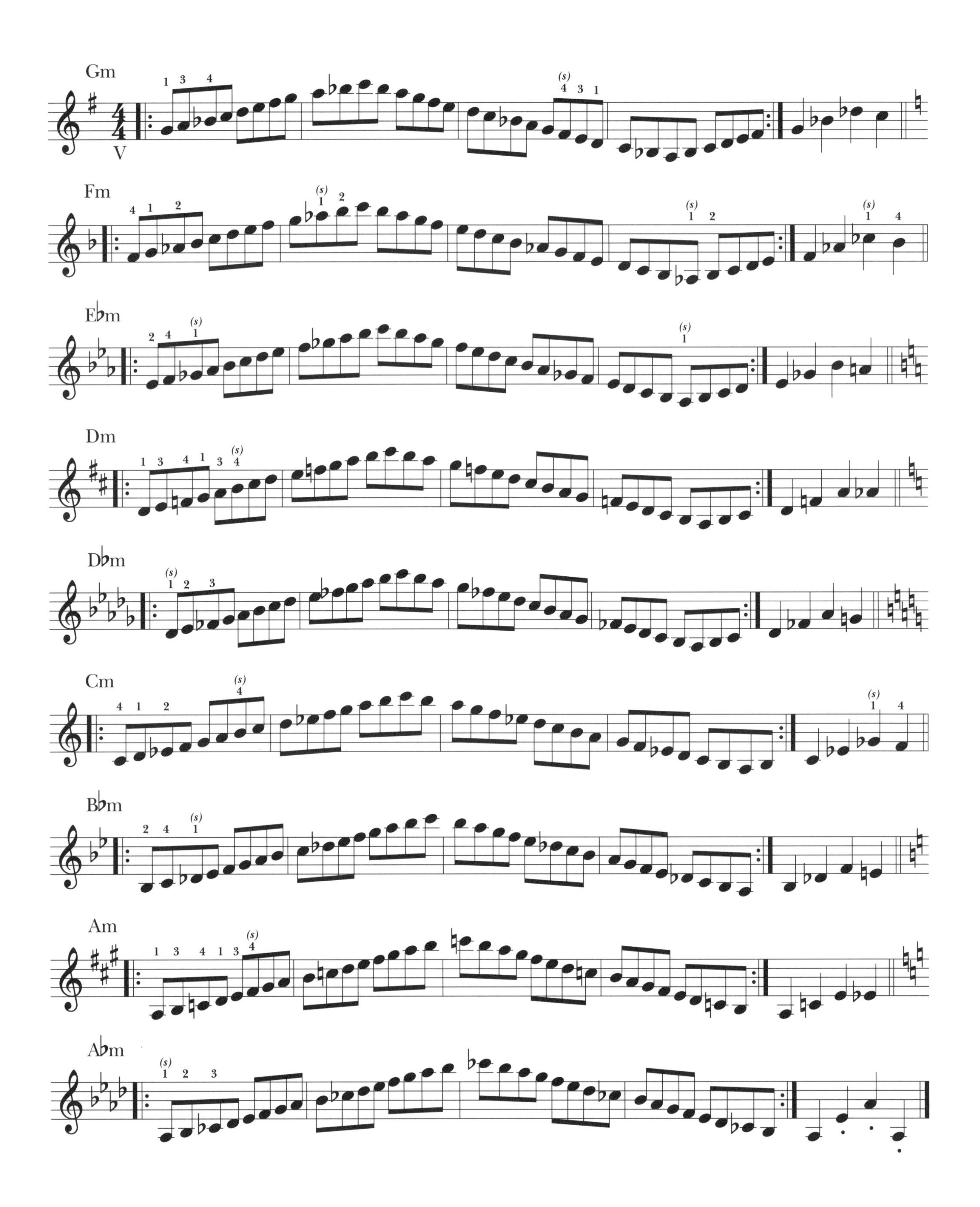

Chord Construction—Three-Note Voicings

Melodization of Tonic Major Chords

Melodic degrees

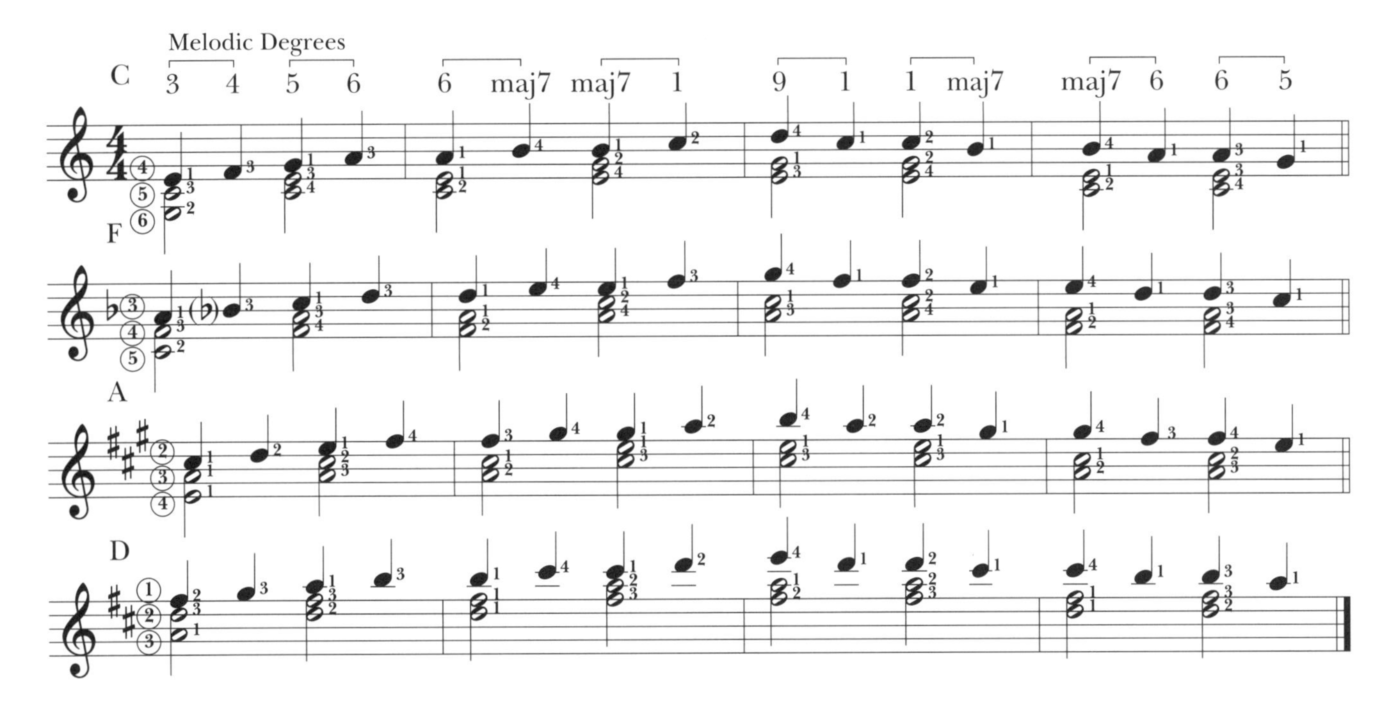

To melodize the above as subdominant (IV) chords, sharp the 4th degree.

Melodization of Tonic and Subdominant Minor 6 Chords

Melodic degrees

Diminished Scales—In Position

The diminished scale is made up of intervals 2, 1, 2, 1, 2, 1, 2, 1, 2, etc. Practice very carefully, as this uniformity produces a rather strange sound. Each fingering pattern contains at least one double stretch, indicated by 1 2 3 4 or 4 3 2 1. This extending of the 1st and 4th fingers may feel awkward at first, but it will prove very valuable for future scale situations. Remember: Stretch the fingers; don't move the hand.

The primary use of diminished scales in improvisation is over diminished 7 chords. When descending, it sounds better if you start on a high degree (or non-chord tone) of the diminished chord. When ascending, start from any note of the scale.

G°/B♭°/D♭°/E°
FINGERING PATTERN 1

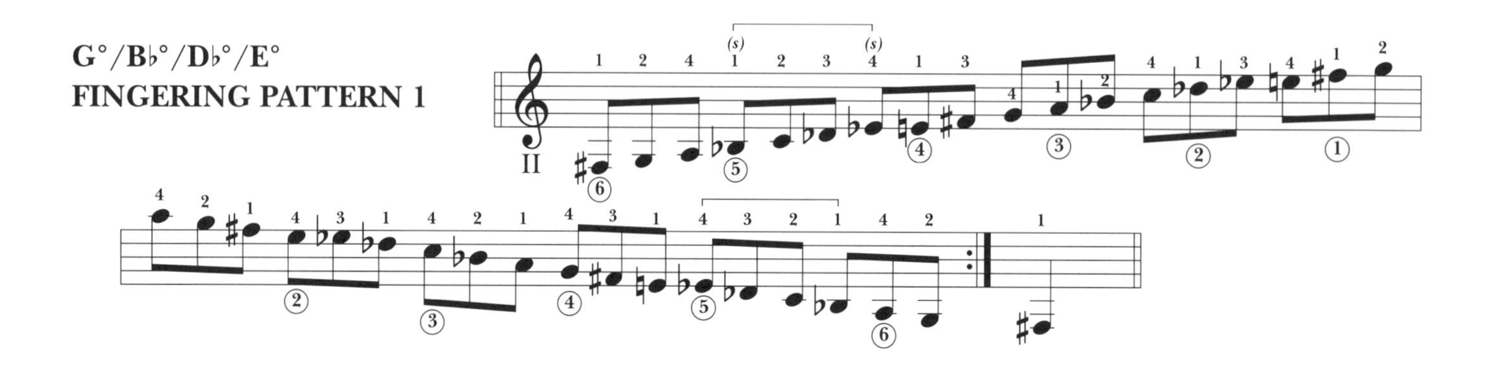

FINGERING PATTERN 2

Fingering pattern 2 employs the double stretch on strings 4 and 2.

G°/B♭°/D♭°/E°

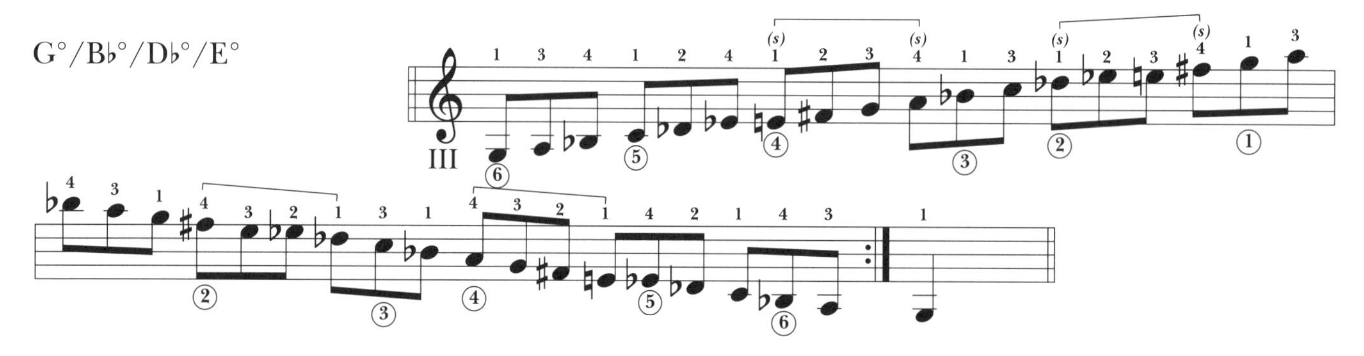

FINGERING PATTERN 3

Fingering pattern 3 employs the double stretch on strings 6 and 1.

G°/B♭°/D♭°/E°

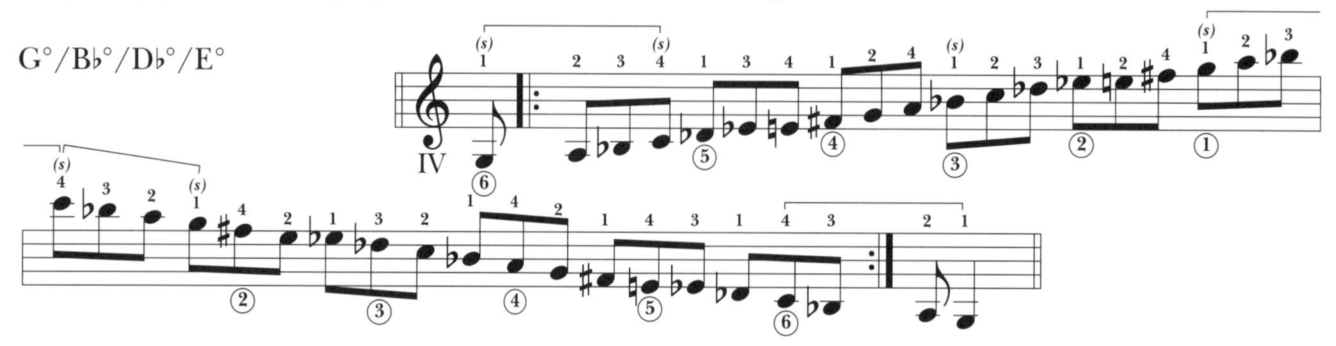

Memorize the fingering patterns. Practice all diminished scales, in all positions.

Practice as follows:

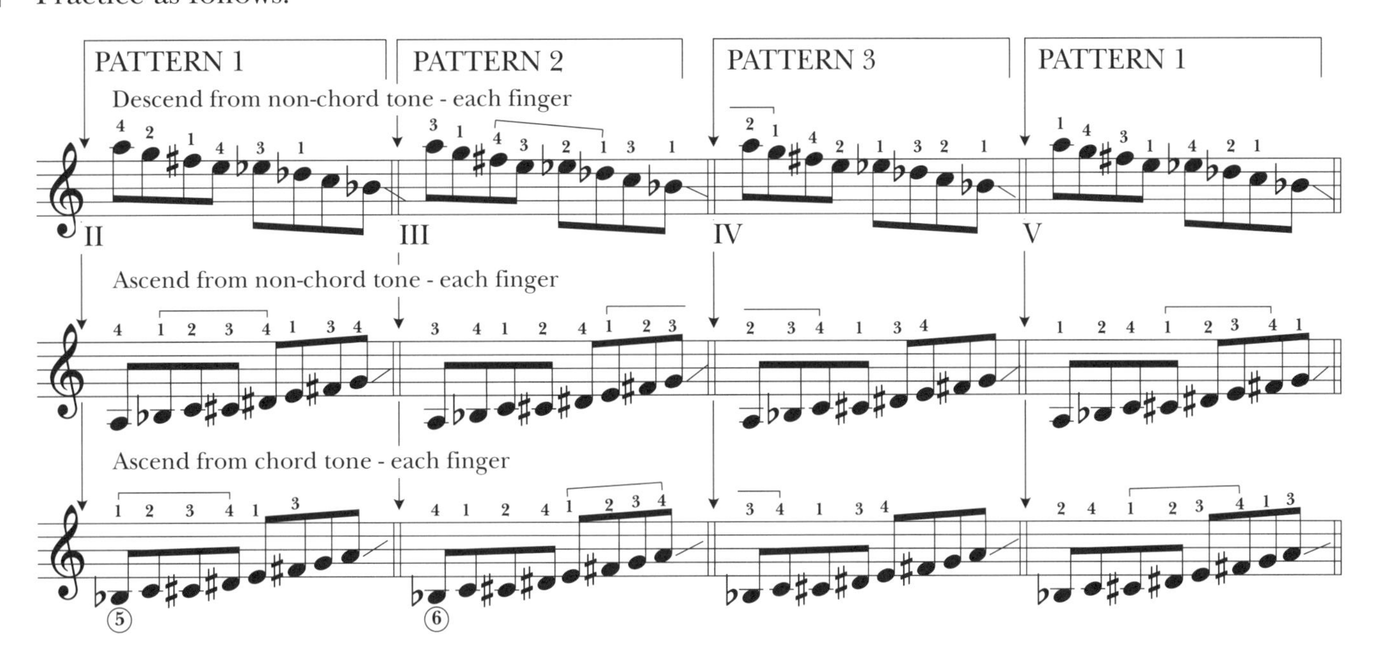

EXAMPLES OF APPLICATION FOR IMPROVISATION:

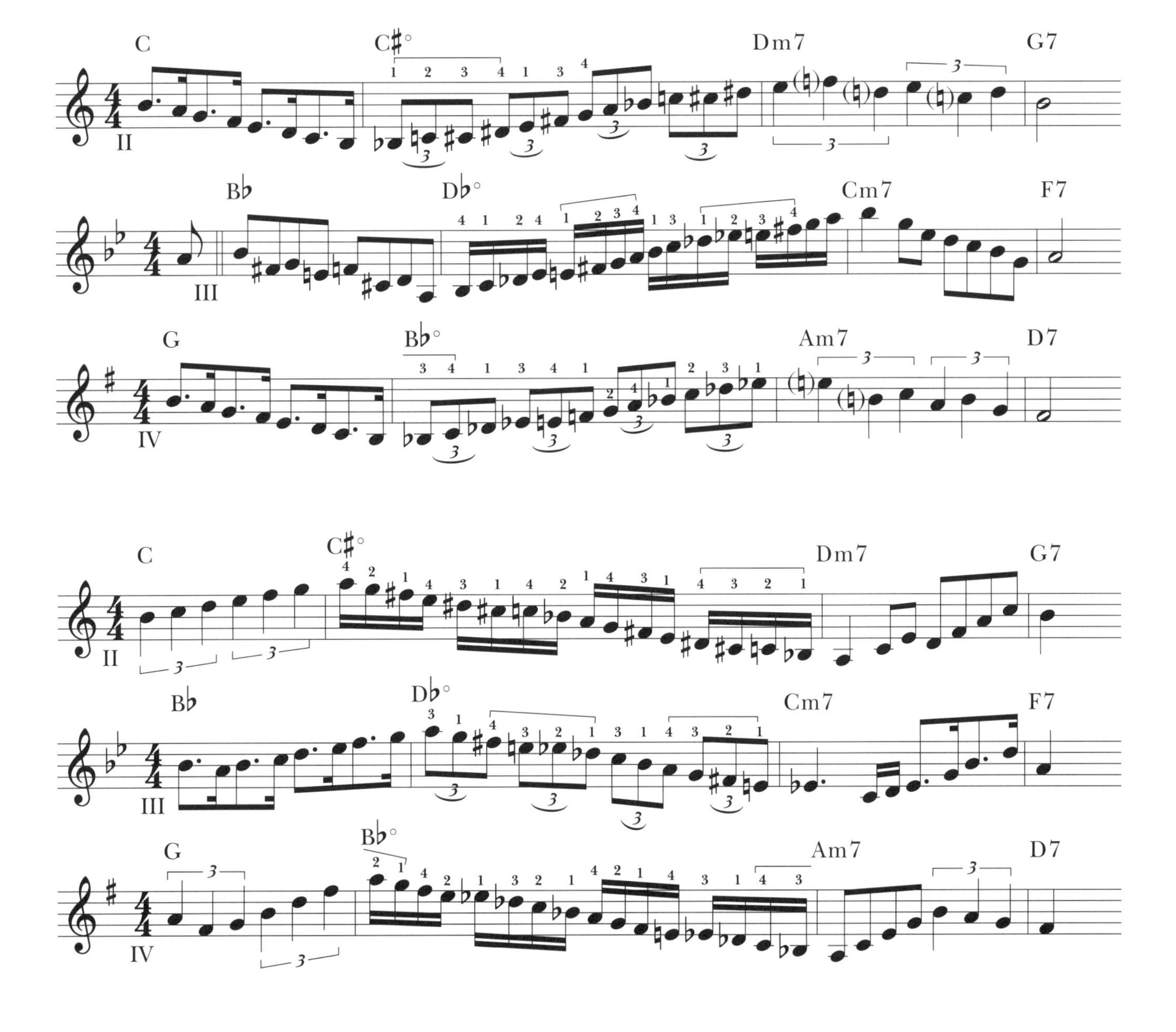

ANOTHER EXAMPLE OF APPLICATION:

- Treating (cycle 5) dominant 7 progressions like a chromatic sequence of diminished 7 chords.

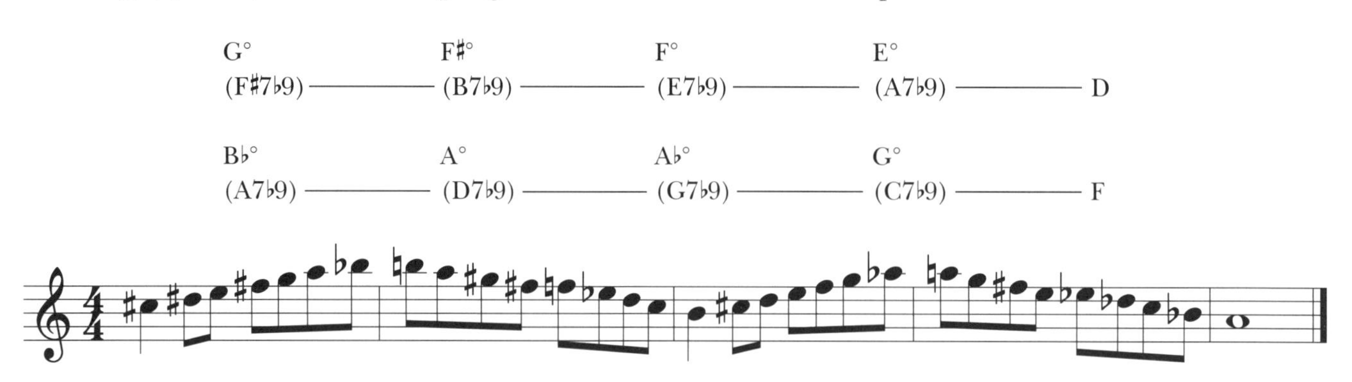

ADDITIONAL DIMINISHED SCALE FINGERINGS:

- Constant fingering: one position change (two octaves; no stretches)

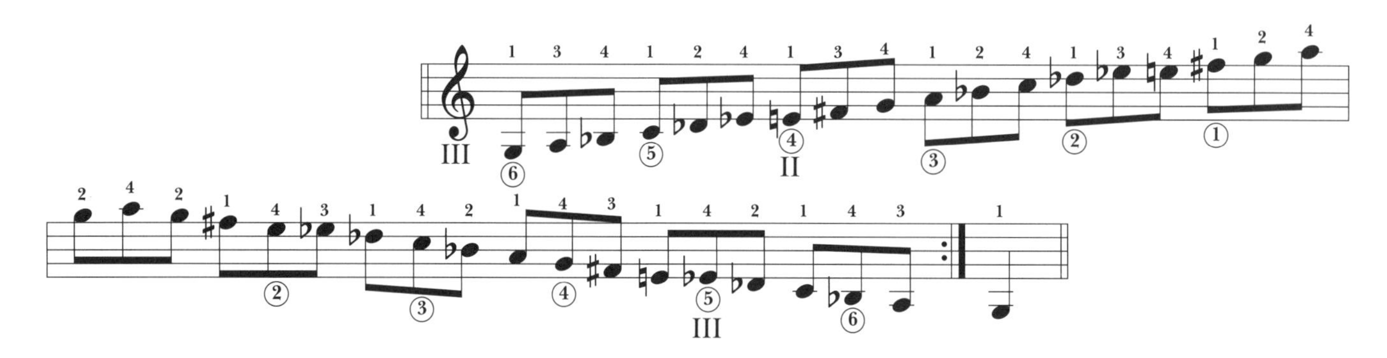

- Constant fingering: double stretch and position change on every string (three octaves)

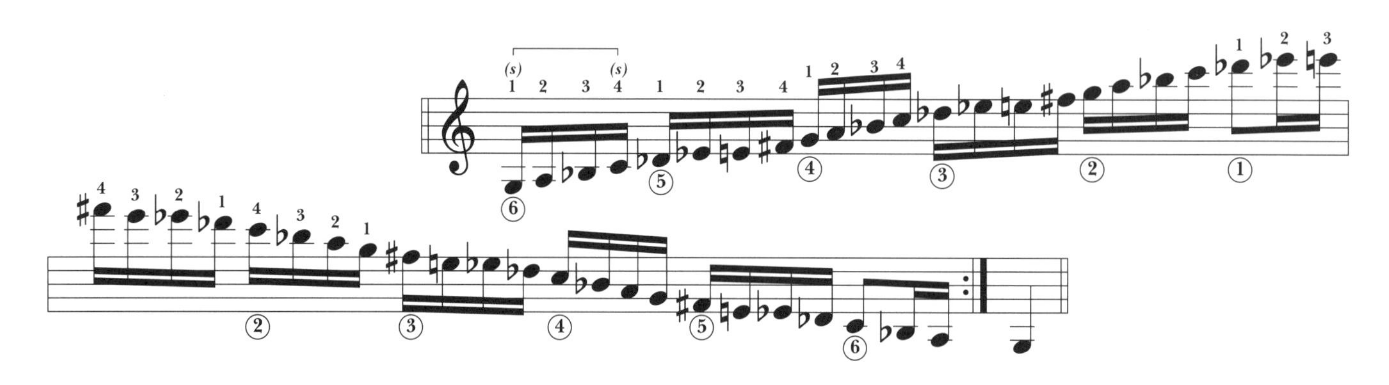

These additional fingerings are less practical for general use.

Chord Construction—Three-Note Voicings

Dominant 7 Chords

A complete dominant 7 chord contains four notes. To construct three-note voicings that accurately represent its sound, chord degrees 3 and ♭7 must be present. These two notes of the dominant 7 chord are called the tritone, as they are three whole steps apart. They form the unstable element that causes the restless sound and the need to resolve by moving on to another chord.

PREPARATION OF CLOSE VOICINGS

Recognition of Melodic Degrees—Dominant 7 Chords

Speed Study

▮ Play thirteen times as written, but each time with a new key signature.

✱ Sequence of key signatures through cycle 5

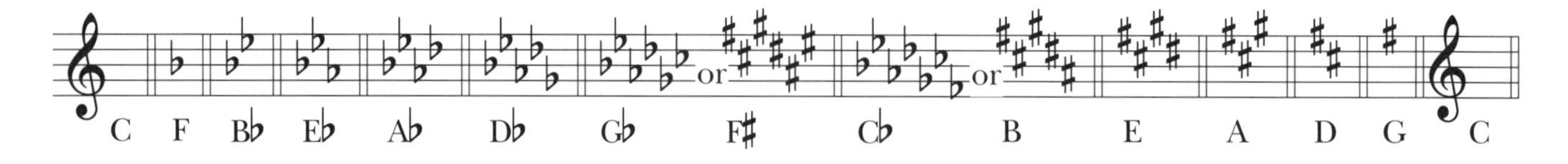

Also practice with minor scales. Nine of each are possible now, but all will be possible later.
Real Melodic Minor: Start with A (major with ♭3), then D, G, etc, through D♭.
Harmonic Minor: Start with (G major) E natural minor and add leading tone.

Arpeggios—Four-Note B♭ Chords

Chord Spelling

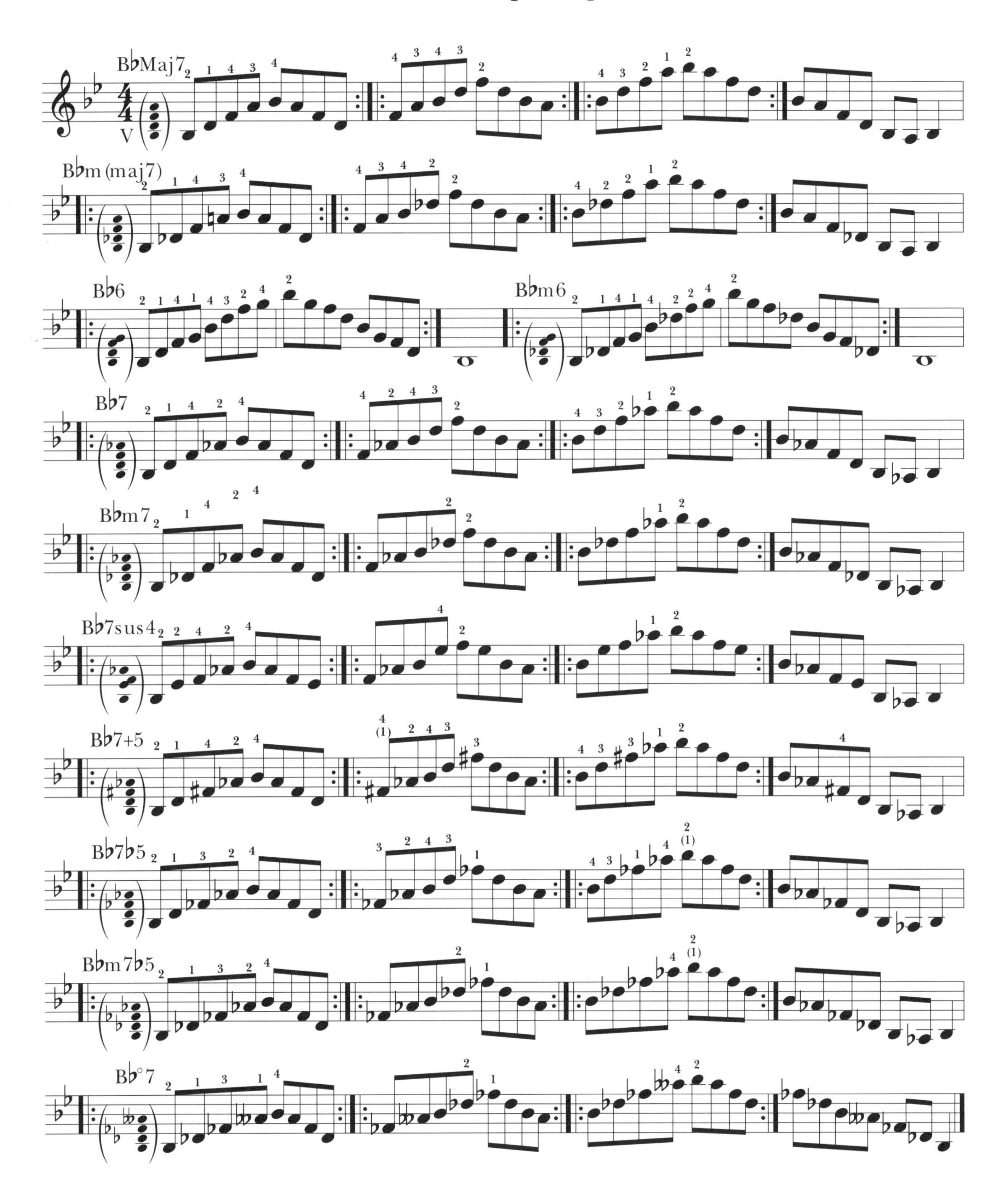

Arpeggios—Four-Note D Chords

Chord Spelling

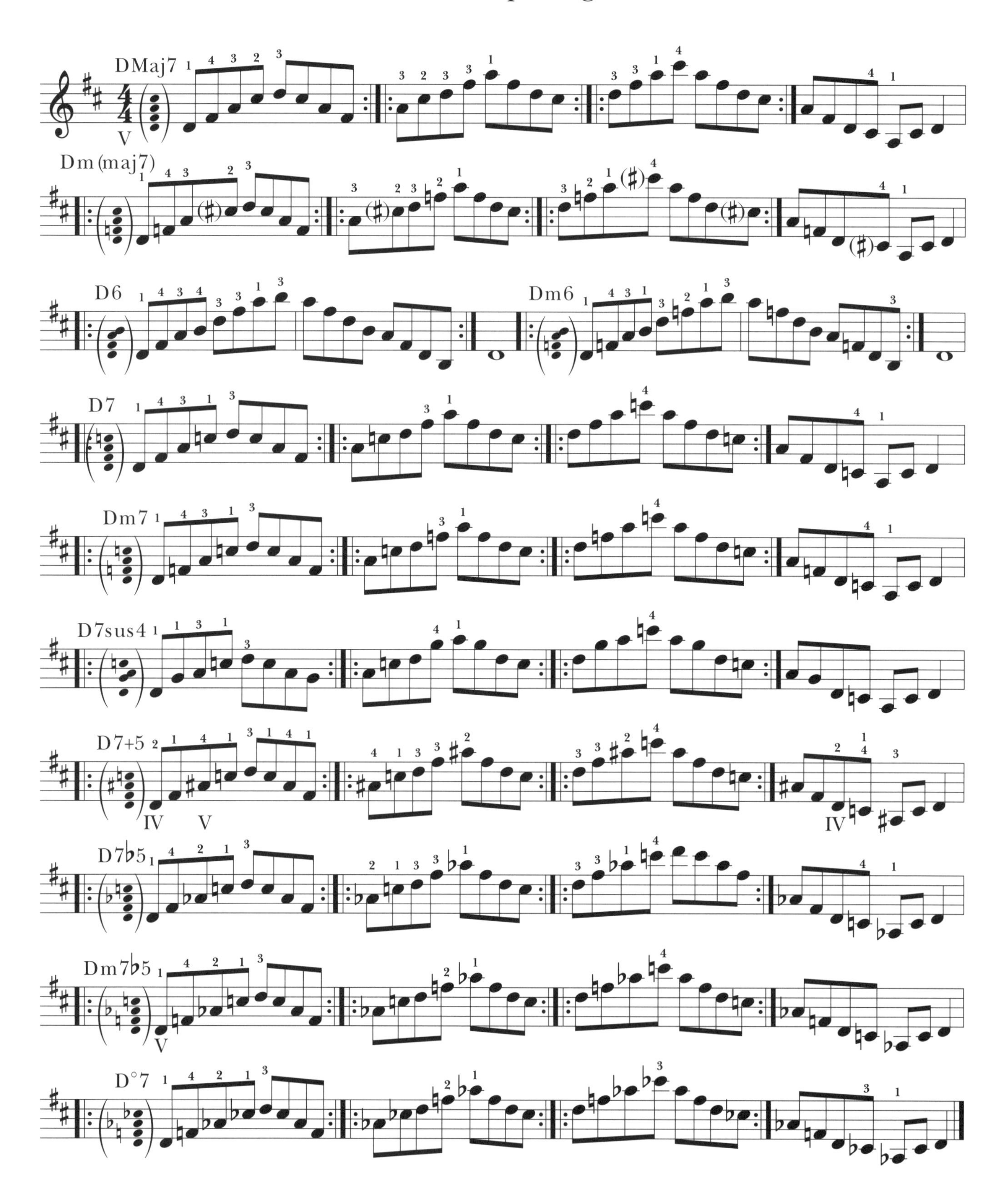

Melodic Rhythm Study No. 9 (duet)

Rhythm Guitar—The Right Hand

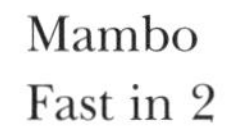

Variation

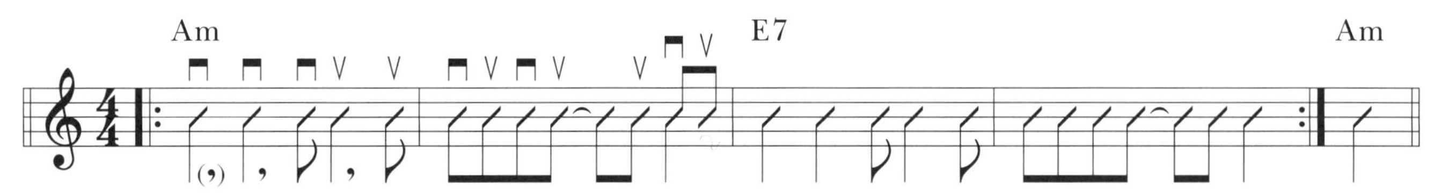

Bolero
Moderate 4

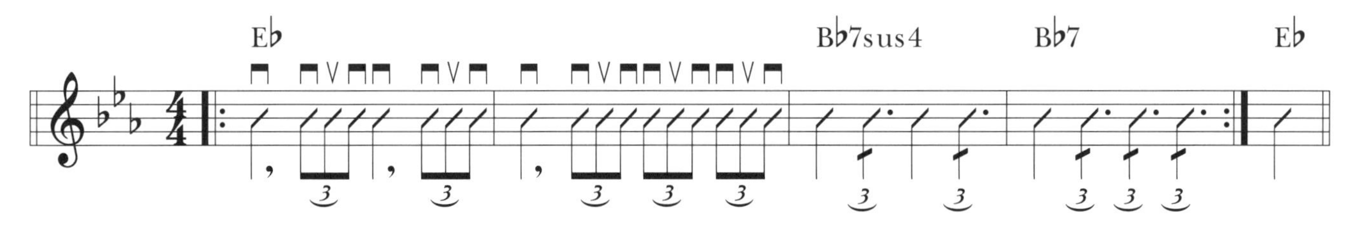

Fast 4

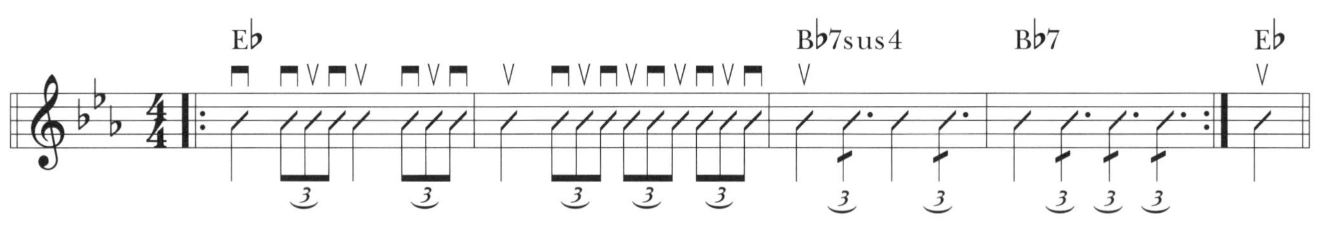

Conga
Moderate 2

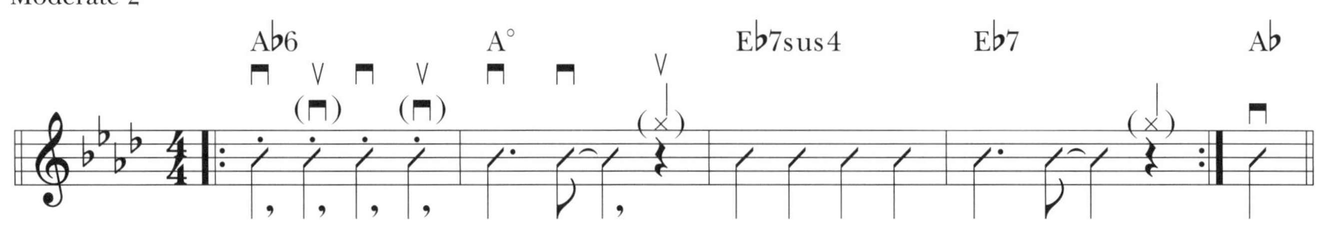

F Major Scale (Twelve Positions)

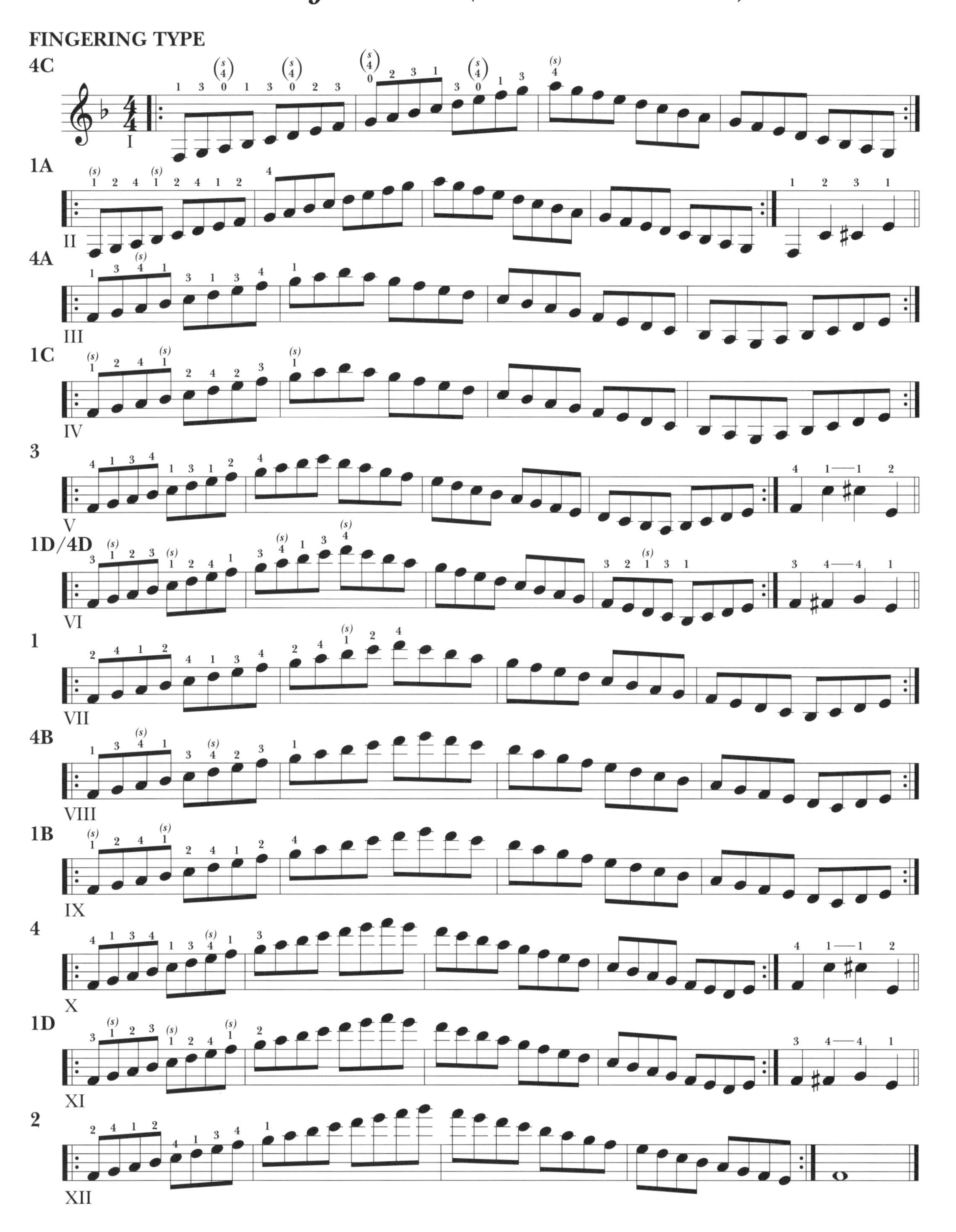

D Harmonic Minor (Nine Positions)

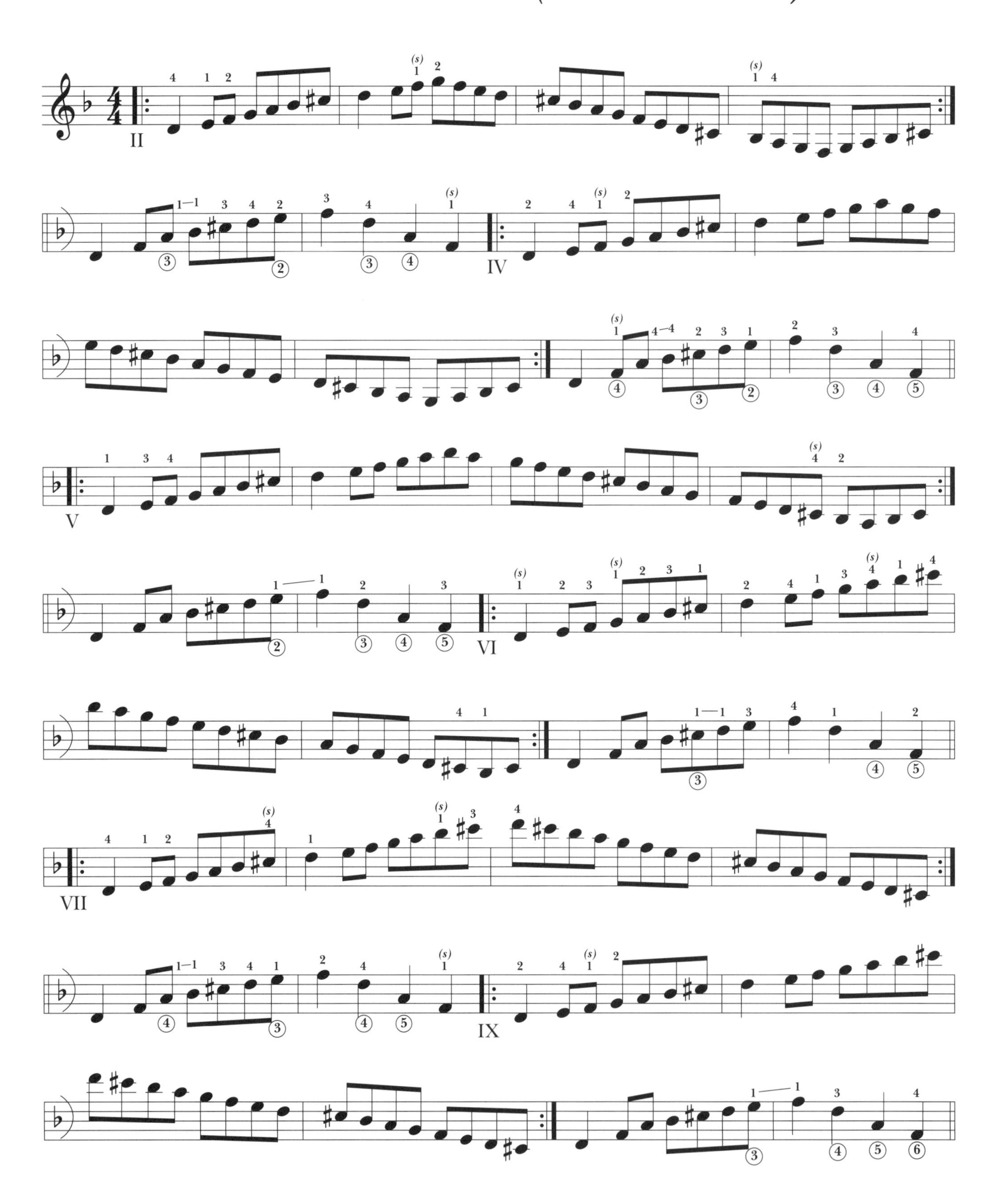

Etude in D Minor (solo)

Melodic Embellishment

For improvisation.

The Appoggiatura: Temporary replacement of a note by a note that is one step above and/or below it.

The following exercises are based on three-note arpeggios. However, by extracting from all chords the smaller structures contained within them, the following has unlimited application.

Practice with all possible fingerings. Use finger stretches as often as possible; use slides only when absolutely necessary.

CHROMATIC APPROACH FROM BELOW: DIRECT RESOLUTION TO CHORD TONE

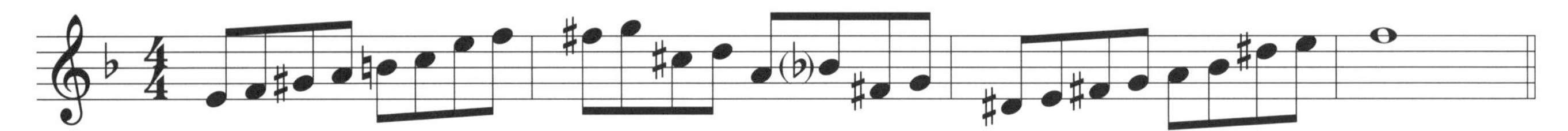

SCALE TONE APPROACH FROM ABOVE: DIRECT RESOLUTION TO CHORD TONE

INDIRECT CHROMATIC APPROACH: RESOLUTION DELAYED BY INSERTION OF SCALE TONE

INDIRECT SCALE TONE APPROACH: RESOLUTION DELAYED BY INSERTION OF CHROMATIC APPROACH

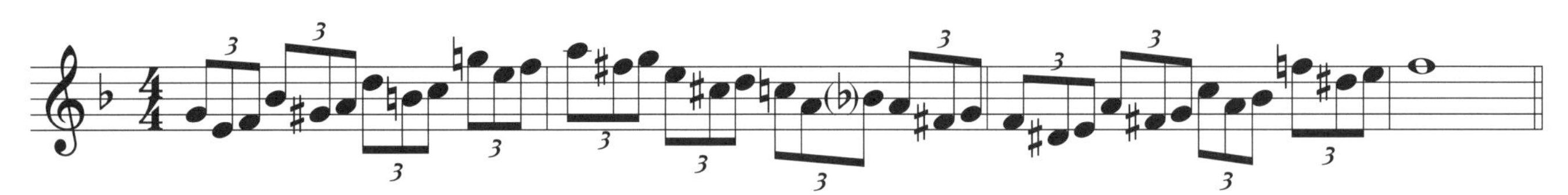

COMBINATION 1: ALTERNATING CHROMATIC AND SCALE TONE APPROACHES

COMBINATION 2: CHORD DEGREES NOT IN CONSECUTIVE ORDER; APPROACHES MIXED

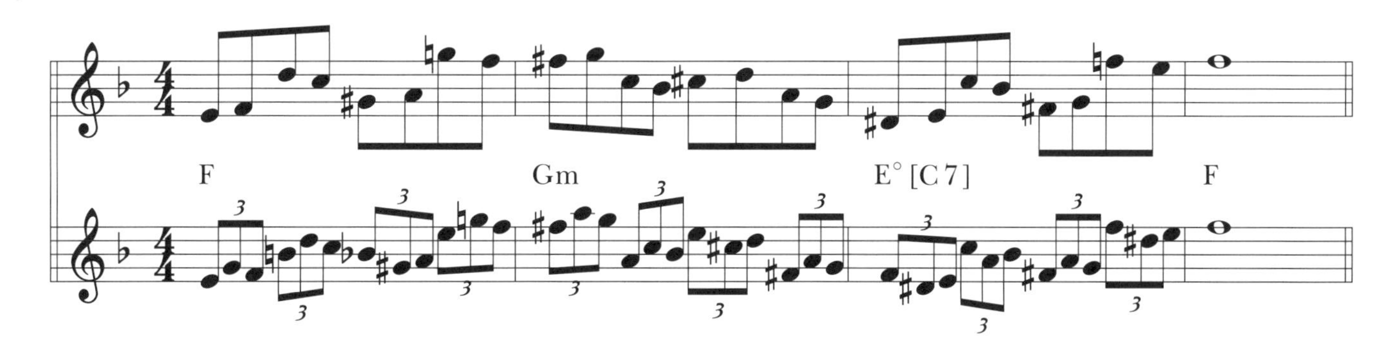

- Many other combinations await your discovery.

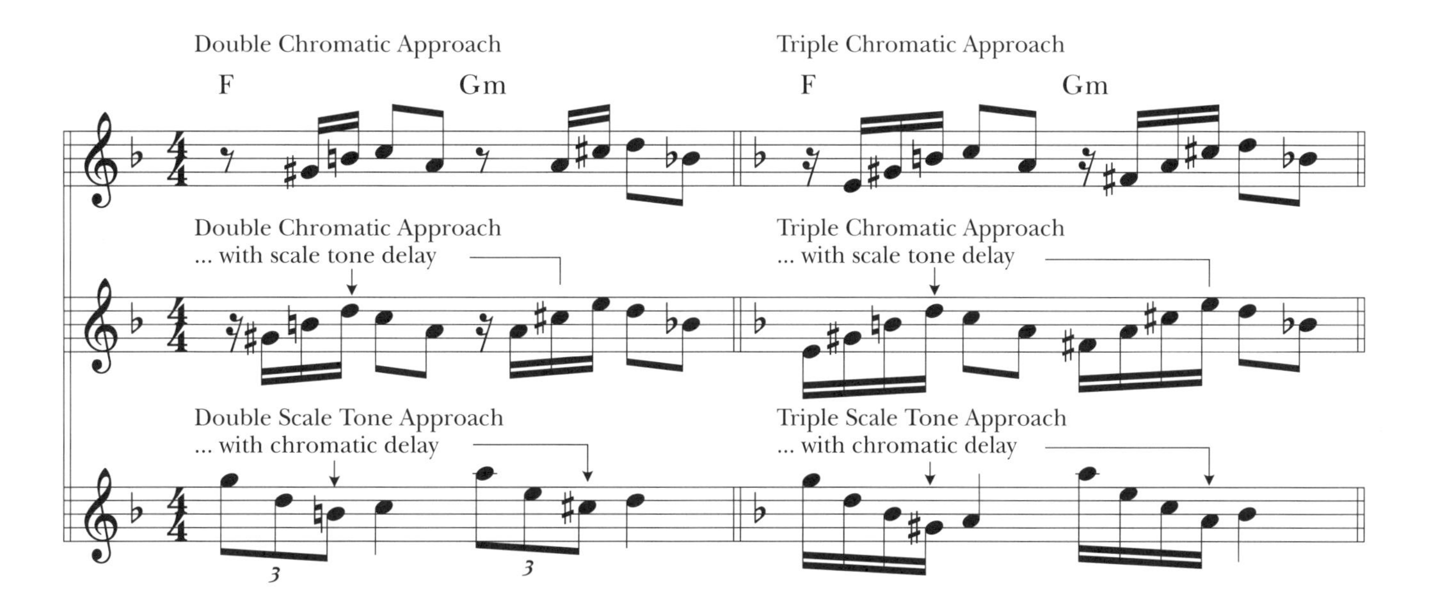

Rhythm Guitar—The Right Hand

5/4 Swing

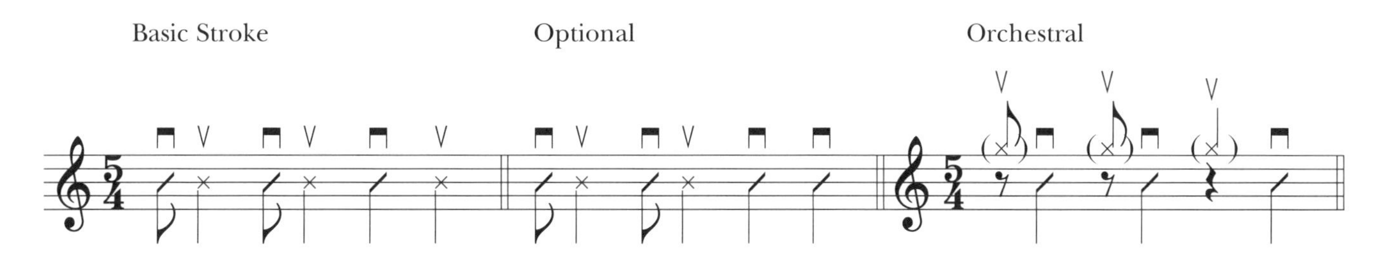

About Altered Chords and Chord Degrees

4th

The sus4 (suspended 4th) means that the 4th degree replaces the 3rd in all major and dominant 7 structures. The 3rd is available only as a melodic passing tone.

With minor chords, sus4 may replace or be used with ♭3. (See 11th, below.)

5th

When the 5th is specifically indicated as sharped or flatted on dominant 7 chords, you might assume that it is truly altered, but this is not so. Rather often the real meaning of a written ♭5 is +11, and ♯5 is ♭13. (See +11 and ♭13.)

When improvising, the player frequently can choose whether to raise or lower the 5th. Sometimes, it may be slightly imperfect theoretically, but ultimately it will be more musical.

For example, when the 5th is sharped, it may be treated melodically as a ♭13, and the normal 5th is used as a passing tone. When the 5th is flatted, it may be treated melodically as a +11, and the 5th is used as a passing tone.

With minor 7 chords, a specifically raised or lowered 5th does in fact represent a truly altered 5th degree.

9th

When the 9th is specifically flatted or sharped, it is truly altered harmonically and melodically. The ♯9 is sometimes melodically treated as ♭3. Alt 9 occurs with dominant 7 chords only.

11th

The 11th with dominant 7 structures is actually an enharmonically named sus4, but it indicates the possible presence of 9 and ♭7 in the voicing. An 11th chord therefore is a dominant 9sus4.

The 11th with minor chords represents the addition of another degree to the total structure, as it may be used with the ♭3 and/or 5, ♭7, and 9.

The augmented 11th (♯11, +11, 11+) exists only with major and dominant 7 chords. It is an added degree to the total structure (of 1, 3, 5, 7, 9) and is used with the 3rd. It does not necessarily replace any chord degree. It is often misleadingly called ♭5.

13th

The ♭13 is actually an enharmonically named ♯5. It cannot be used harmonically with a normal 5th, but it does not represent an altered 5th.

It is called ♭13 to indicate that the normal 5th is to be used as a melodic passing tone. The ♭13 is often misleadingly named ♯5. (13ths can occur only in dominant 7 chords.)

Whenever ♭13 seems to exist on a minor 7 chord, you are actually dealing with a I-for-IIIm7 situation. The appearance of an open voicing of the I chord with the 3rd in the bass, the root in the lead, and the sound brightened up with the 9th inside may mislead you into thinking otherwise. Probably the best name for this structure is minor 7 (add ♭6).

Arpeggios—Four-Note E♭ Chords

Chord Spelling

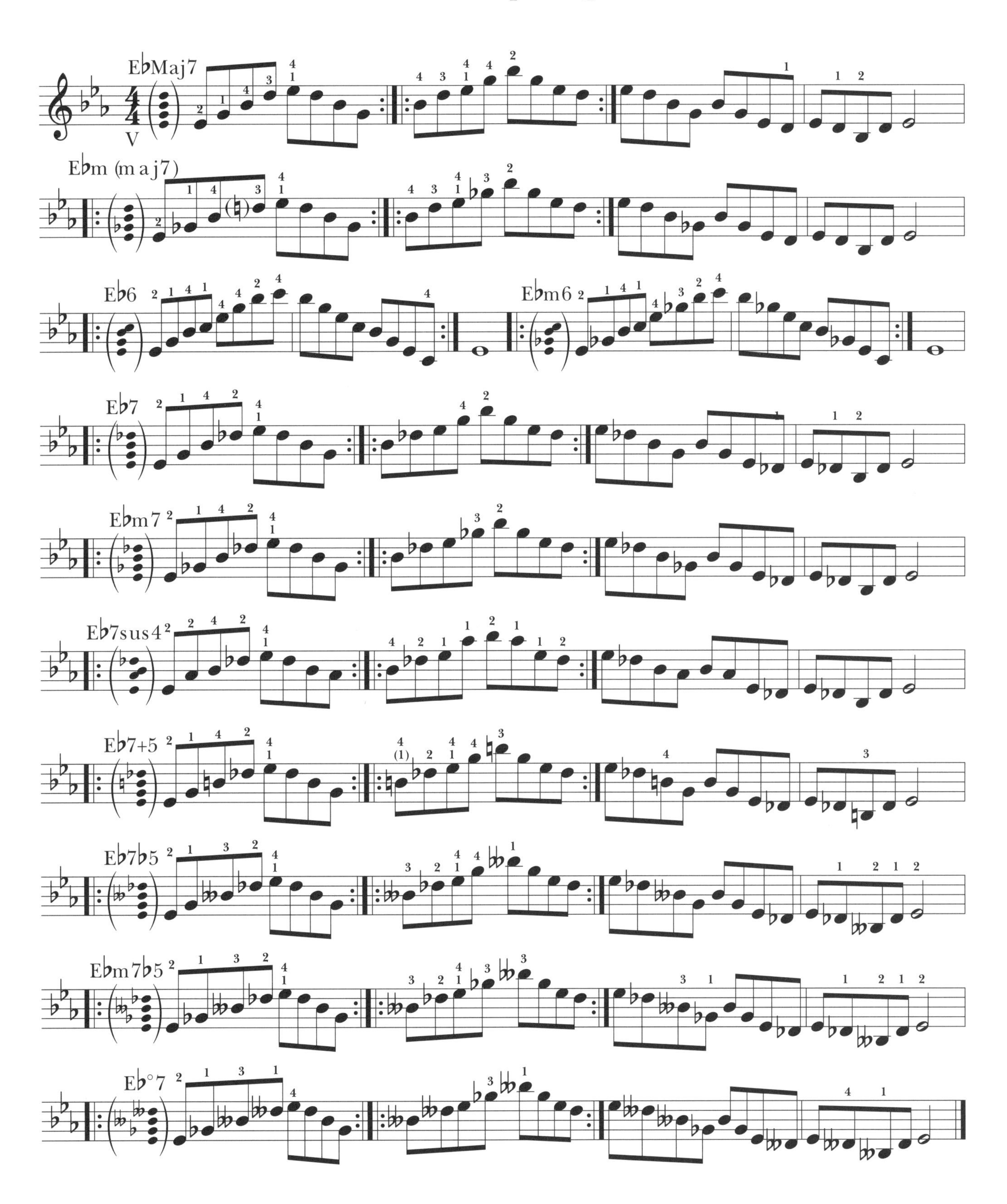

Arpeggios—Four-Note A Chords

Chord Spelling

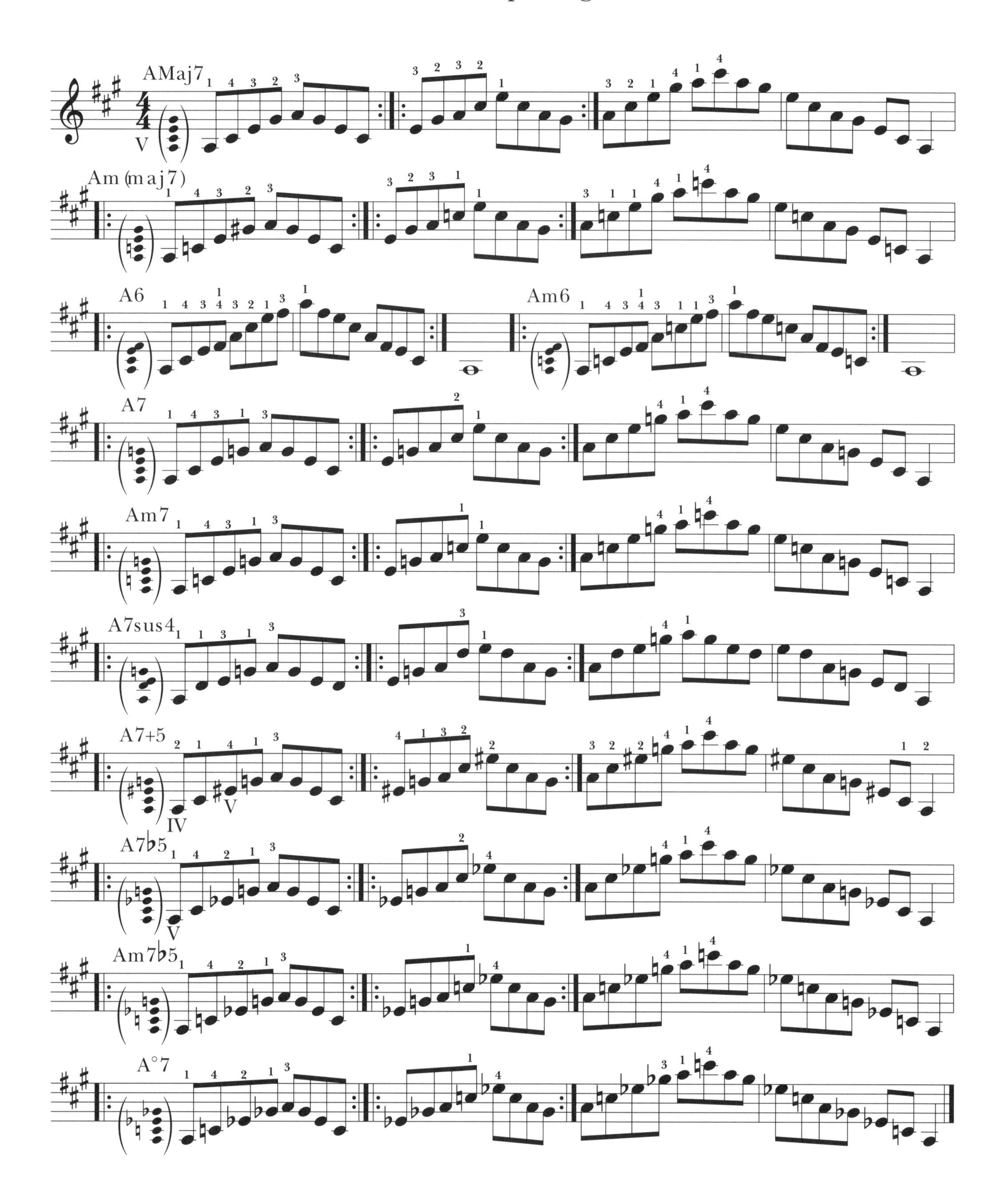

Chord Construction—Three-Note Voicings

Melodization of Dominant 7 Chords

Melodic degrees: Major scale from intended tonic

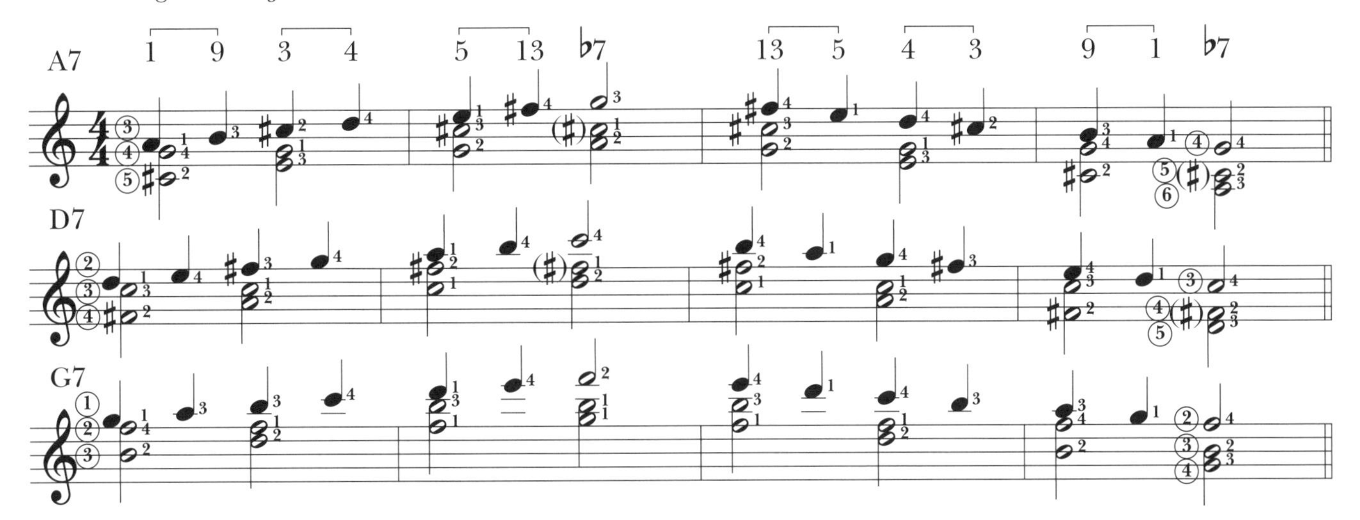

Once the dominant 7 sound has been established, voicings may be used in passing that do not contain the 3 and ♭7. The ear has a tendency to retain this sound.

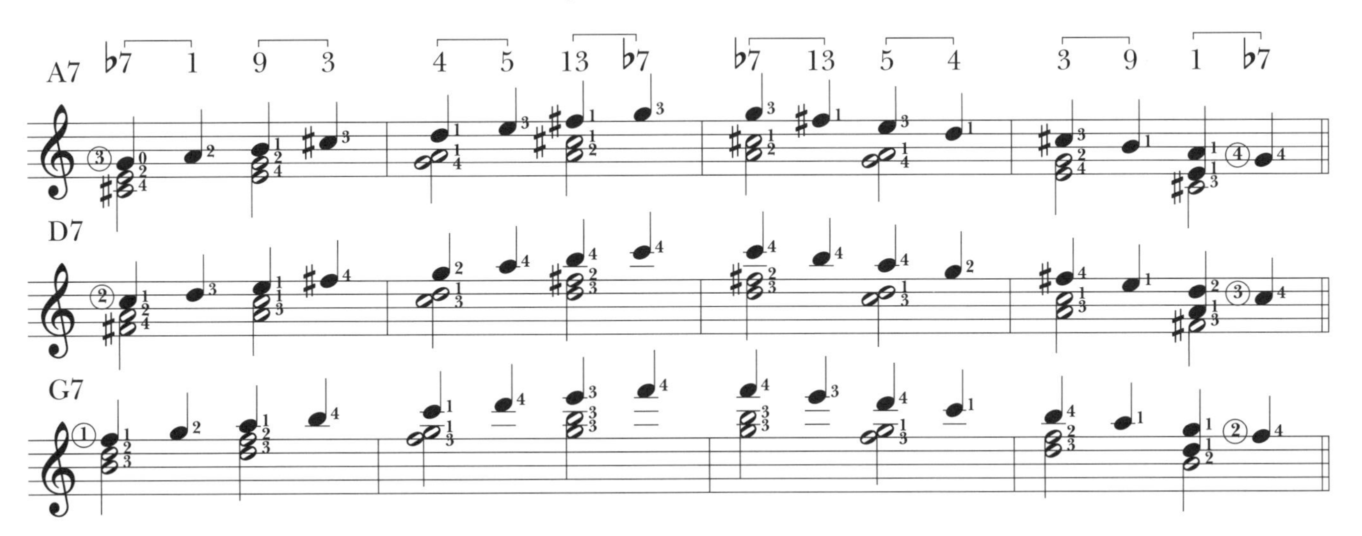

Important: Because of their mobility, three-note voicings are very valuable for chord melody playing, for harmonized fills, and for comping. They are shown melodized according to chord-scale relationships and can really open up the harmonic/melodic potential of the guitar.

Melodization of I Minor Chords with Harmonic Minor Scale

Melodic degrees: Harmonic minor scale from chord name

Arpeggio Study—Seventh Chords

- Play from all fingers, but stay in position throughout the entire sequence.

* Also play the first chord of each measure as a minor 7 chord.

Melodic Rhythm Study No. 10 (duet)

Major Scales—Position VII

Twelve keys—ascending chromatically.

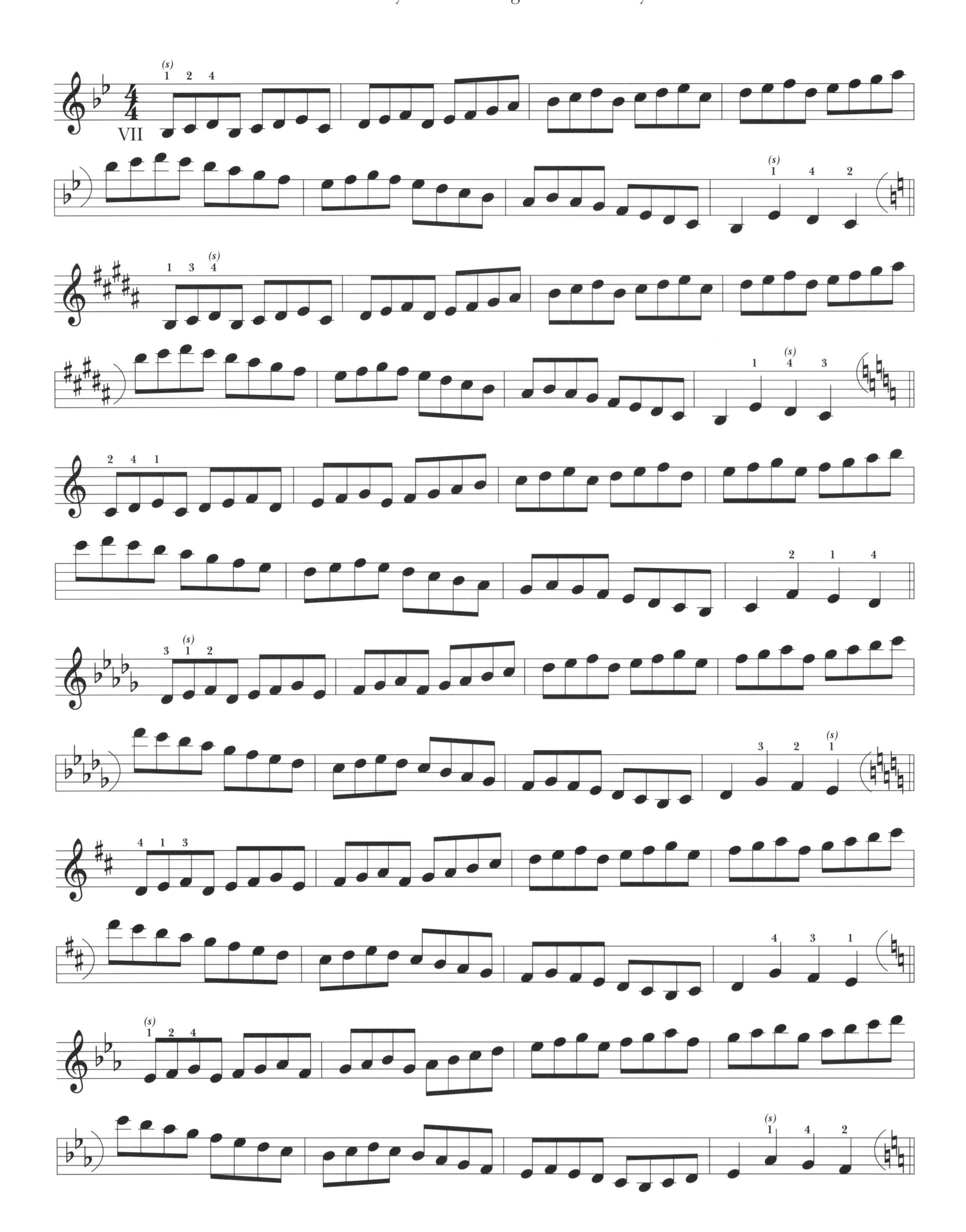

Principal Real Melodic Minor Scales—Position VII

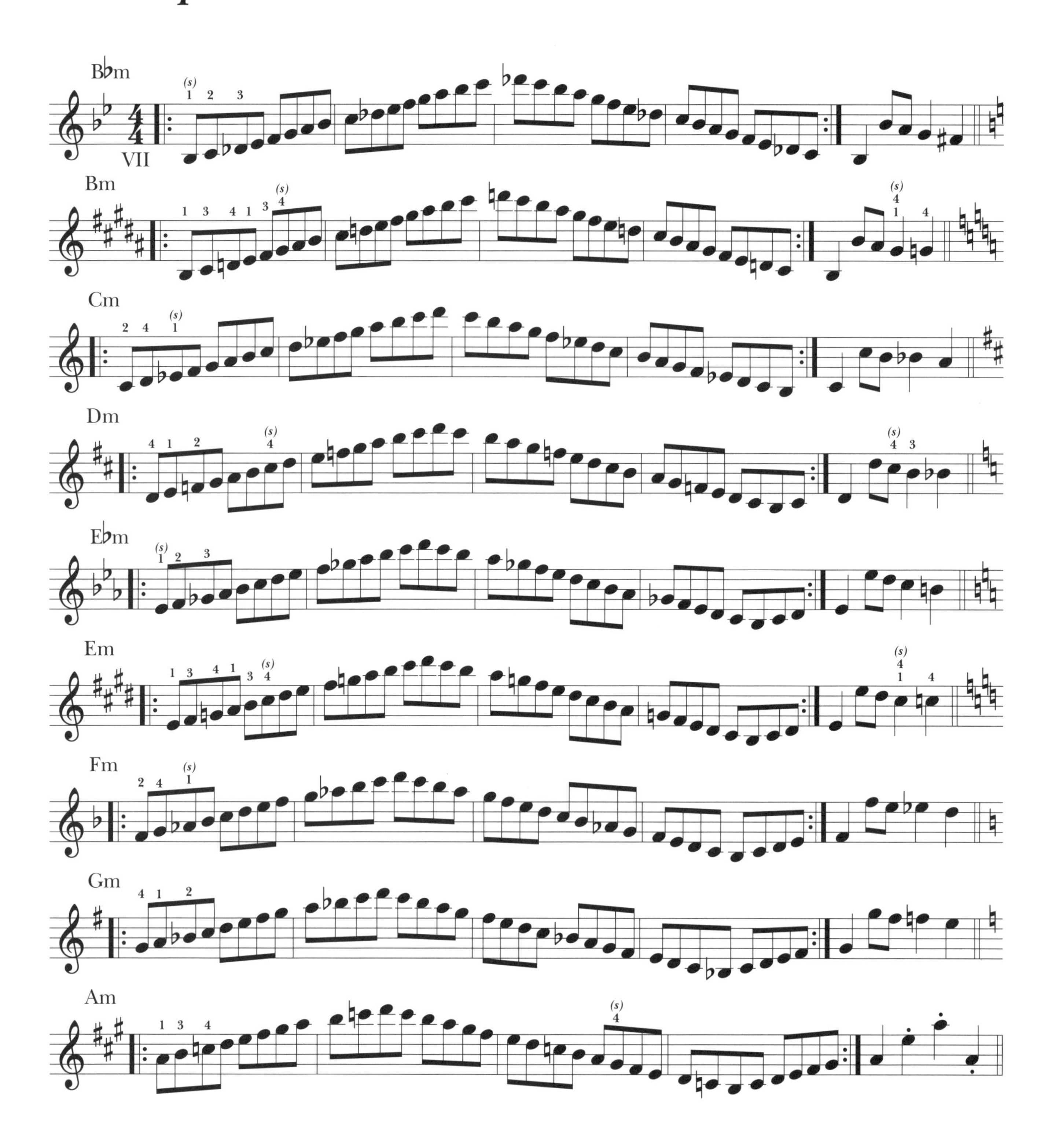

Chords—Three-Note Voicings

Melodization of Diminished Triads

Melodic degrees: Diminished scale (chord tones plus notes a whole step above and/or a half step below them).

- Fingering is constant if the sequence is played on the same set of strings.

Open Voicings

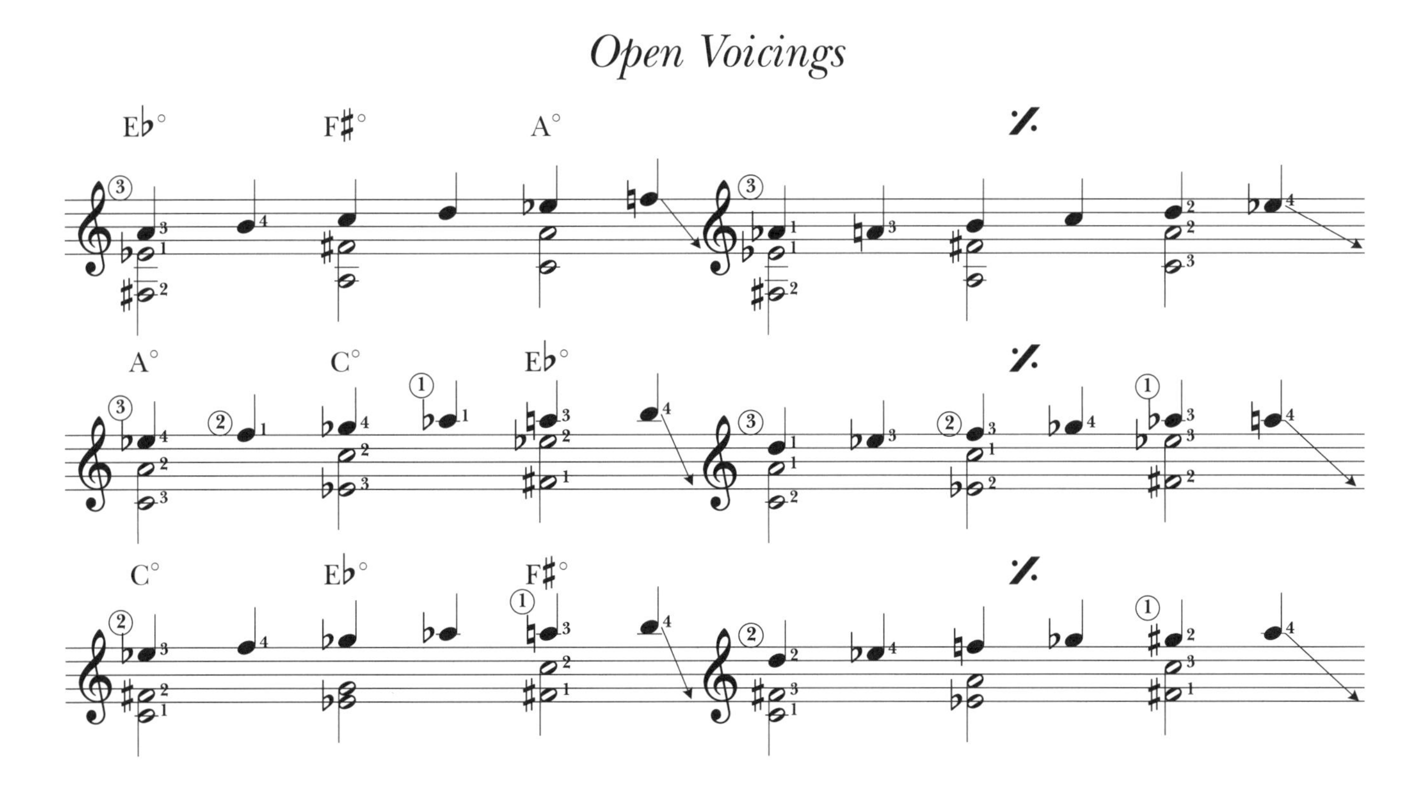

As we deal almost exclusively with diminished 7 chords, all of the preceding sequences may be played with any of the letter names that make up the four-note diminished 7 structure.

Melodization of Augmented Triads

Melodic degrees: Whole tone scale (chord tones plus notes a whole step above and/or below them—1, 9, 3, ♭5, +5, ♭7).

Fingering is constant if the sequence is played on the same set of strings. Note: These sequences also apply to dominant 7(+5) chords.

Open Voicings

As an augmented chord primarily represents the whole tone scale, the entire structure may move in whole steps.

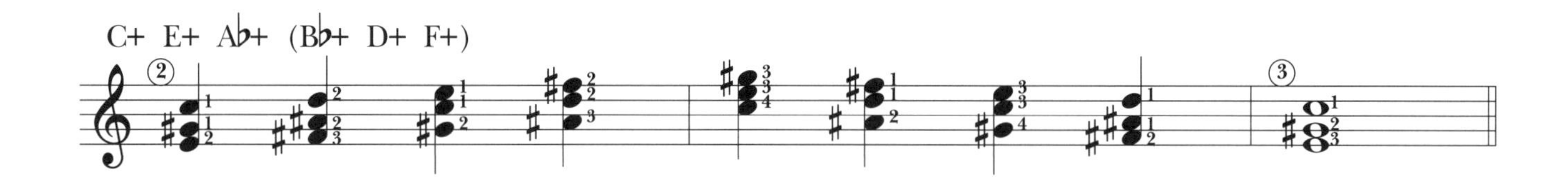

Arpeggios—Four-Note A♭ Chords

Chord Spelling

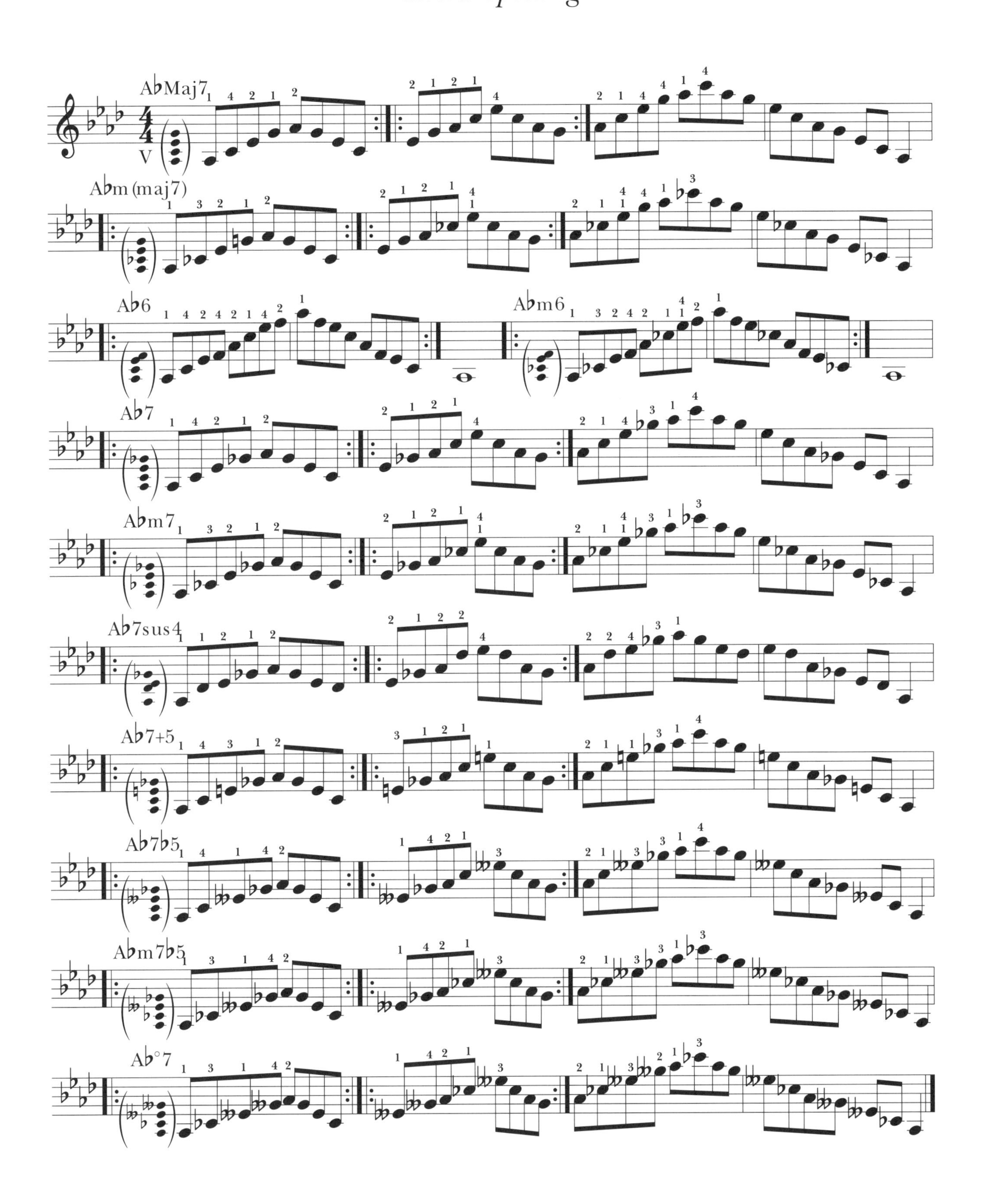

Arpeggios—Four-Note E Chords

Chord Spelling

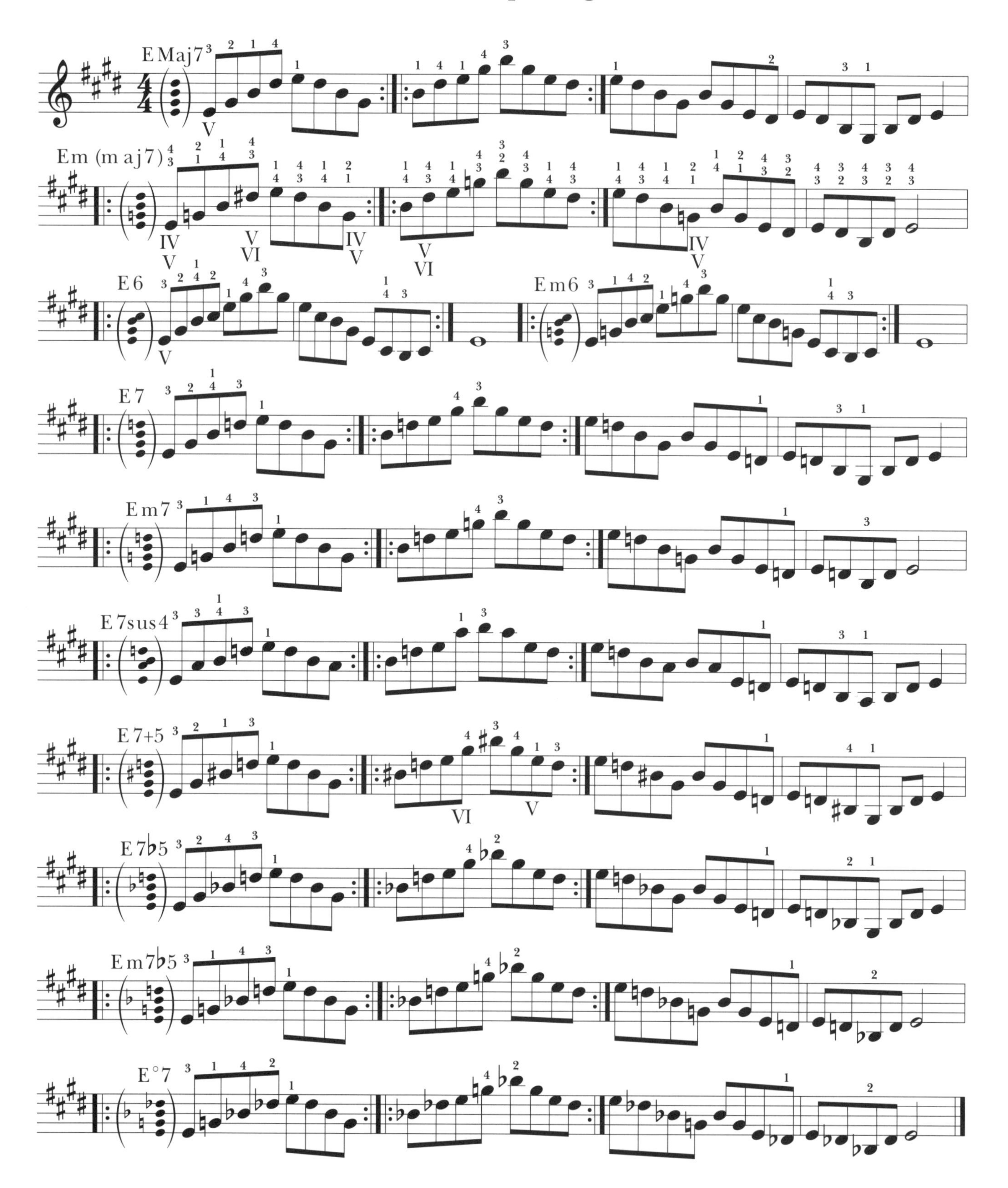

G Major Scale (Twelve Positions)

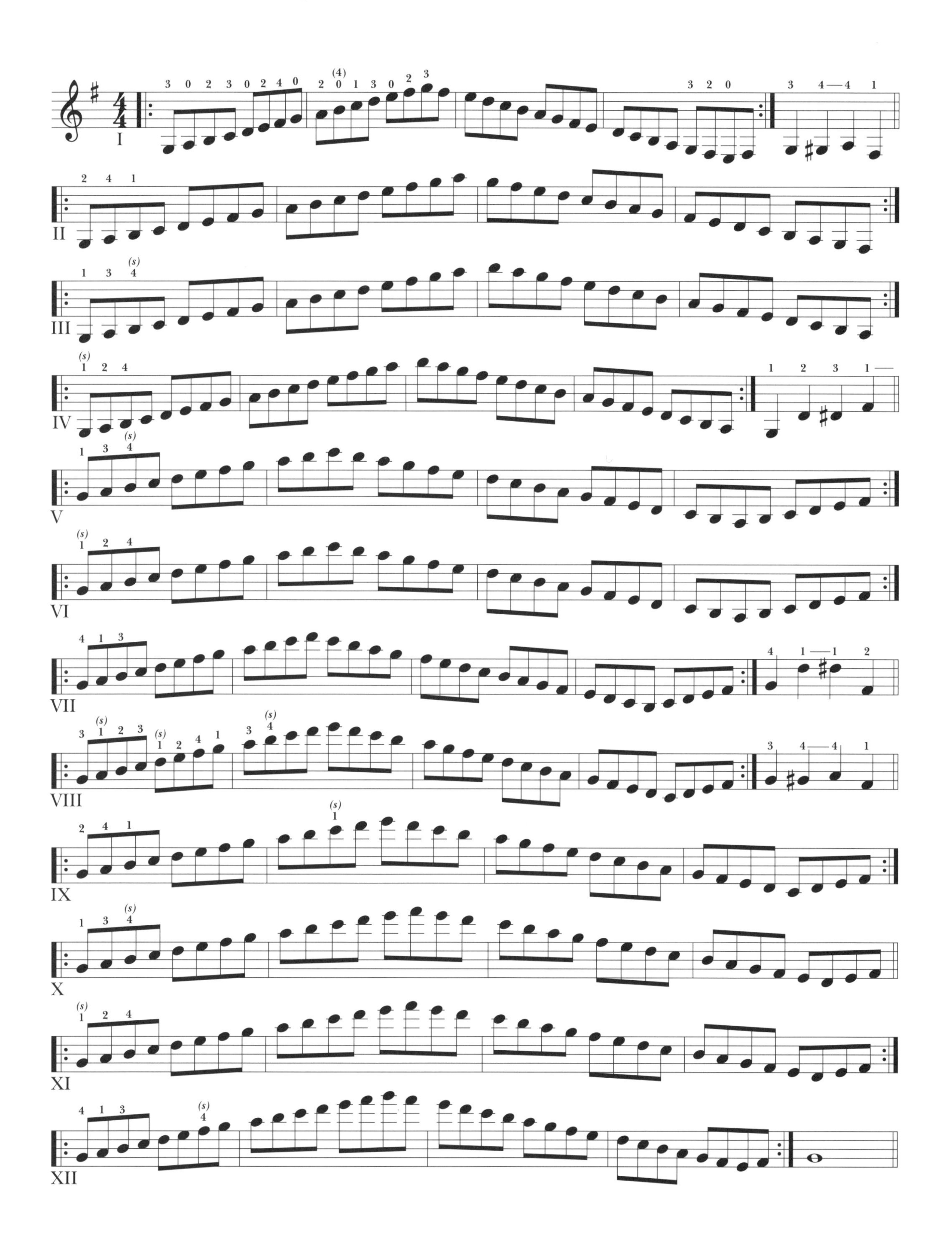

E Harmonic Minor—Nine Positions

E Minor Etude (solo)

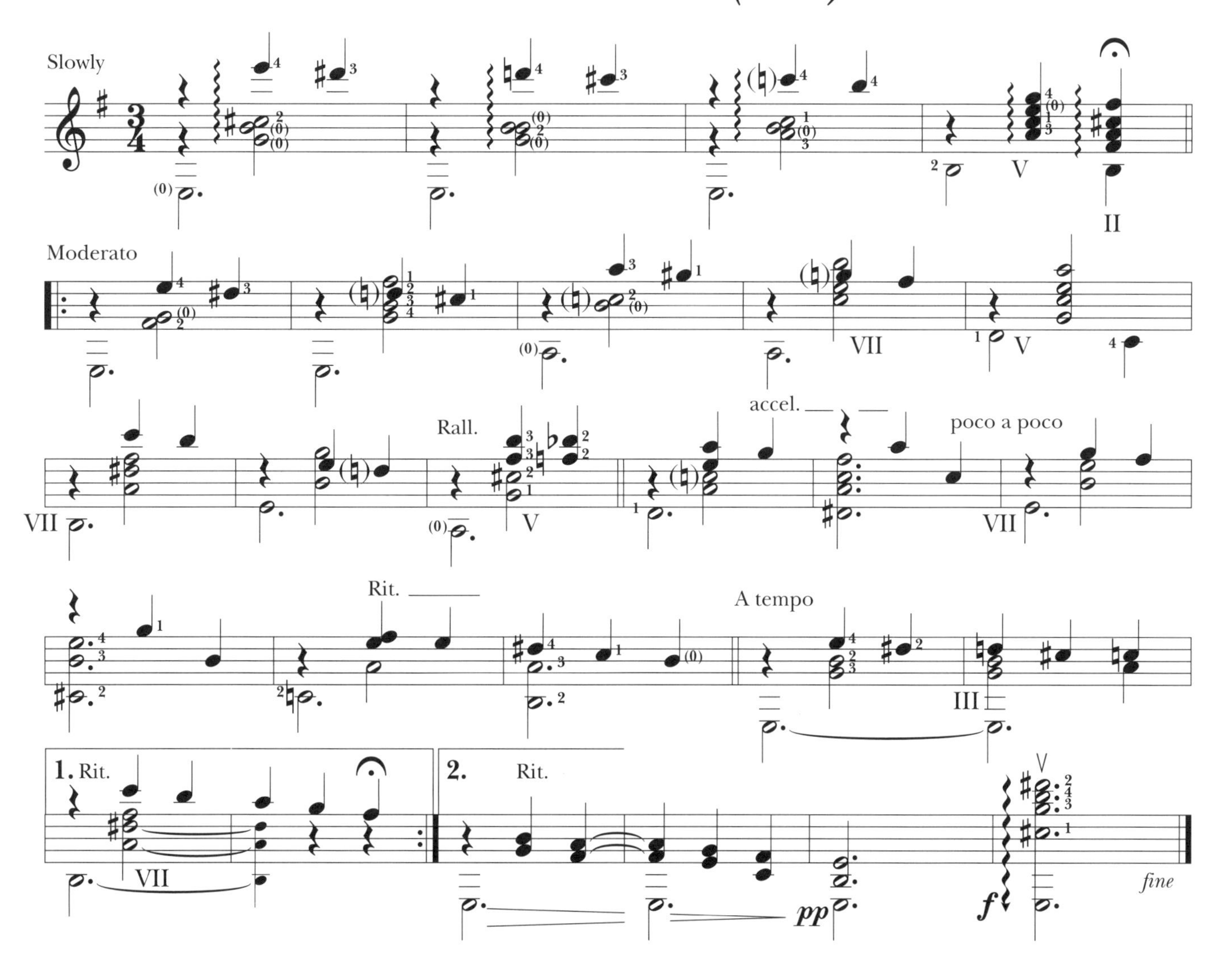

Chord-Scale Relationships—Dominant 7 Chords

For improvisation.

1. The condition of the three highest degrees (tensions 9, 11, 13) on all dominant 7 chords with scale tone roots is controlled by the preceding scale.

I7, II7, V7	1, 3, 5, ♭7, 9, (11), 13	Major scale from intended tonic
VI7	1, 3, 5, ♭7, 9, (11), (♭13)	Real melodic minor scale from intended tonic
III7, VII7	1, 3, 5, ♭7, ♭9, (11), (♭13)	Harmonic minor scale from intended tonic
IV7	1, 3, 5, ♭7, 9, +11, 13	Real melodic minor scale from 5th

✱ The III7 and VII7 chords have a "built-in" ♭9. When the 9 is flatted, it is truly altered and ♯9 is compatible with it. By treating the ♯9 melodically as ♭3, the natural minor scale is the result. This is a second choice of related scale. All eight notes of the combined harmonic and natural minor scales are also used.

2. These three high degrees on all dominant 7 chords with non-scale tone roots are constant (9, +11, 13) and they are all treated the same as the IV7 chord.

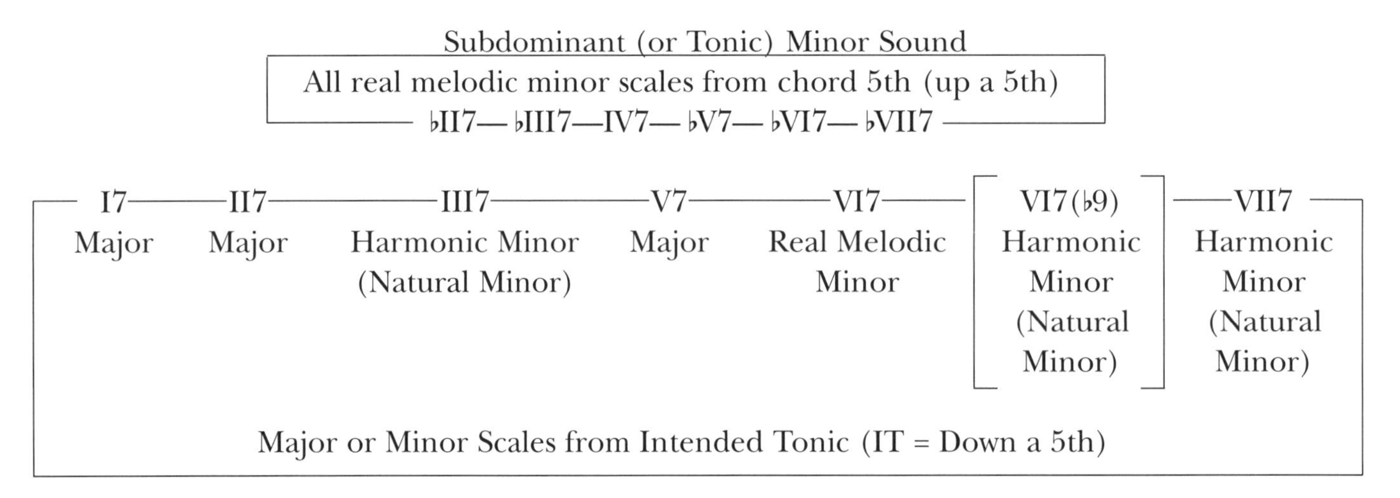

There is one structure containing an added alteration (not forced on it by the preceding scale sound): VI7(♭9). That chord has been included here, because it is encountered so often that we have become conditioned to hear it as the "norm." The VI7 with unaltered 9 is usually found only as a result of the melody being this note.

Have someone play the progressions for you (or use a tape recorder) and practice the proper scales over the following chord sequences.

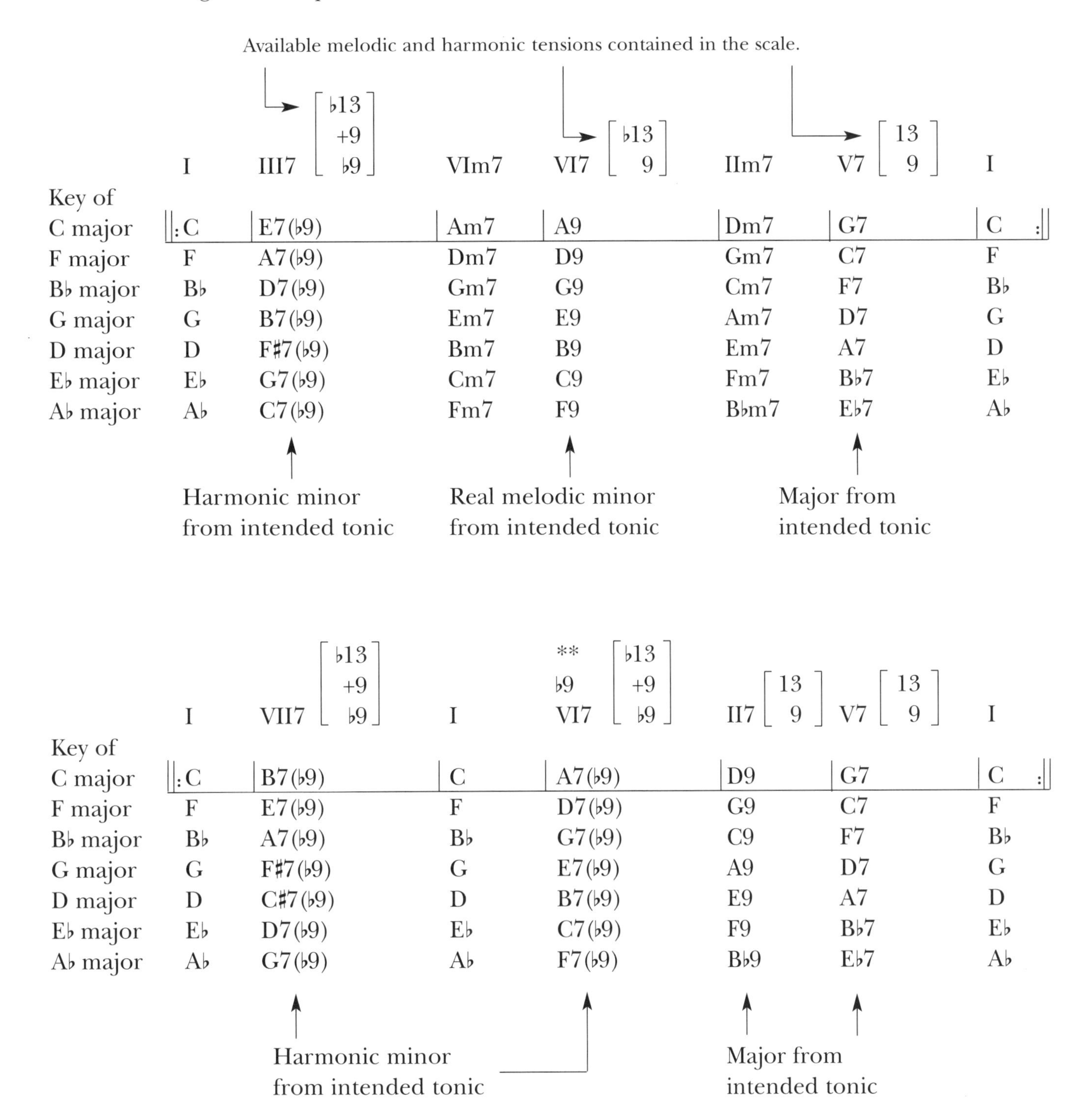

Available melodic and harmonic tensions contained in the scale.

Key of	I	III7 [♭13, +9, ♭9]	VIm7	VI7 [♭13, 9]	IIm7	V7 [13, 9]	I
C major	C	E7(♭9)	Am7	A9	Dm7	G7	C
F major	F	A7(♭9)	Dm7	D9	Gm7	C7	F
B♭ major	B♭	D7(♭9)	Gm7	G9	Cm7	F7	B♭
G major	G	B7(♭9)	Em7	E9	Am7	D7	G
D major	D	F♯7(♭9)	Bm7	B9	Em7	A7	D
E♭ major	E♭	G7(♭9)	Cm7	C9	Fm7	B♭7	E♭
A♭ major	A♭	C7(♭9)	Fm7	F9	B♭m7	E♭7	A♭

Key of	I	VII7 [♭13, +9, ♭9]	I	** ♭9 VI7 [♭13, +9, ♭9]	II7 [13, 9]	V7 [13, 9]	I
C major	C	B7(♭9)	C	A7(♭9)	D9	G7	C
F major	F	E7(♭9)	F	D7(♭9)	G9	C7	F
B♭ major	B♭	A7(♭9)	B♭	G7(♭9)	C9	F7	B♭
G major	G	F♯7(♭9)	G	E7(♭9)	A9	D7	G
D major	D	C♯7(♭9)	D	B7(♭9)	E9	A7	D
E♭ major	E♭	D7(♭9)	E♭	C7(♭9)	F9	B♭7	E♭
A♭ major	A♭	G7(♭9)	A♭	F7(♭9)	B♭9	E♭7	A♭

Key of	I	IV7 [13, +11, 9]	IIIm7	♭III7 [13, +11, 9]	IIm7	♭II7 [13, +11, 9]	I
C major	‖: C	F9	Em7	E♭9	Dm7	D♭9	C :‖
F major	F	B♭9	Am7	A♭9	Gm7	G♭9	F
B♭ major	B♭	E♭9	Dm7	D♭9	Cm7	C♭9 (B9)	B♭
G major	G	C9	Bm7	B♭9	Am7	A♭9	G
D major	D	G9	F♯m7	F9	Em7	E♭9	D
E♭ major	E♭	A♭9	Gm7	G♭9	Fm7	F♭9 (E9)	E♭
A♭ major	A♭	D♭9	C7	C♭9 (B9)	B♭m7	A9	A♭

Real melodic minor from chord 5th (IV7, ♭III7, ♭II7)

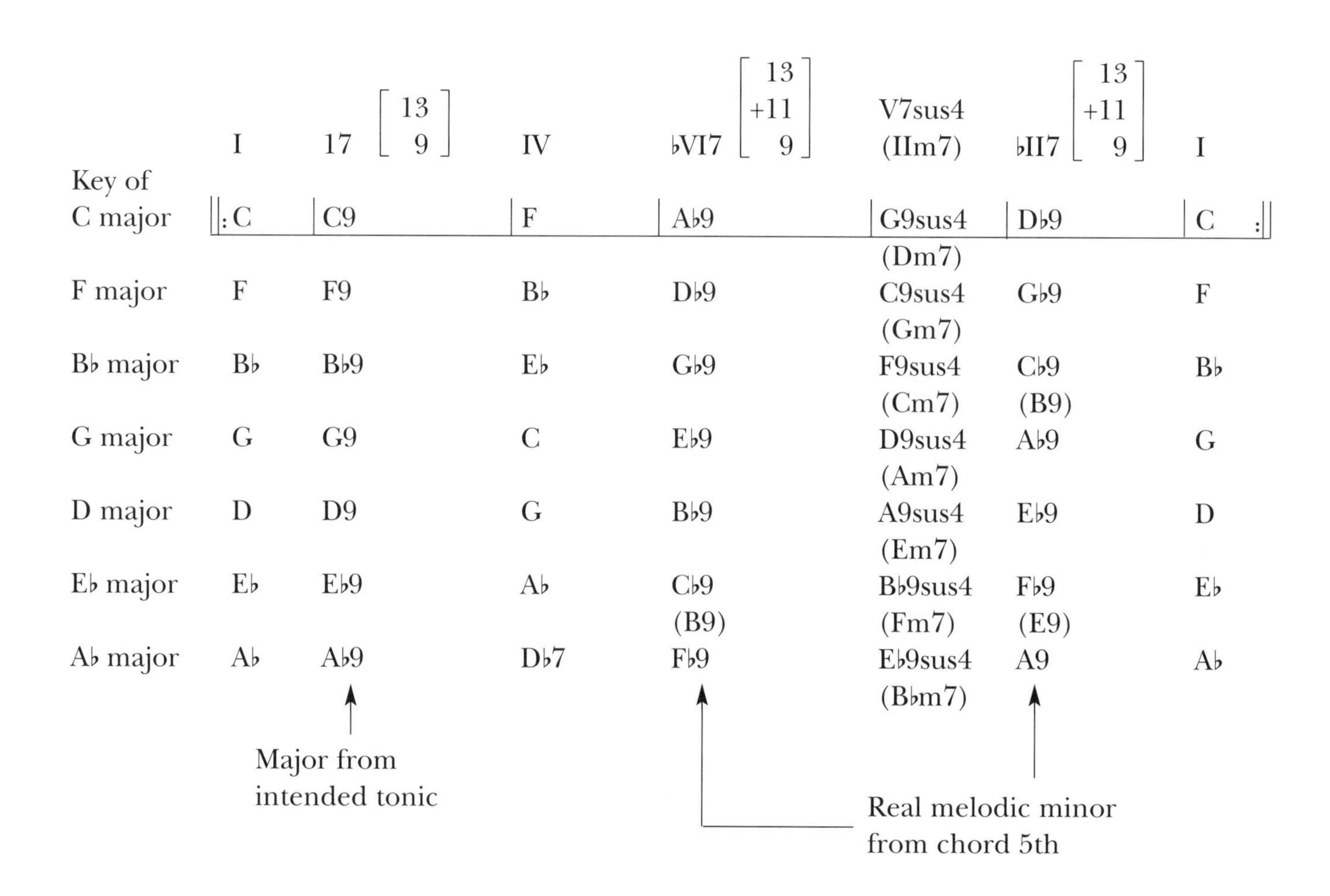

Key of	I	I7 [13, 9]	IV	♭VI7 [13, +11, 9]	V7sus4 (IIm7)	♭II7 [13, +11, 9]	I
C major	‖: C	C9	F	A♭9	G9sus4 (Dm7)	D♭9	C :‖
F major	F	F9	B♭	D♭9	C9sus4 (Gm7)	G♭9	F
B♭ major	B♭	B♭9	E♭	G♭9	F9sus4 (Cm7)	C♭9 (B9)	B♭
G major	G	G9	C	E♭9	D9sus4 (Am7)	A♭9	G
D major	D	D9	G	B♭9	A9sus4 (Em7)	E♭9	D
E♭ major	E♭	E♭9	A♭	C♭9 (B9)	B♭9sus4 (Fm7)	F♭9 (E9)	E♭
A♭ major	A♭	A♭9	D♭7	F♭9	E♭9sus4 (B♭m7)	A9	A♭

Major from intended tonic (I7)

Real melodic minor from chord 5th (♭VI7, ♭II7)

Key	I	♭V7 [13, +11, 9]	IV	♭VII7 [13, +11, 9]	I	B7 [13, 9]	I
C major	‖: C	G♭9	F	B♭9	C	G7	C :‖
F major	F	C♭9 (B9)	B♭	E♭9	F	C7	F
B♭ major	B♭	F♭9 (E9)	E♭	A♭9	B♭	F7	B♭
G major	G	D♭9	C	F9	G	D7	G
D major	D	A♭9	G	C9	D	A7	D
E♭ major	E♭	A9	A♭	D♭9	E♭	B♭7	E♭
A♭ major	A♭	D9	D♭7	G♭9	A♭	E♭7	A♭
		↑		↑			

Real melodic minor from chord 5th

It is necessary that you know (very well) the normal condition of tensions on all dominant 7 structures so you will instantly recognize any alterations that may be present. The effect of specially altered degrees on dominant 7 chord-scale relationships will be discussed later.

From this point on, all chord-scale pages consist of a great deal of information applicable to composition, spontaneous or otherwise, presented very concisely. As this concerted presentation can be confusing, the material must be worked out by the interested student very gradually over a considerable period of time.

Determine the scale for a chord by its effect on the scale preceding it.

Practical Fingerings for Moving from Position to Position

4-4 AND 1-1 FINGER SLIDES EMPLOYING THE HALF STEP

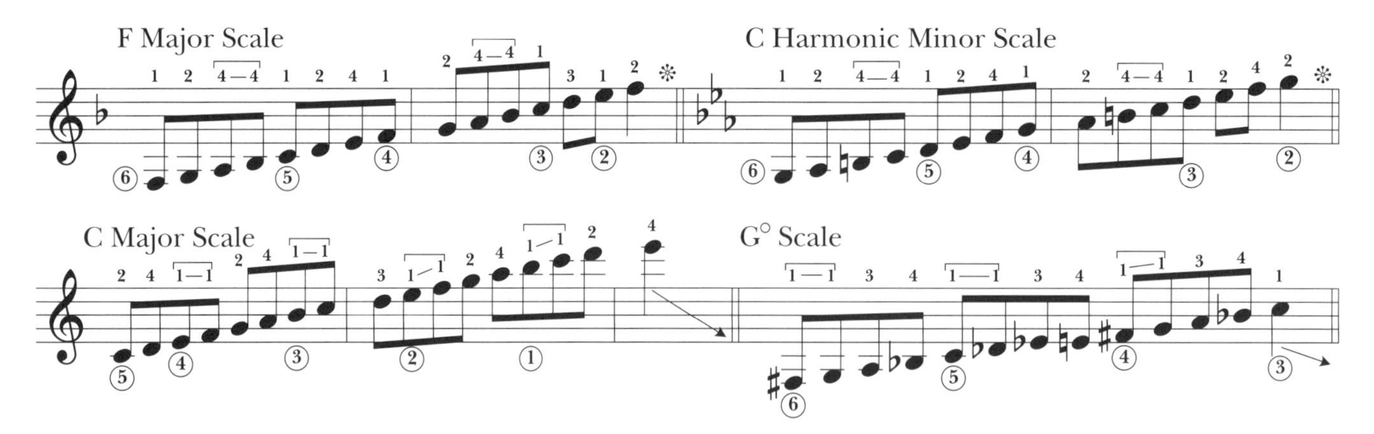

* No descent with 4th finger slides

The preceding 1st and 4th finger slides are also possible (and practical) for distances of from two to three frets.

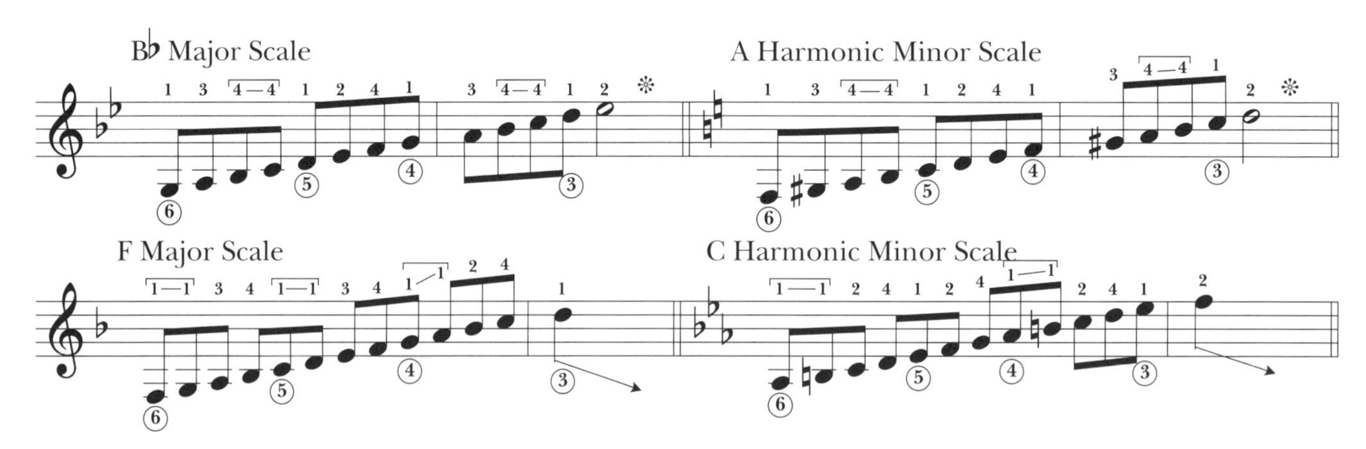

13-13 EMPLOYING THE HALF STEP 12-13, 12-12 VARIATIONS

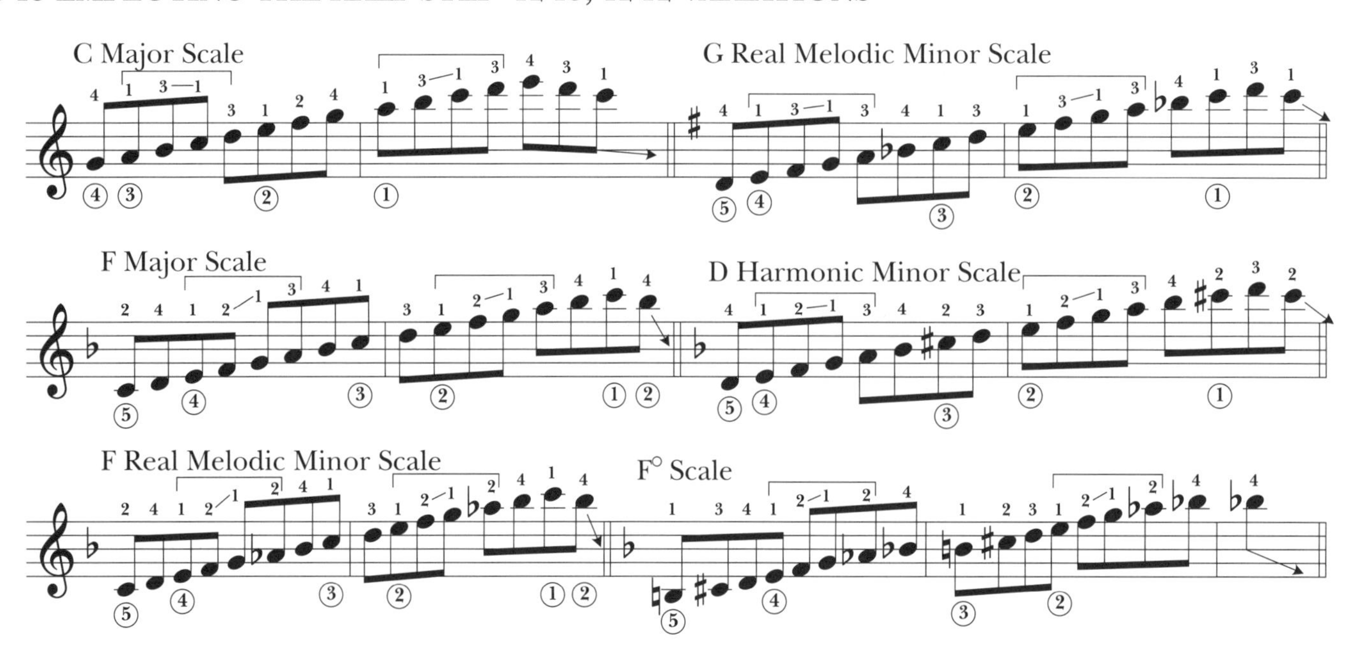

1-2 3-4 THE DOUBLE STRETCH—EMPLOYING THE HALF STEP

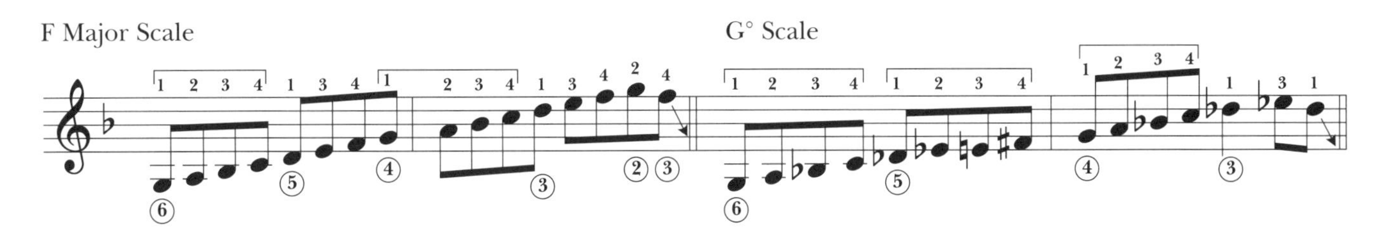

13-24 FINGER EXCHANGE—EMPLOYING THE HALF STEP

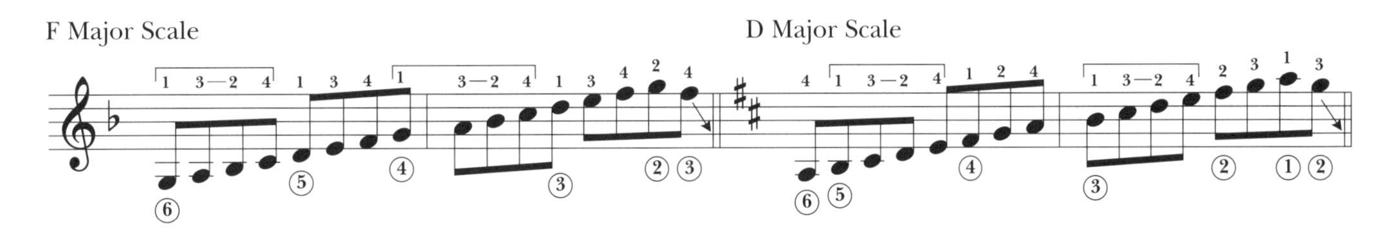

124-124 REPEATED FINGERING—SEPARATED BY A WHOLE STEP

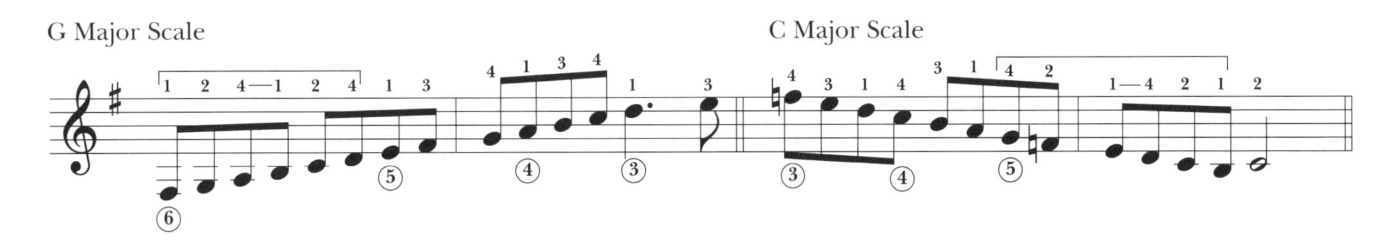

134-134 REPEATED FINGERING—SEPARATED BY A WHOLE STEP

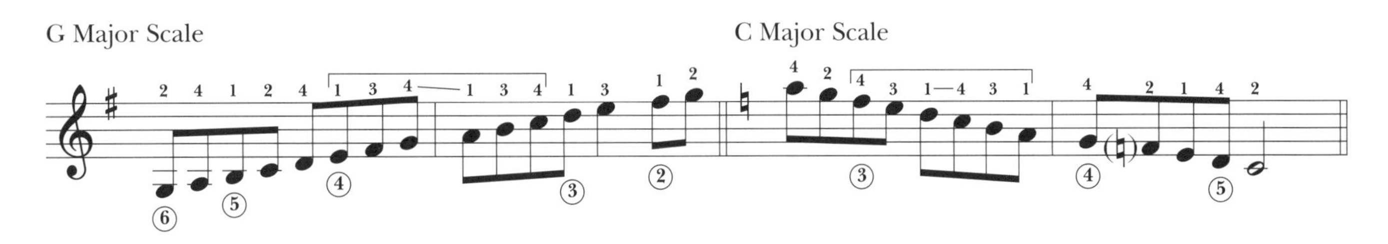

13-134 VARIATION OF ABOVE, 13-124 VARIATION OF ABOVE

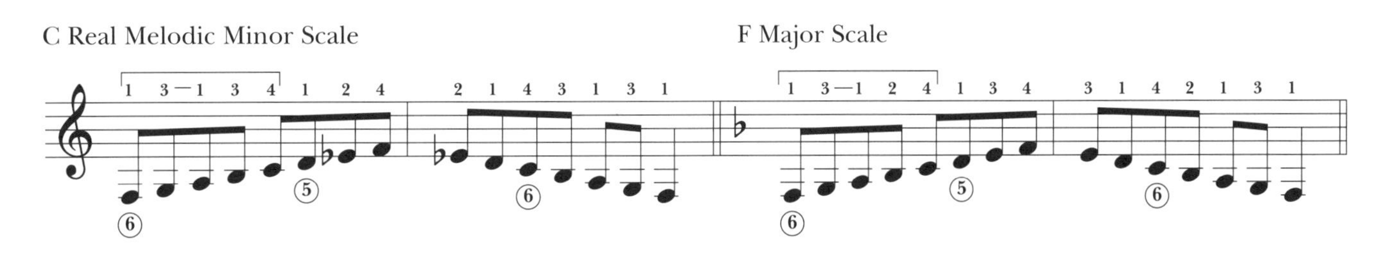

Analyze the intervals involved in the preceding position-to-position fingerings. You will find many other possibilities for application, especially when used in combinations.

All of the fingerings employing the half step are very reliable, as they do not require looking at the fingerboard. The others are sometimes dangerous when the music and/or conductor demand your full attention.

Chord Construction—Three-Note Voicings

Dominant 7 Chords—Preparation of Close and Open Voicings

The distance between the 3rd and ♭7th chord degrees of a dominant structure is called a tritone. This tritone interval (an augmented 4th or a diminished 5th) divides our twelve-tone (chromatic) scale exactly in half. Therefore, each tritone by itself represents the sound of two dominant 7 chords, their roots being separated by the same ♯4 or ♭5 interval. A third note must be added to a tritone to remove this ambiguity.

In a cycle 5 chord progression, tritones move chromatically downward. The ♭7 of the first chord moves to 3 of the next chord, which moves to ♭7 of the next, and so on.

In the following studies, root and 5th chordal degrees are added to chromatic tritone sequences (representing cycle 5 progressions as follows: 1) below, 2) above, and 3) between.

1

TRITONE ON 3RD AND 4TH STRINGS (♭7, 3 IN THE LEAD)

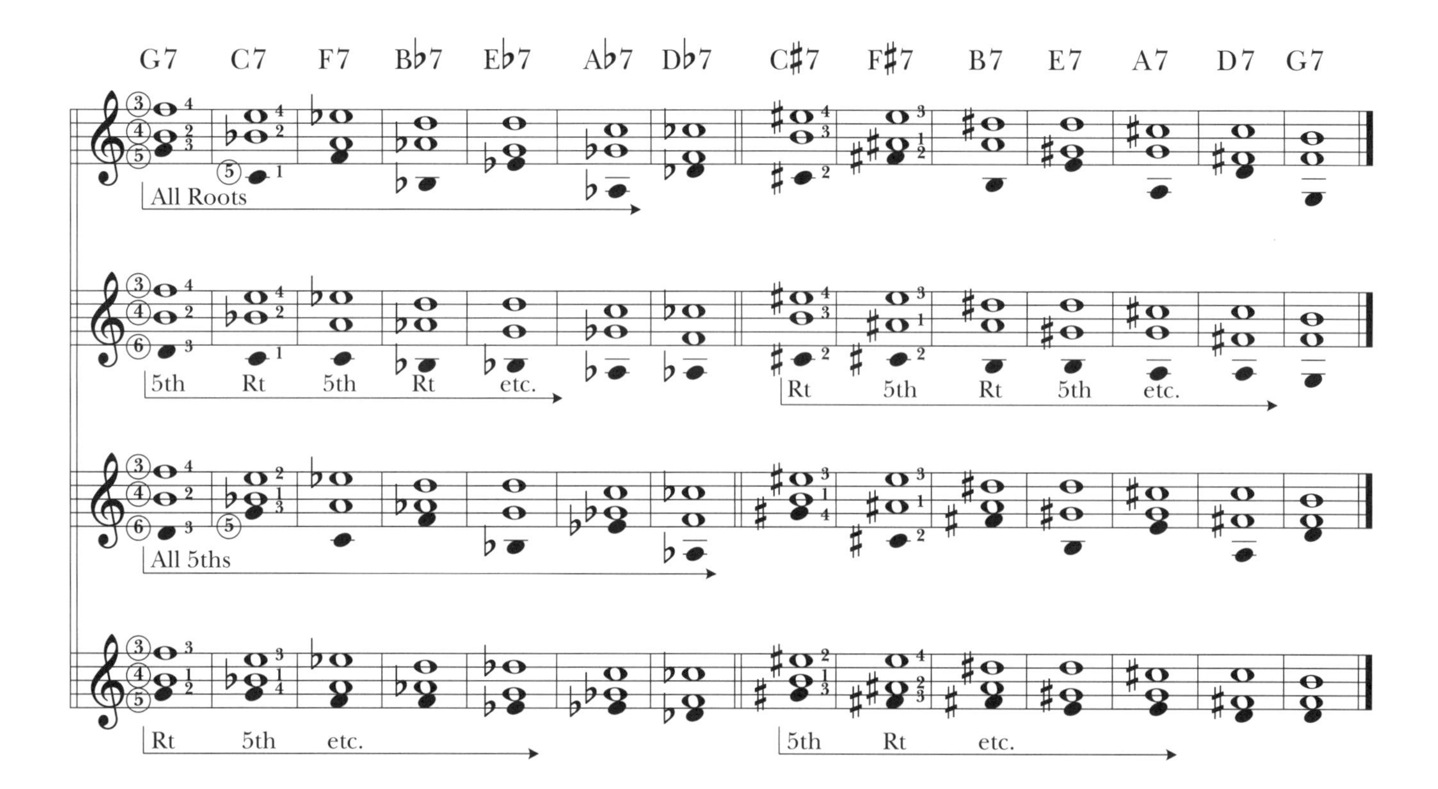

TRITONE ON 2ND AND 3RD STRINGS (♭7, 3 IN THE LEAD)

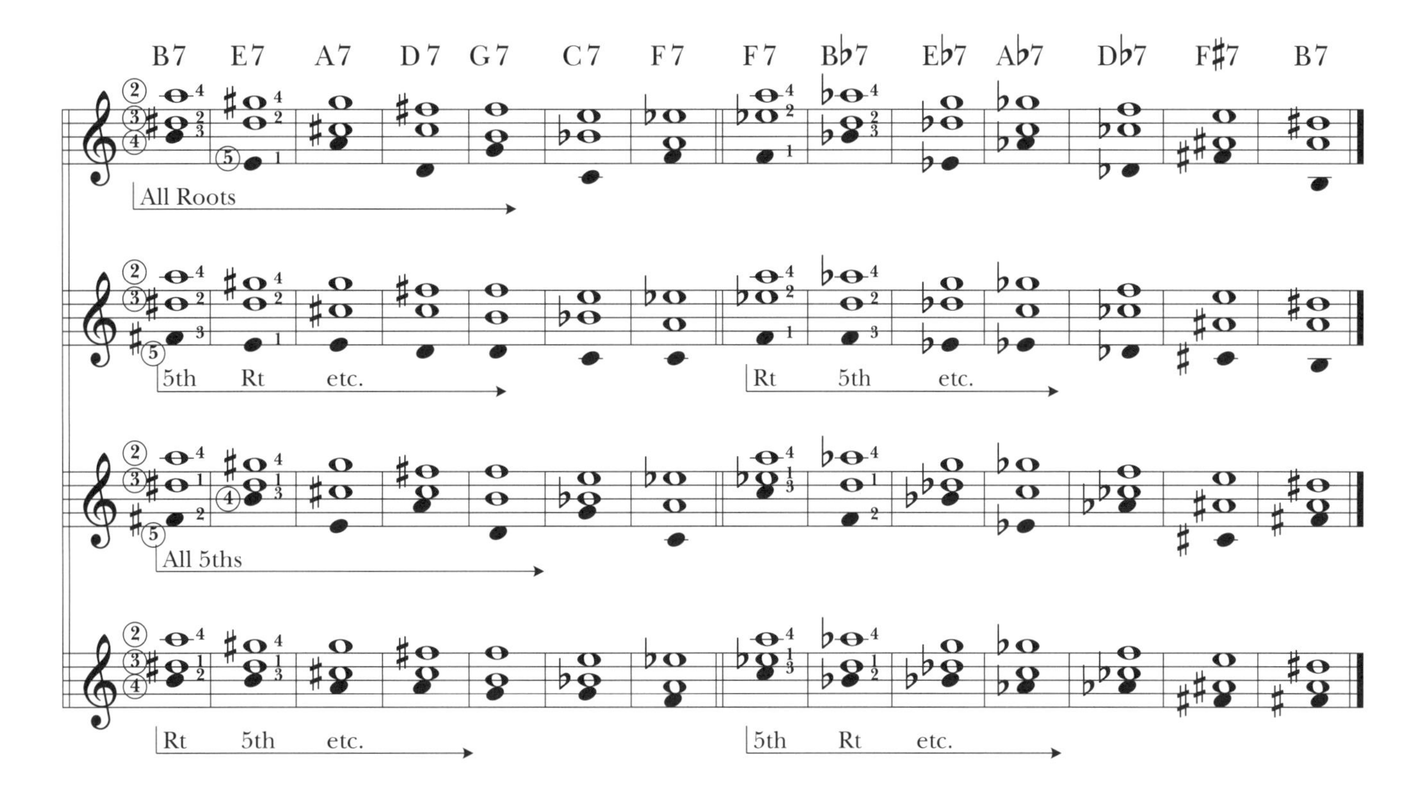

2

TRITONE ON 4TH AND 5TH STRINGS (ROOT, 5 IN THE LEAD)

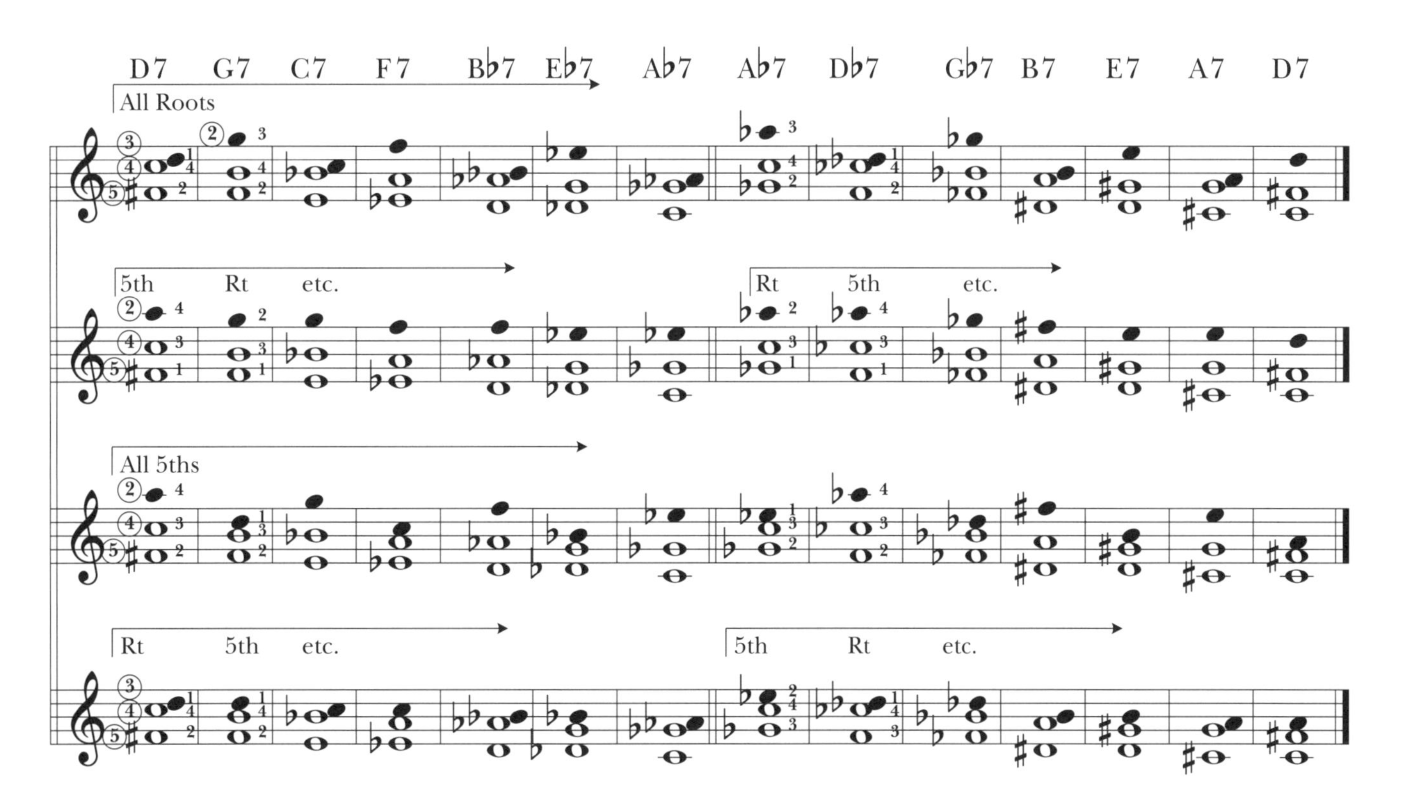

TRITONE ON 3RD AND 4TH STRINGS (ROOT, 5 IN THE LEAD)

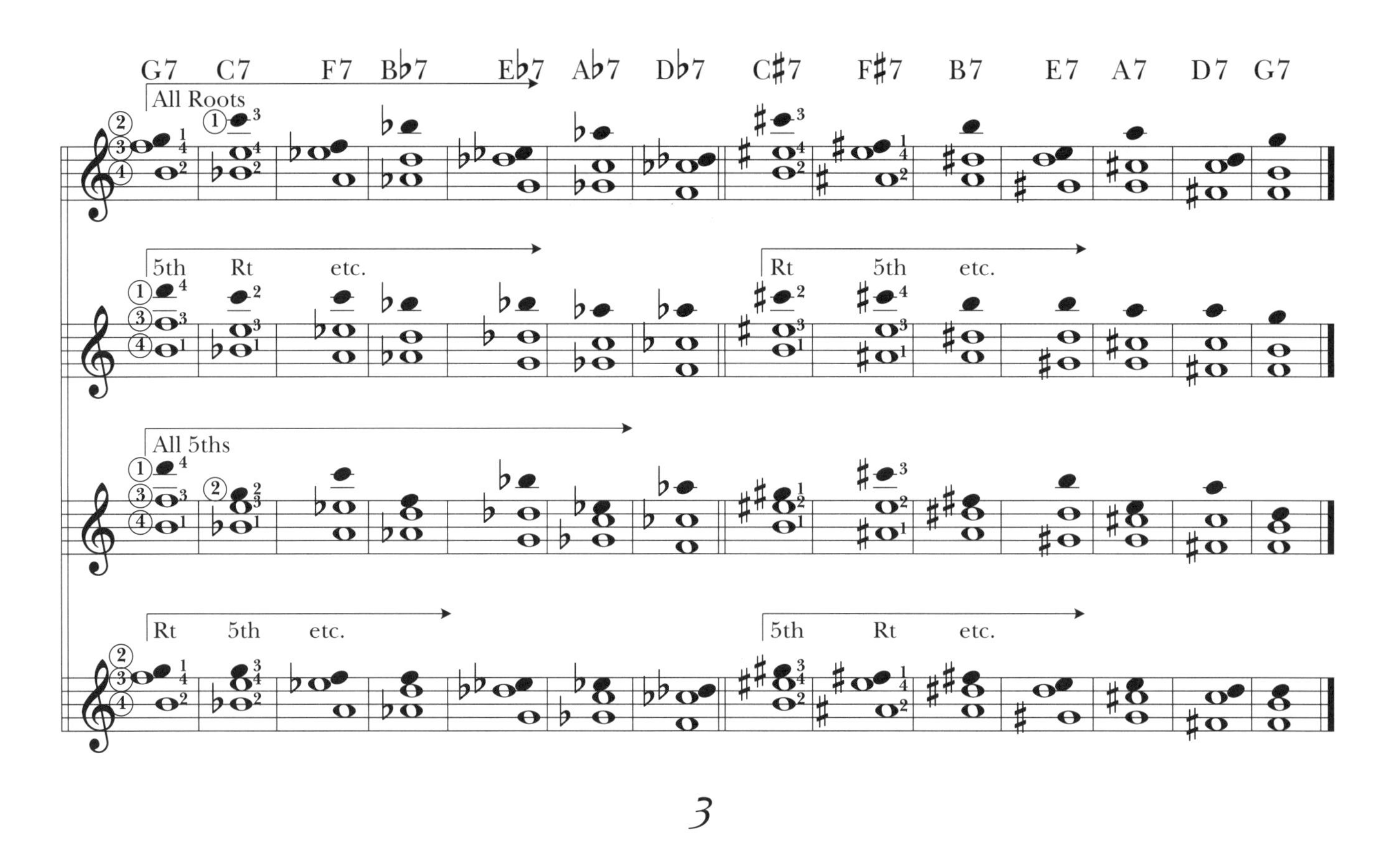

3

TRITONE ON 2ND AND 4TH STRINGS (3, ♭7 IN THE LEAD)

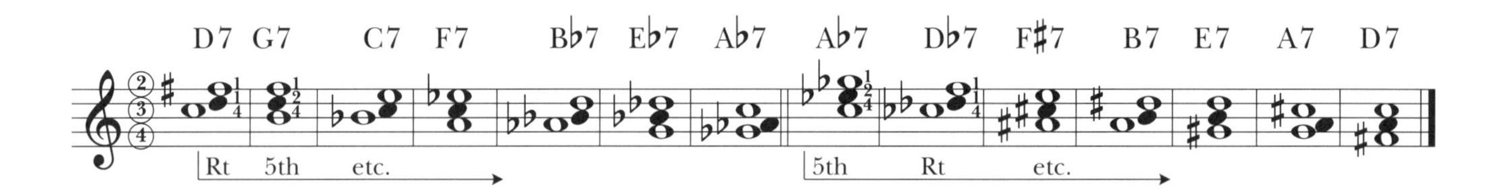

TRITONE ON 3RD AND 4TH STRINGS (3, ♭7 IN THE LEAD)

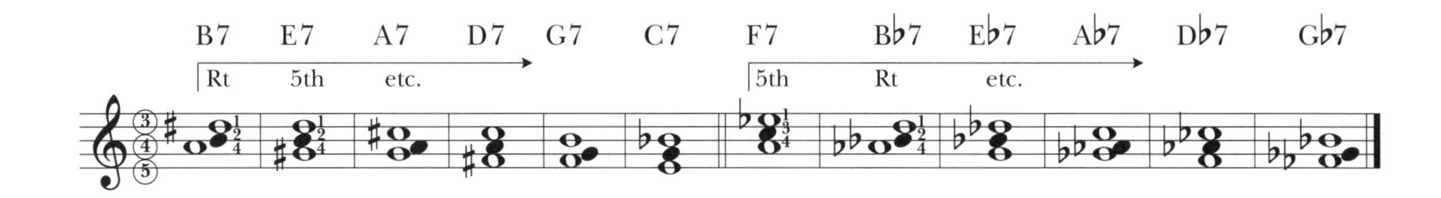

The tritone (interval of ♯4 or ♭5) should not be used below B–F as found on the 5th and 4th strings, respectively. The sound becomes cloudy in pitch from this point on down.

Arpeggios—Four-Note D♭ Chords

Chord Spelling

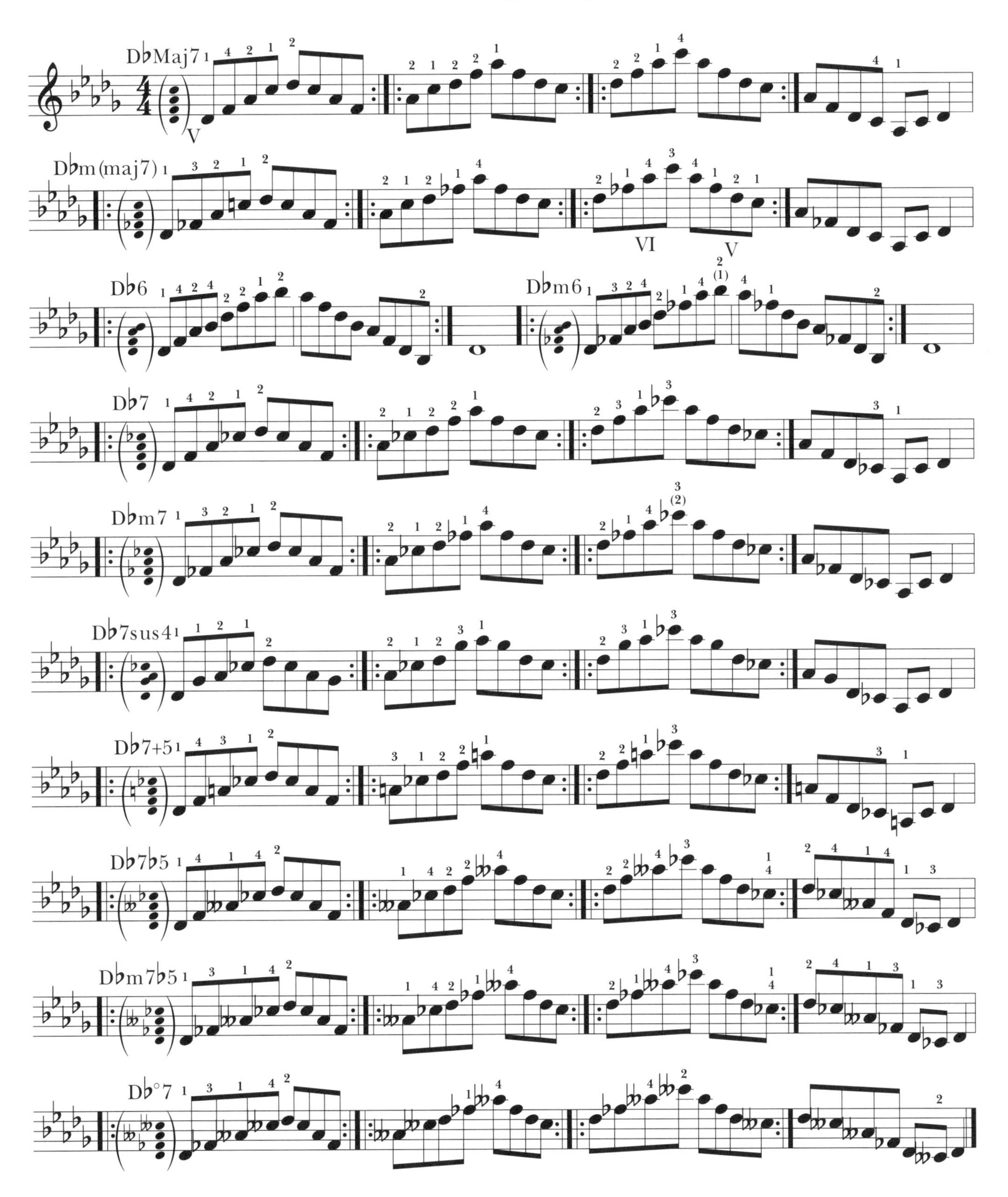

Arpeggios—Four-Note B Chords

Chord Spelling

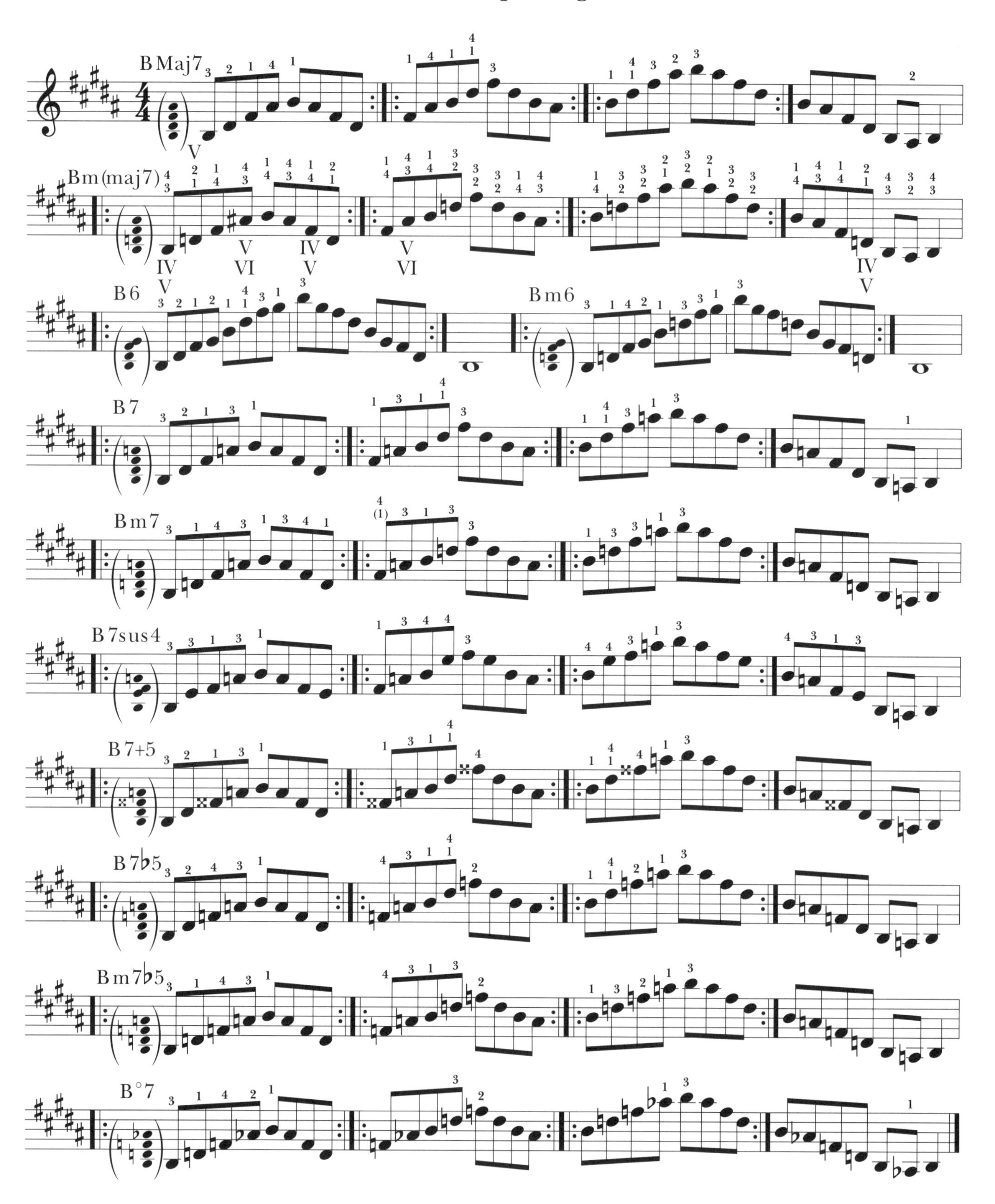

Rhythm Guitar—The Right Hand

Polka Dot (Polka-Duet)

D
VII
C7 F C7 F
VIII
C7
X IX VIII
F G7[♭5] C7
1. 2.
VII VII
F [B♭m] F
E
V
Dm C Dm6 Am
Em F E7 A7 E7 Am
VII
Dm C D7 G7
F
C G7 C C
IX
A7 D7 G7 C C F C C
VII
fine

Major Scales—Position VIII

Twelve Keys—Through Cycle 5

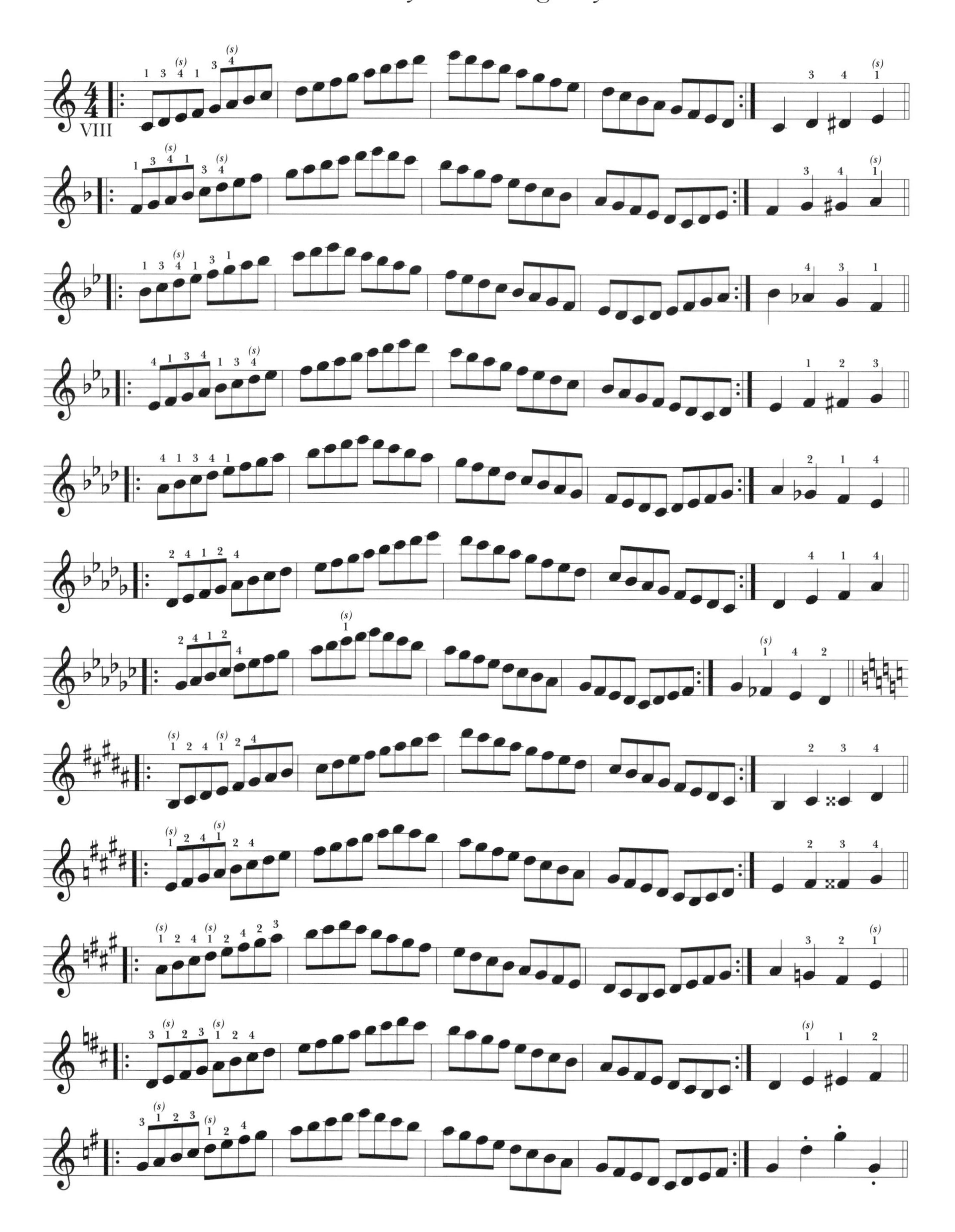

Chords—Three-Note Voicings

Melodization of Tonic Major Chords

Melodic degrees: Major scale from chord name

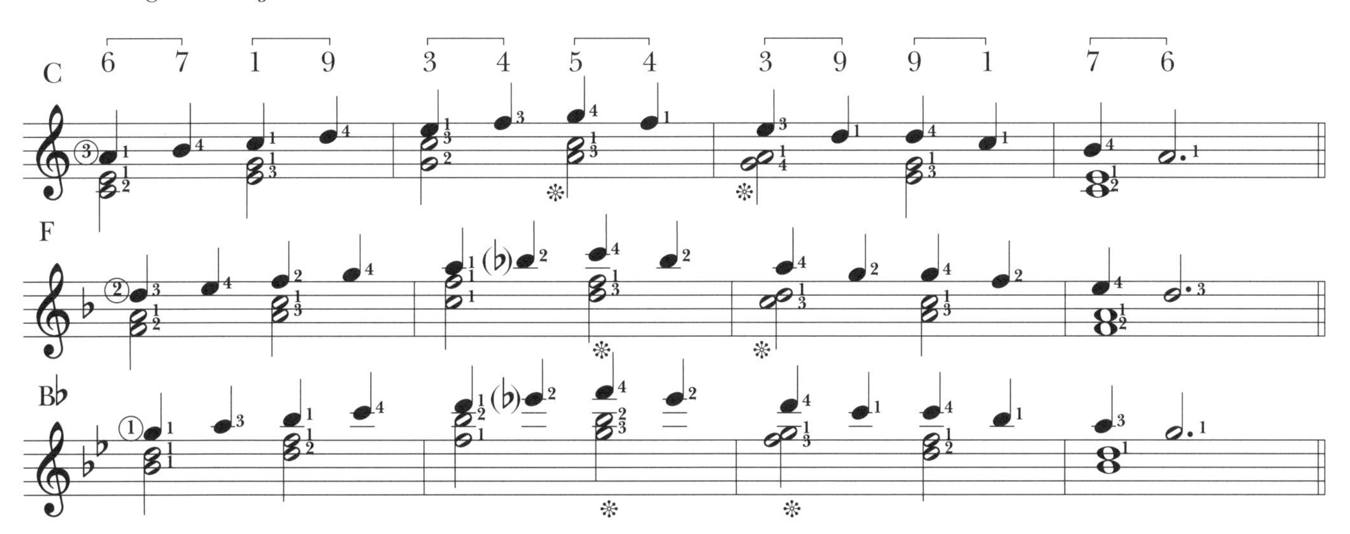

✱ 6th degree necessary as an undervoice

Melodization of Minor 7 Chords as VIm7

Melodic degrees: Major scale from ♭3 of chord

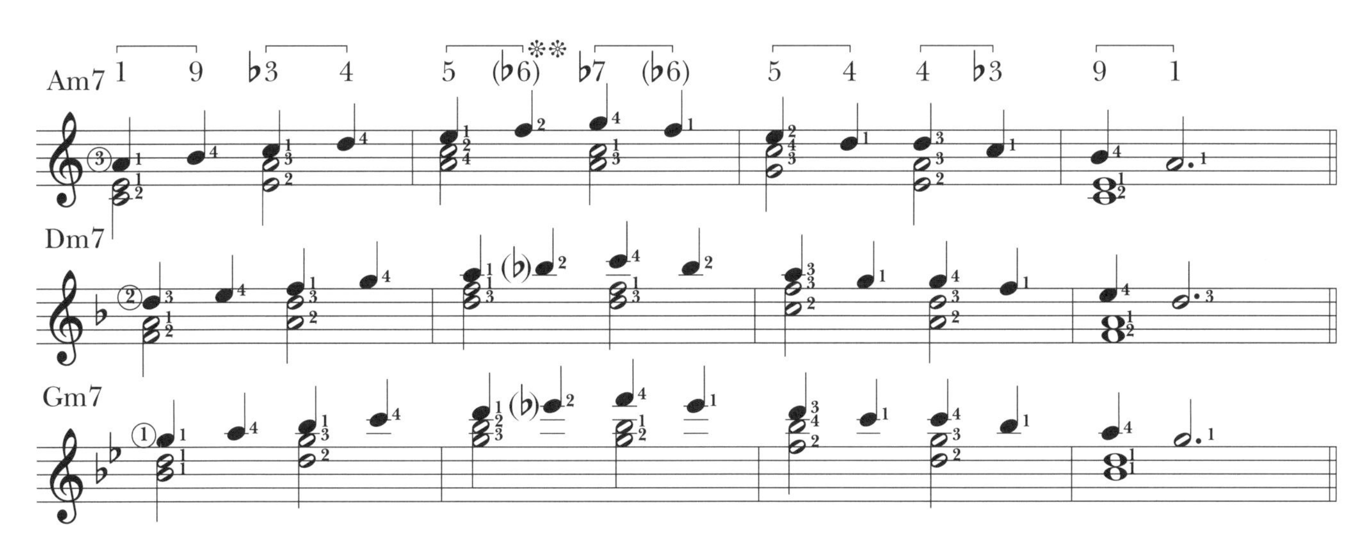

✱✱ Melodic degrees shown in parentheses must be used only in passing.

As the preceding I major and VIm7 chords produce the same tonic major sound, their voicings are interchangeable (C = Am7, F = Dm7, B♭ = Gm7). This is called **diatonic substitution**, or the replacement of one chord with another that represents the sound of the same scale and chord function (tonic, subdominant, and dominant) and whose chord tones are derived from higher or lower scale degrees.

Melodization of Subdominant Major Chords

Melodic degrees: Major scale from 5th of chord

✻ ♯4 is a diatonic tension on IV chords.

Melodization of Minor 7 Chords as IIm7

Melodic degrees: Major scale from ♭7 of chord

As the preceding IVmaj and IIm7 chords produce the same subdominant sound, their voicings are interchangeable (A♭ = Fm7, C = Am7, F = Dm7).

Arpeggios—Four-Note F♯ Chords

Chord Spelling

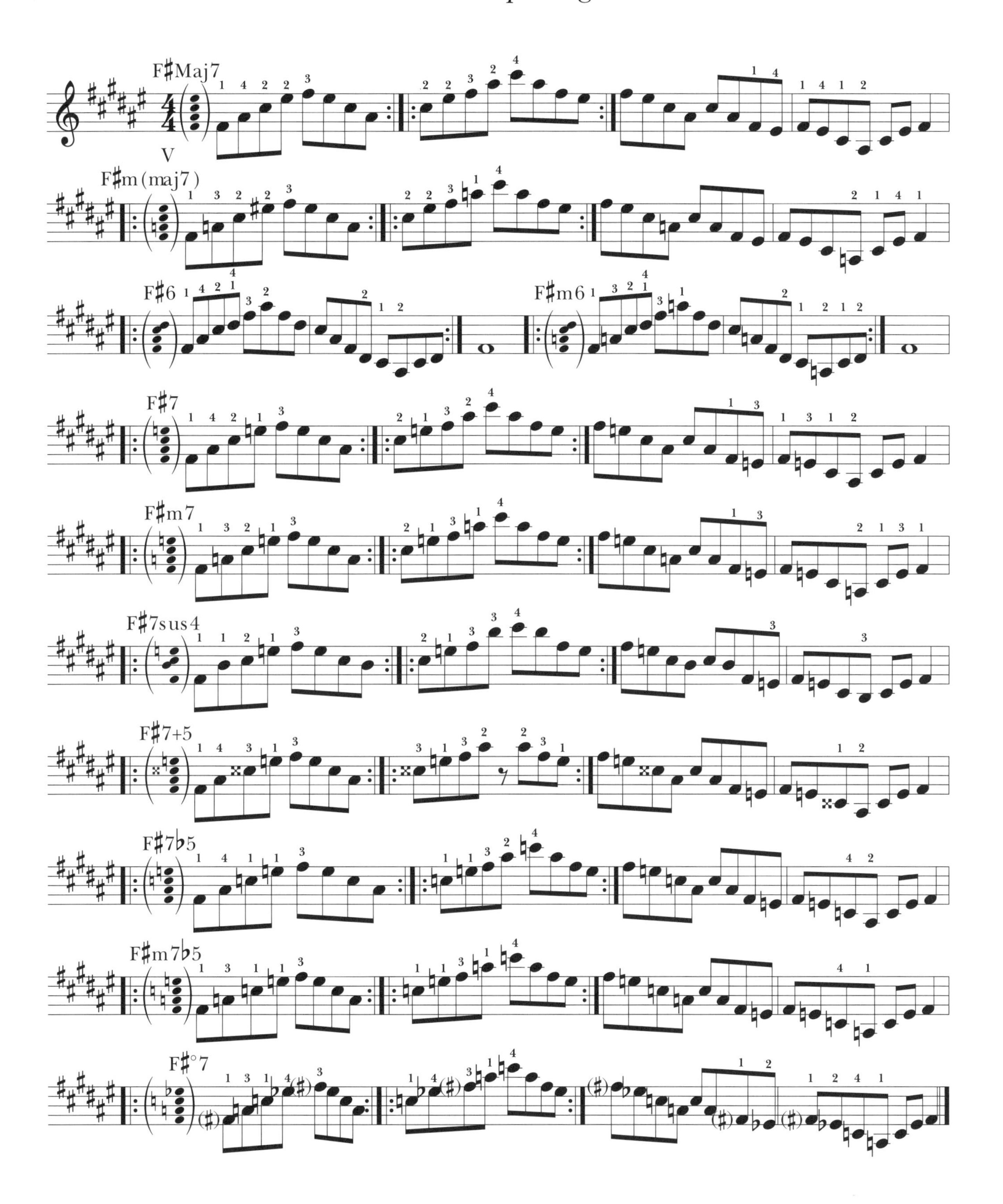

Arpeggios—Four-Note G♭ Chords

Chord Spelling

All fingering from preceding F♯ arpeggios.

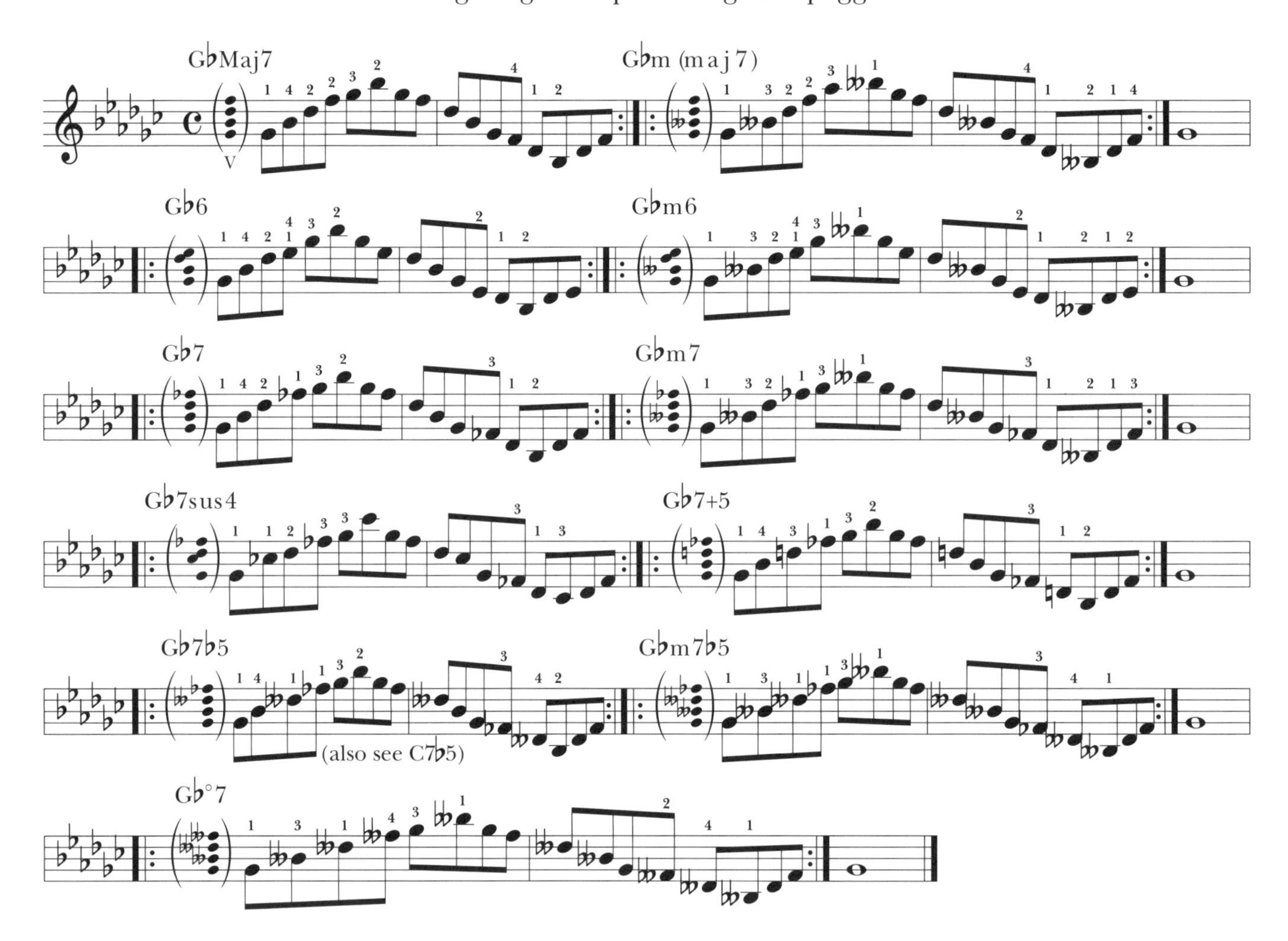

Four-Note C♯ Chords

Fingering from preceding D♭ arpeggios.

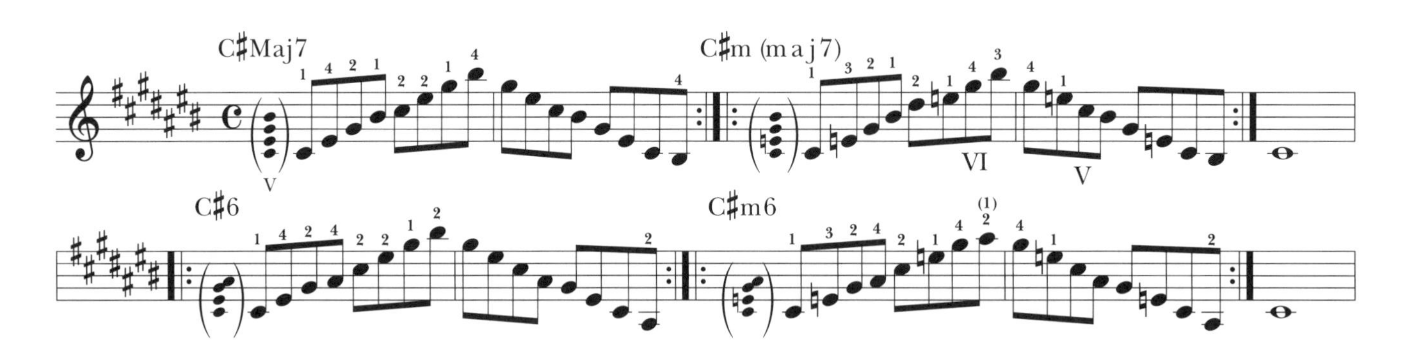

Four-Note C♭ Chords

Fingering from preceding B arpeggios.

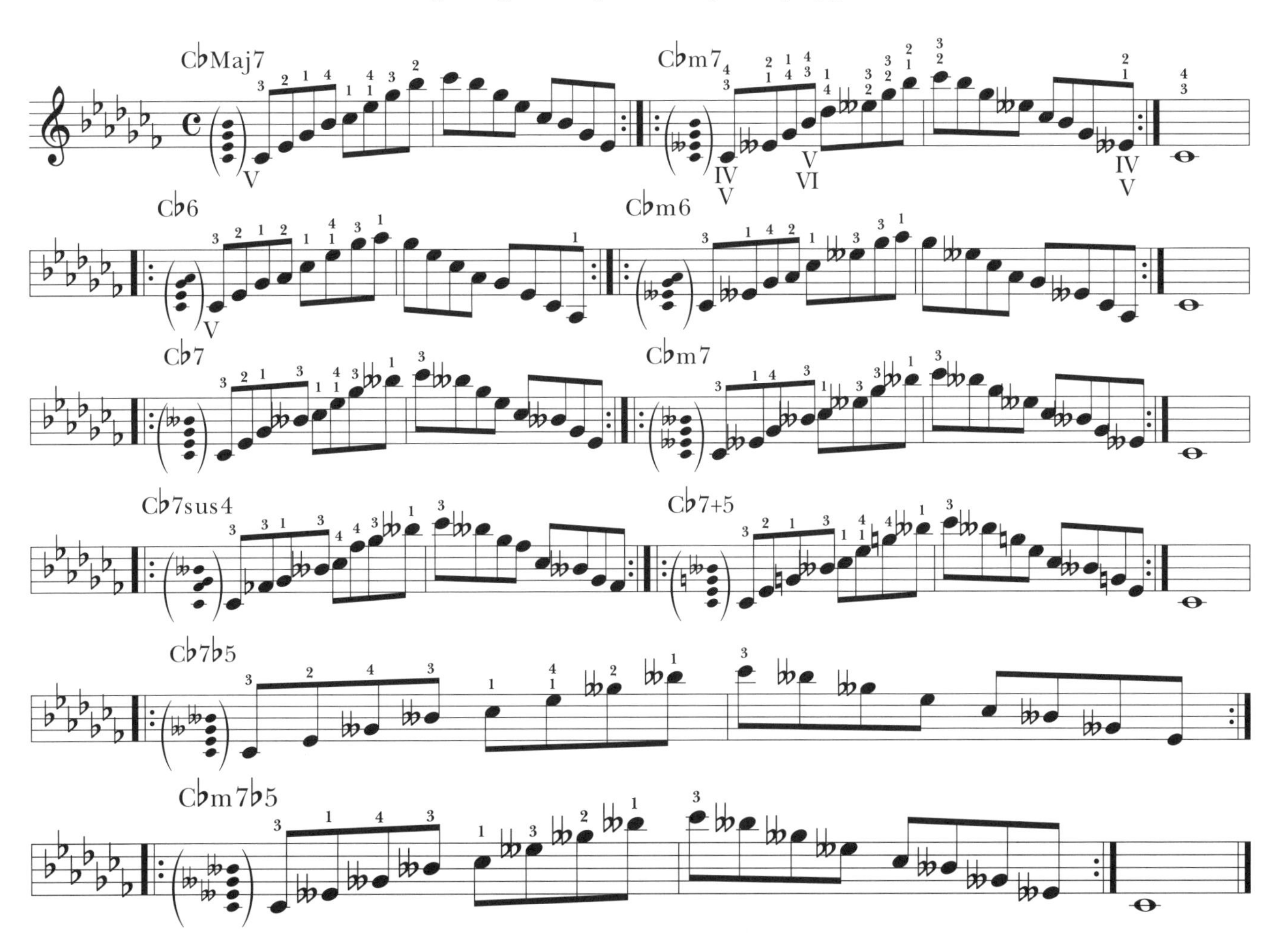

Chords—Three-Note Voicings

Dominant 7 Chords—Open Voicings, All Inversions

- Chord voicings notated here as (●) should be used only in passing for the following reasons:
  - Incomplete structure (indefinite sound)
  - Weak degree in the "bass"

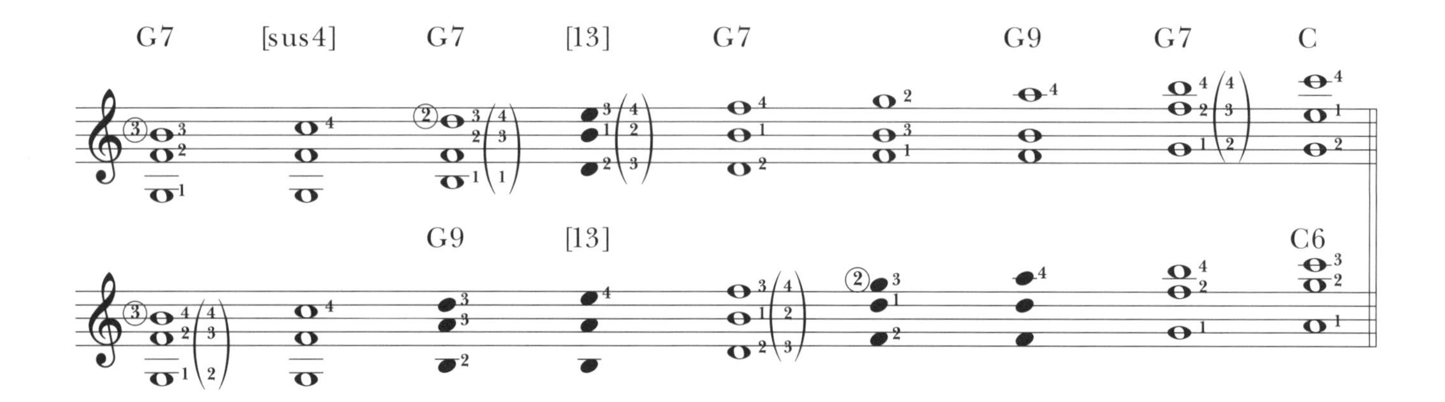

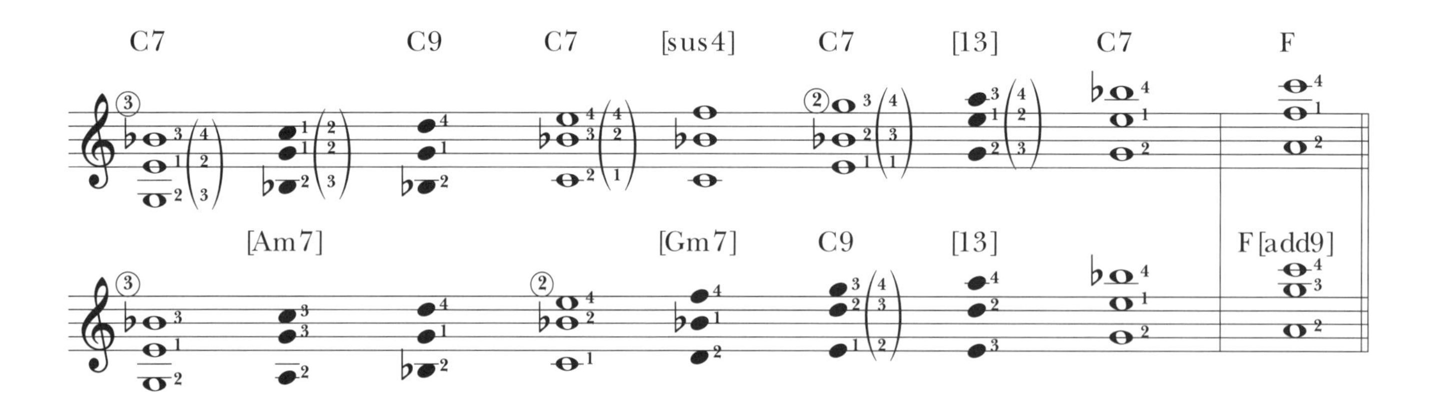

Most three-part chord voicings without the root do not have a well-defined sound, unless 1) they follow a strong voicing (including the root) of the same chord, or 2) they are the second chord of a strong cadence, closely voice led from the first chord (which has set the tonality), or 3) they are a spread voicing with the 5th degree on the bottom, sounding in the low register.

B♭ Major Scale (Twelve Positions)

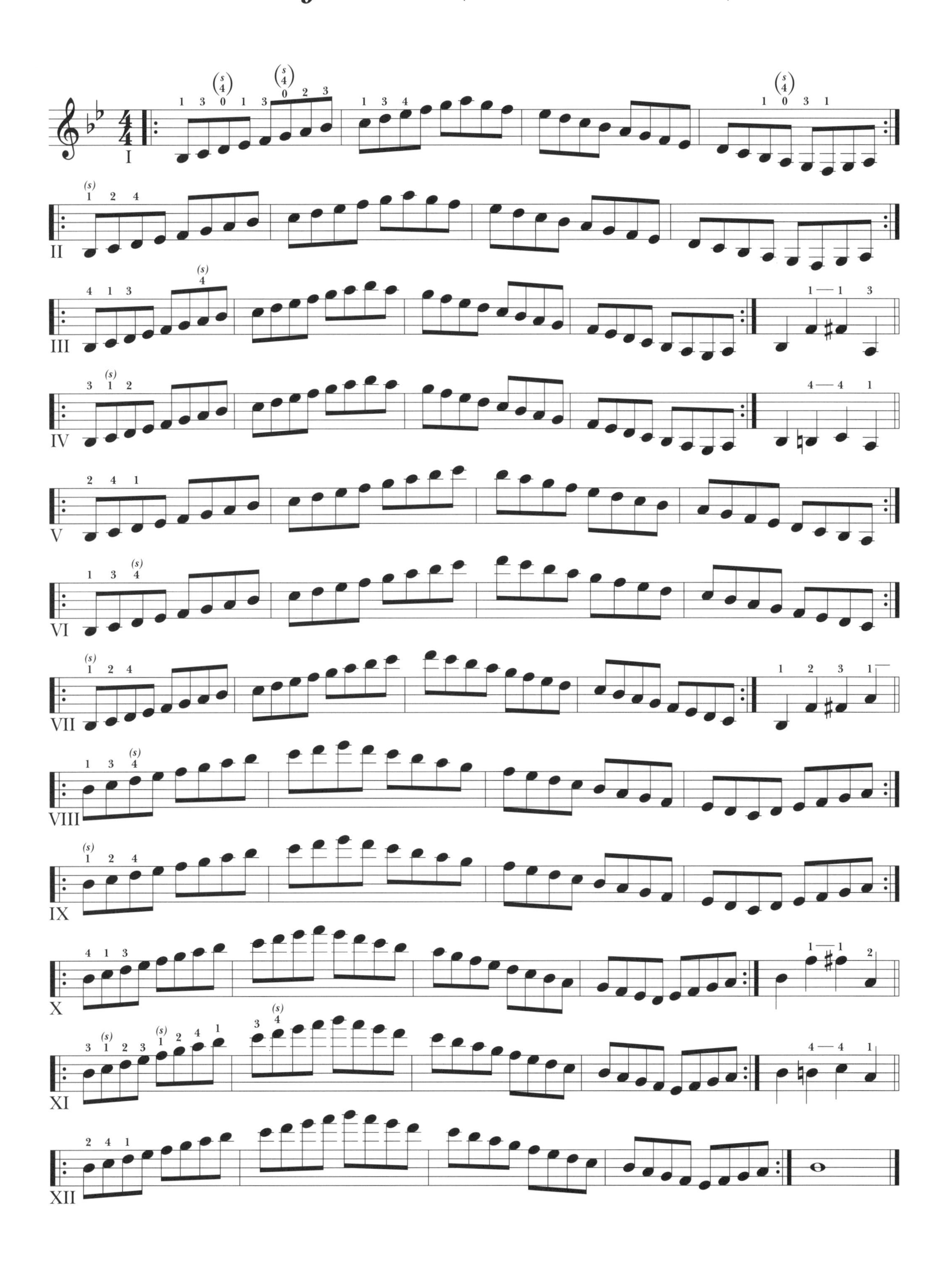

G Harmonic Minor (Nine Positions)

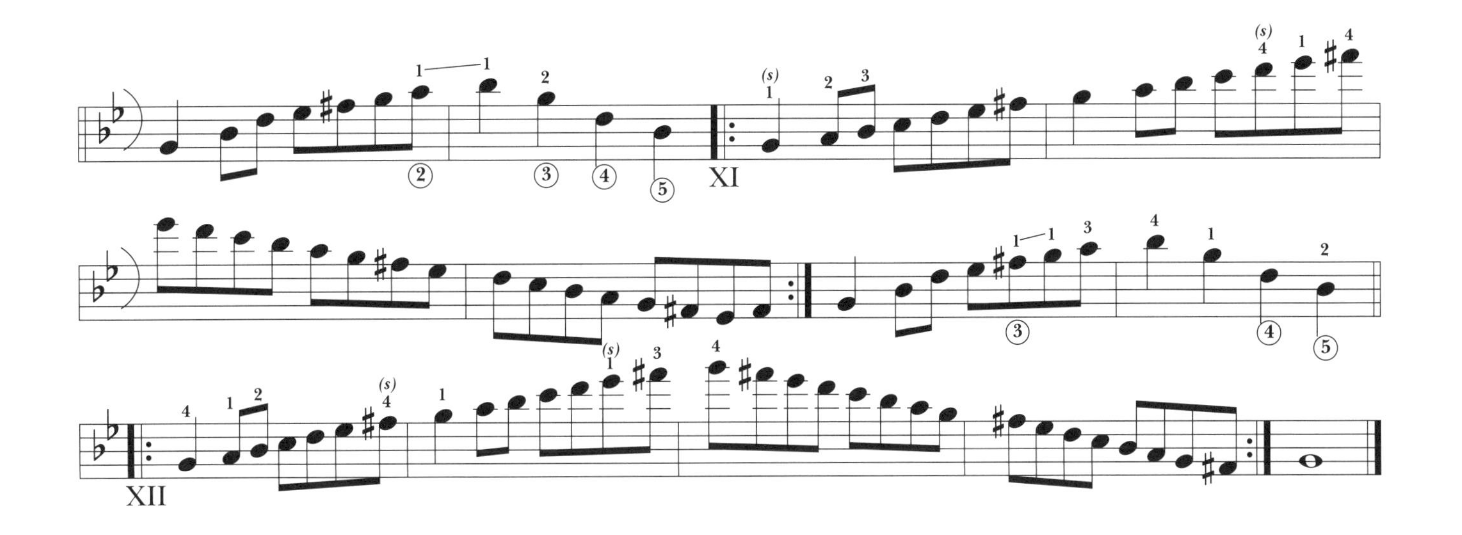

Etude in G Minor (solo)

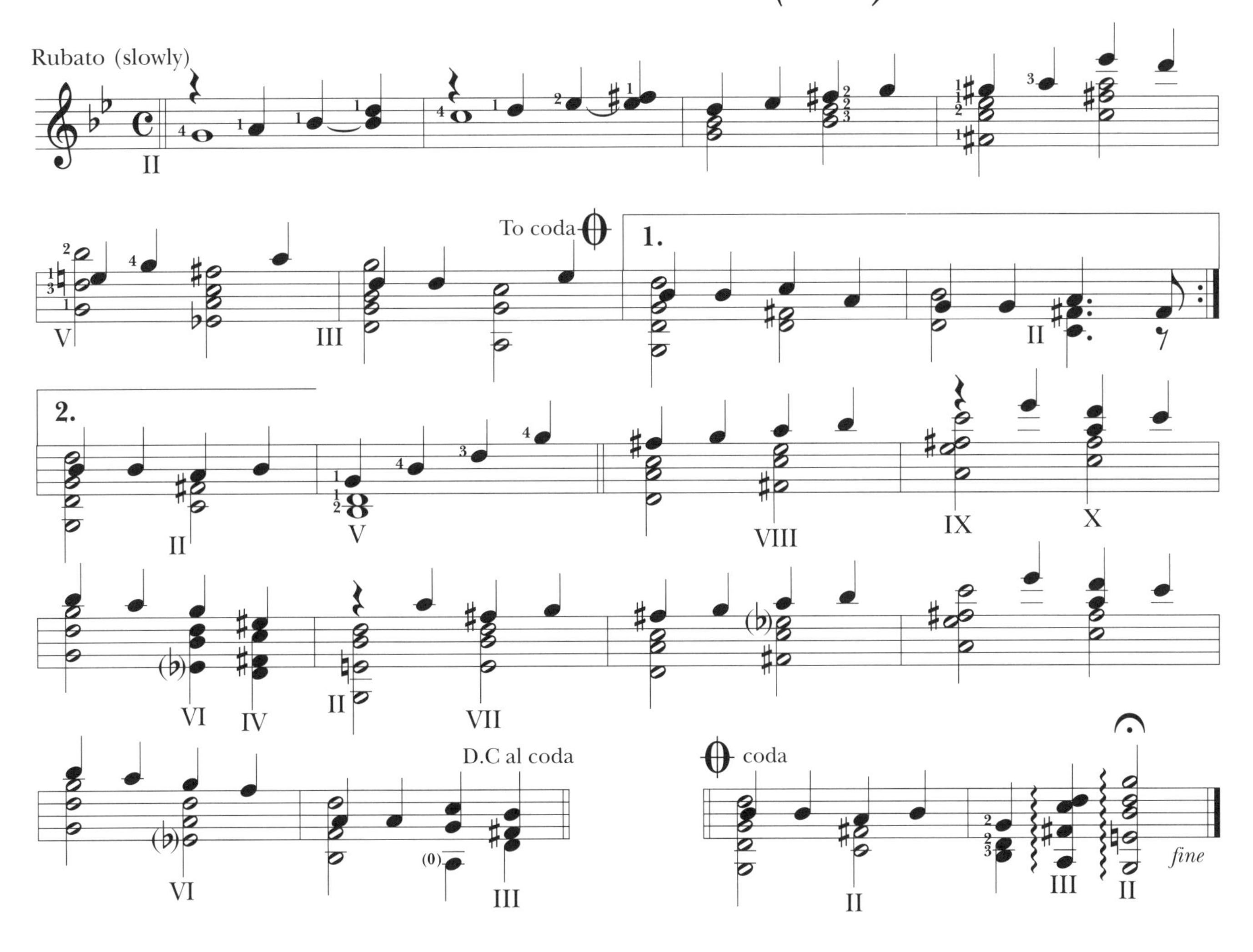

Arpeggios—Diminished 7 Chords

Chord Spelling Most Used

Because the notes of the diminished 7 chord divide the chromatic scale into four equal parts (all minor 3rd intervals), any chord tone may be considered the root. To eliminate the use of double flats in notation, chord spelling varies. Diminished 7 chords are often notated as if they were constructed from major scale degrees 1, ♭3, ♭5/♯4, and 6, as well as 1, ♭3, ♭5, ♭♭7. The number 7 is not usually used with diminished chord symbols. The 7th chordal degree is always assumed (unless a three-note structure is specified by the word "triad").

Scale degrees from chord name.

Arpeggios—Dominant 7(♭5) Chords

Because the notes of the dominant 7(♭5) chord divide the chromatic scale into two like parts (each consisting of four half steps and two half steps), the structure can be named from the ♭5 as well as the root.

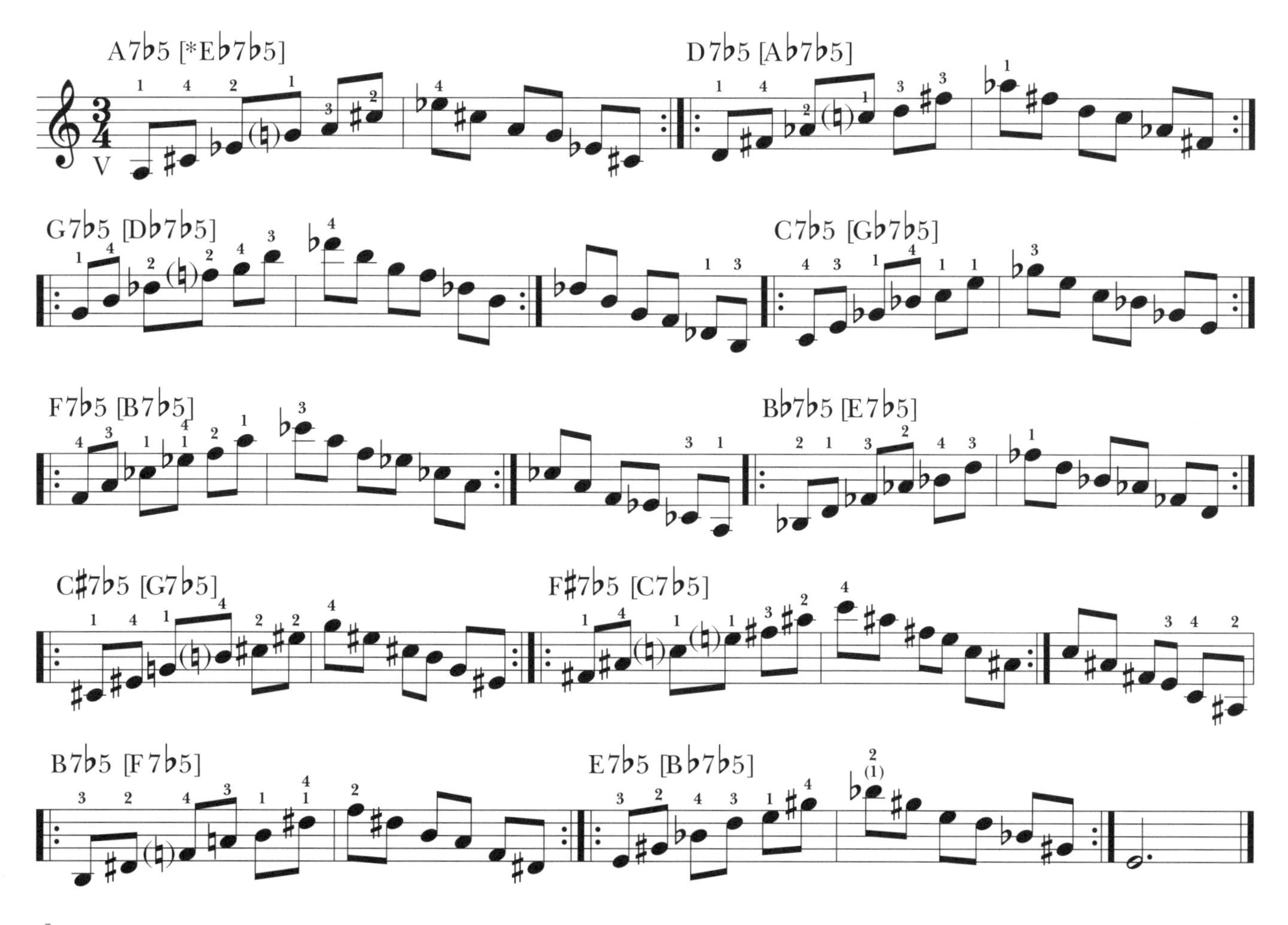

* Enharmonic spelling: same sound but different notation.

Theory: Diatonic 7th Chords—Harmonic Minor

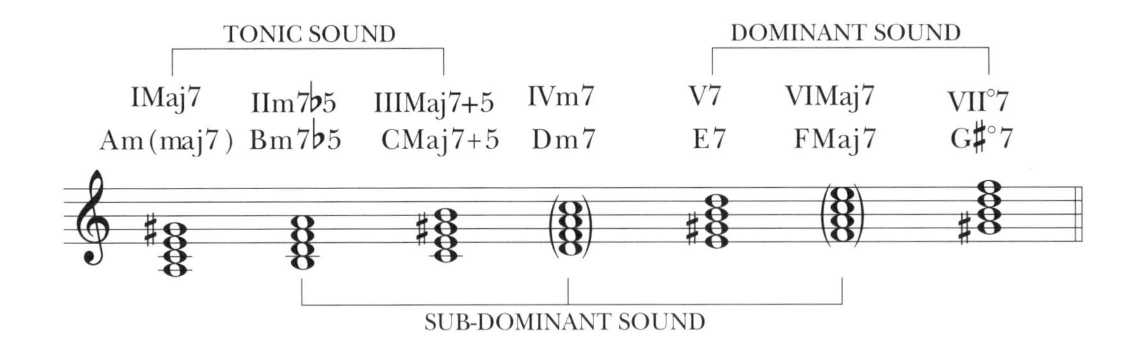

- Note the following:
  - The tonic chord is usually a minor triad. However it is sometimes found brightened up with the 6th degree borrowed from the melodic minor scale.
  - The II chord is always a minor 7(♭5).
  - IIm7(♭5) is often (and misleadingly) referred to as IVm6 (Bm7(♭5) = Dm6).
  - The 9th degree on V7 is always ♭9.
  - IVm7 and VIMaj7 usually occur as passing chords, for they tend to suggest the sound of the relative major (or natural minor).

Expect anything to happen in minor keys, from the most basic diatonic harmonic minor relationships to a conglomeration of (temporary) sounds borrowed from real or traditional melodic and natural minor scales.

Arpeggio and Scale Study

- Play in all possible areas of the fingerboard.

Play the entire sequence without changing position; don't "baby" your fingers.

Chords—Three-Note Voicings

Melodization of Subdominant Minor 6 Chords

Melodic degrees: Real melodic minor scale from chord name.

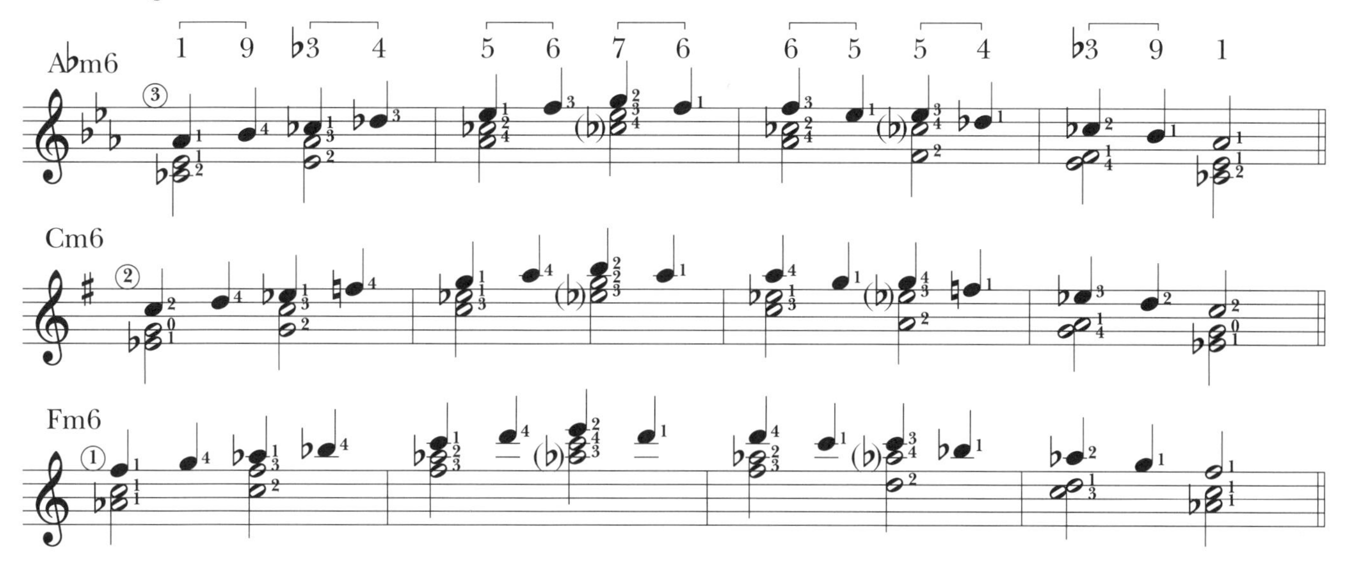

Melodization of Minor 7(♭5) as Altered IIm7 Chords

Melodic degrees: Real melodic minor scale from ♭3 of chord.

As the preceding IVm6 and IIm7(♭5) chords produce the same subdominant minor sound, their voicings are interchangeable (A♭m = Fm7(♭5), etc.).

Melodization of Dominant 7 Chords as IV7 and ♭VII7

Melodic degrees: Real melodic minor scale from 5th degree of chord.

Melodization of Dominant 7 Chords as VI7

Melodic degrees: Real melodic minor scale from intended tonic.

Major Scales—Position X

Twelve keys—through cycle 5.

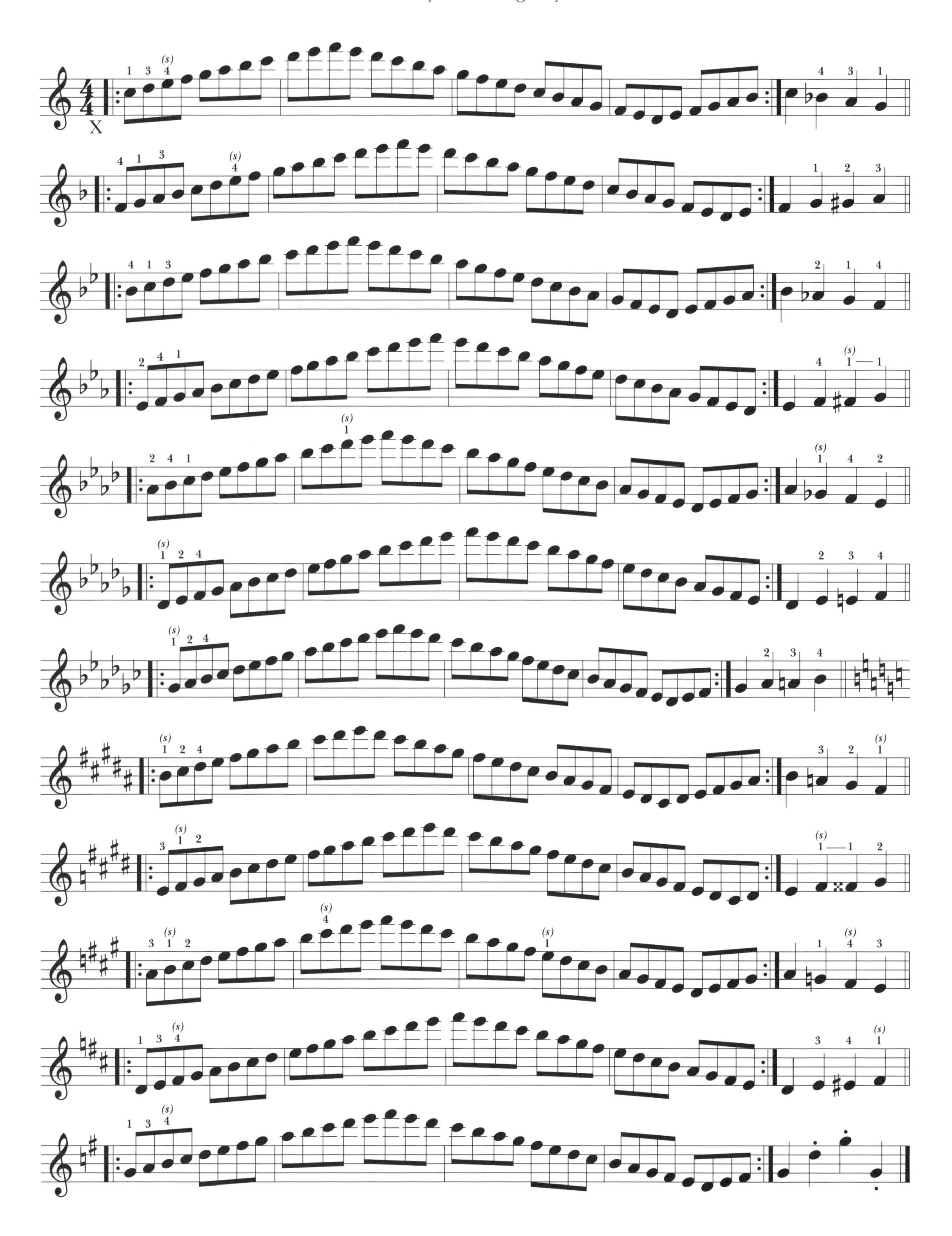

Principle Real Melodic Minor Scales—Position X

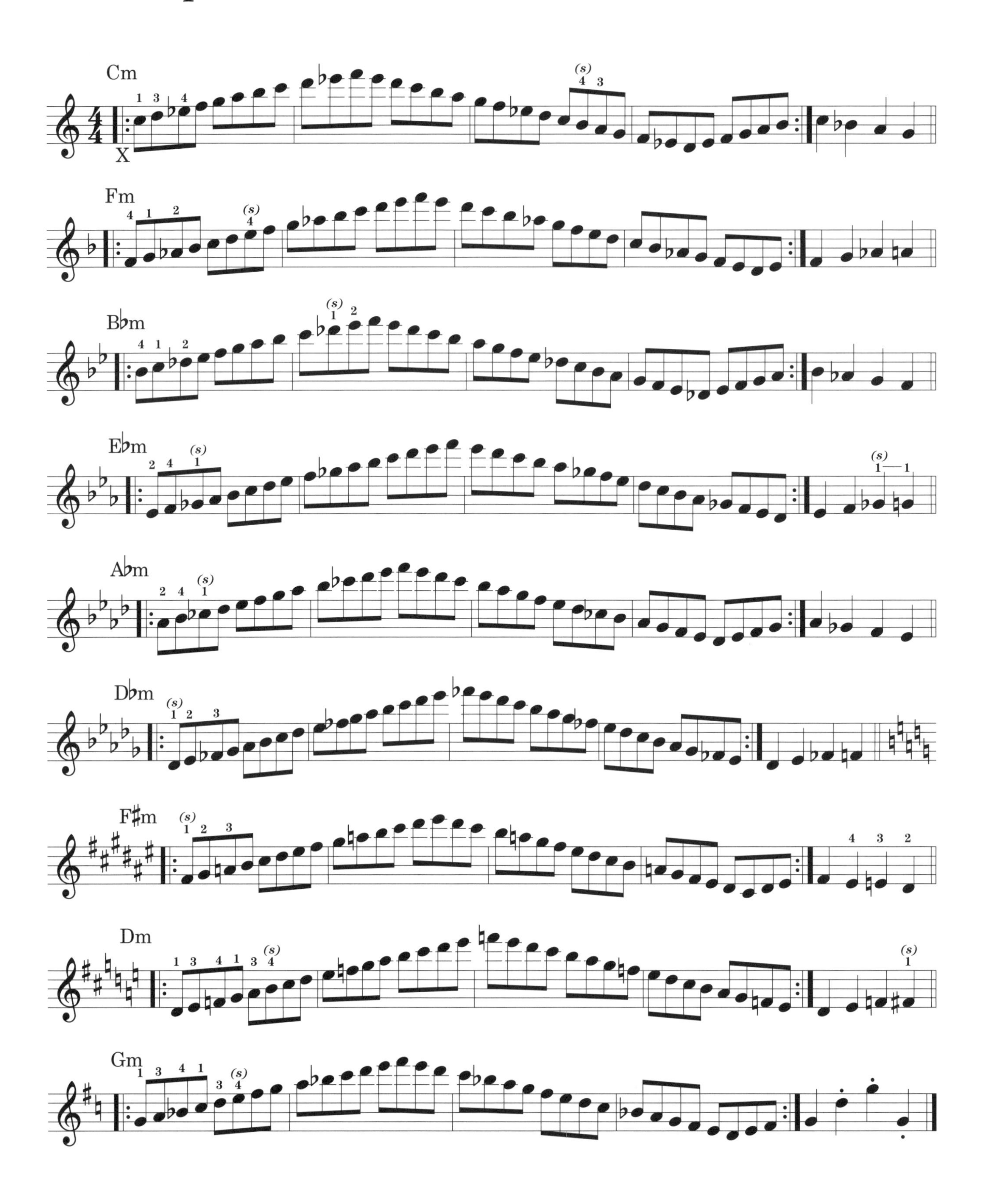

Chords—Three-Note Voicings

Major 6th Chords—Close and Open Voicings

6TH AND 3RD IN THE LEAD

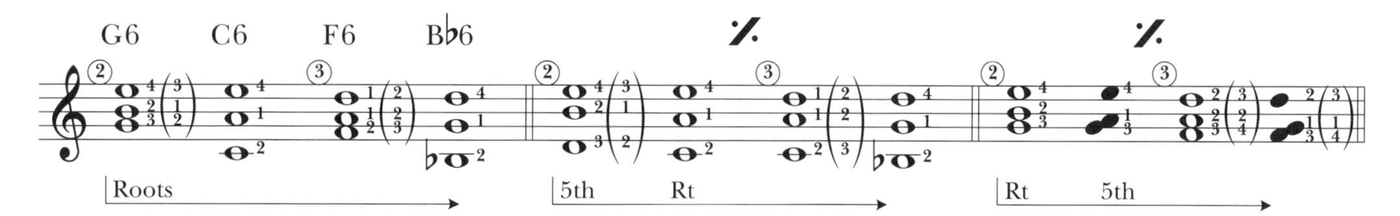

3RD AND 6TH IN THE LEAD
(ROOT, 5TH, INSIDE VOICE)

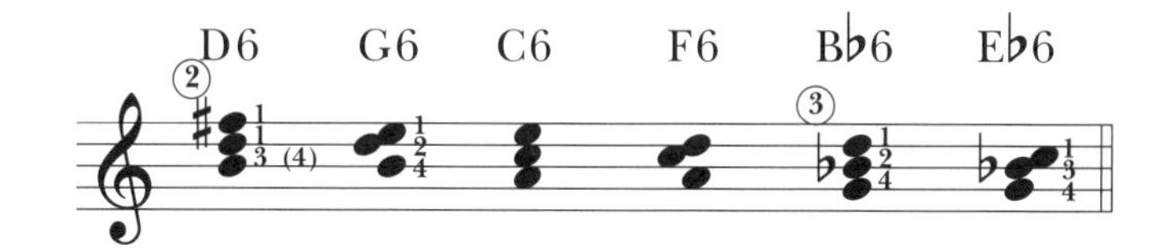

ROOT AND 5TH IN THE LEAD

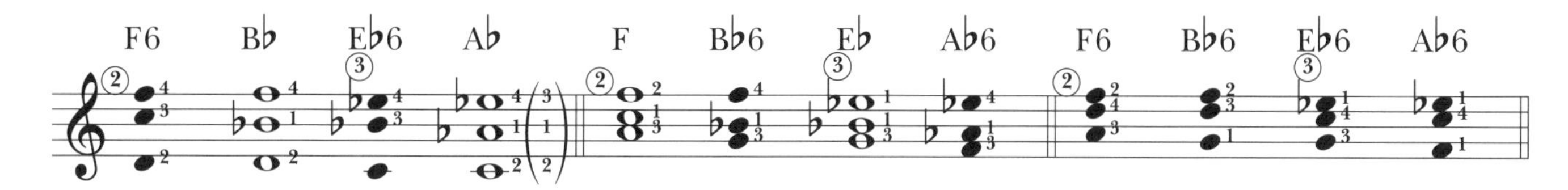

Major 7th Chords

3RD AND MAJOR 7TH IN THE LEAD

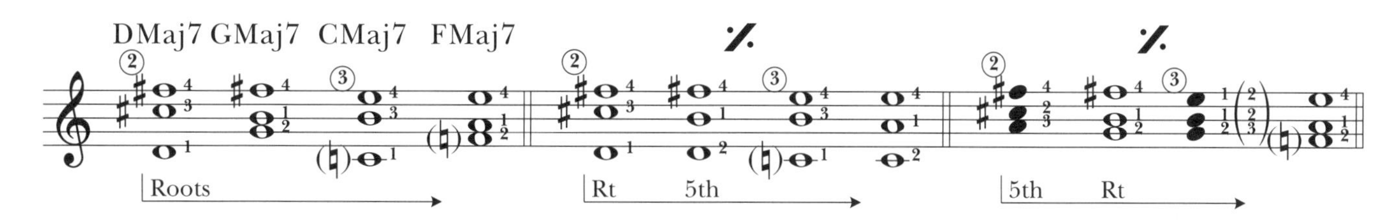

3RD AND MAJOR 7TH IN THE LEAD
(ROOT, 5TH, INSIDE VOICE)

NO ROOT, LEAD WITH MAJOR 7TH

5TH IN THE LEAD

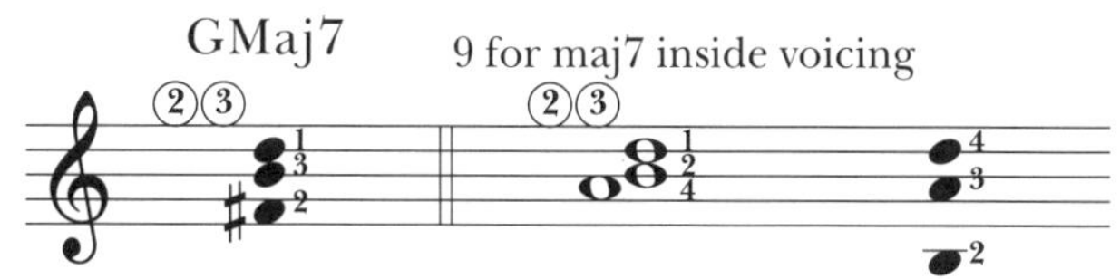

Major 6 and 7 Chords—Open Voicings, All Inversions

Chord Construction—Five-Part Harmony

- A 9th chord (five notes) is built by adding another note a 3rd above the four-part structure.

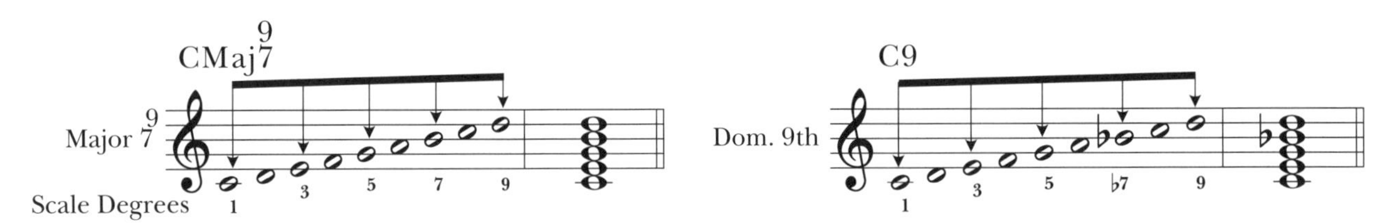

Only dominant 7 and sus4 chords will accept an alteration of a half step up or down to this added 9th, i.e. C7(♭9), C7(♯9), or +9.

Five-Note Arpeggios

Major 7 (9) and Dominant 9 Chords—Chord Spelling

Fingering for all five-note chords is shown in the fifth position with temporary changes to adjacent positions when necessary. After learning as written, transpose and play all structures from all letter names existing from position II through position X.

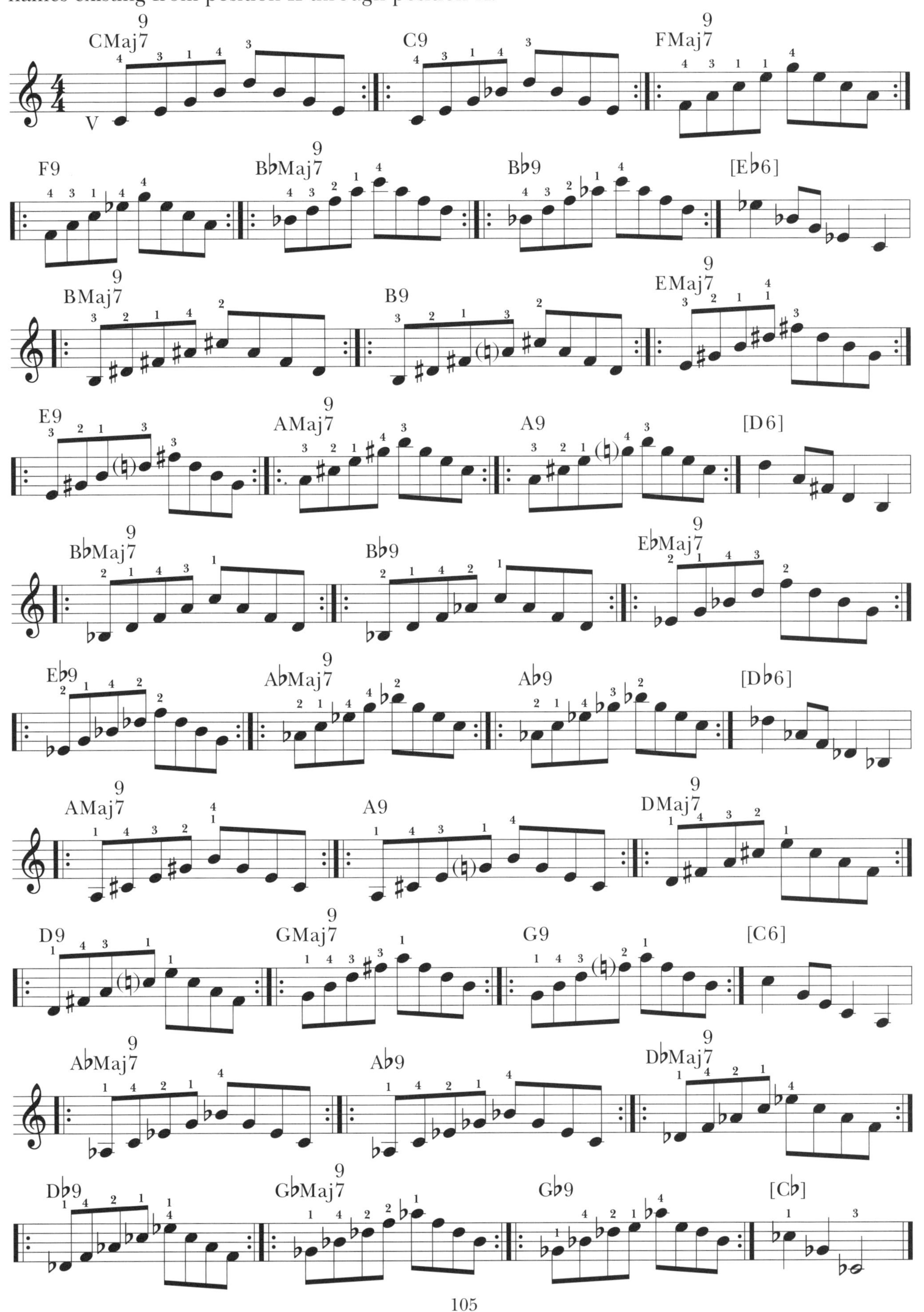

Daydreams (duet)

Slow 4

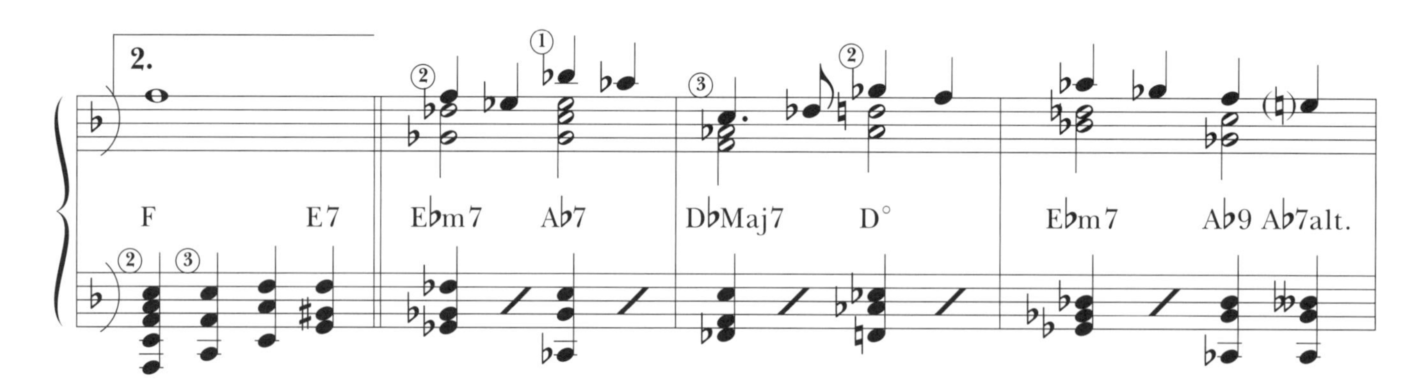

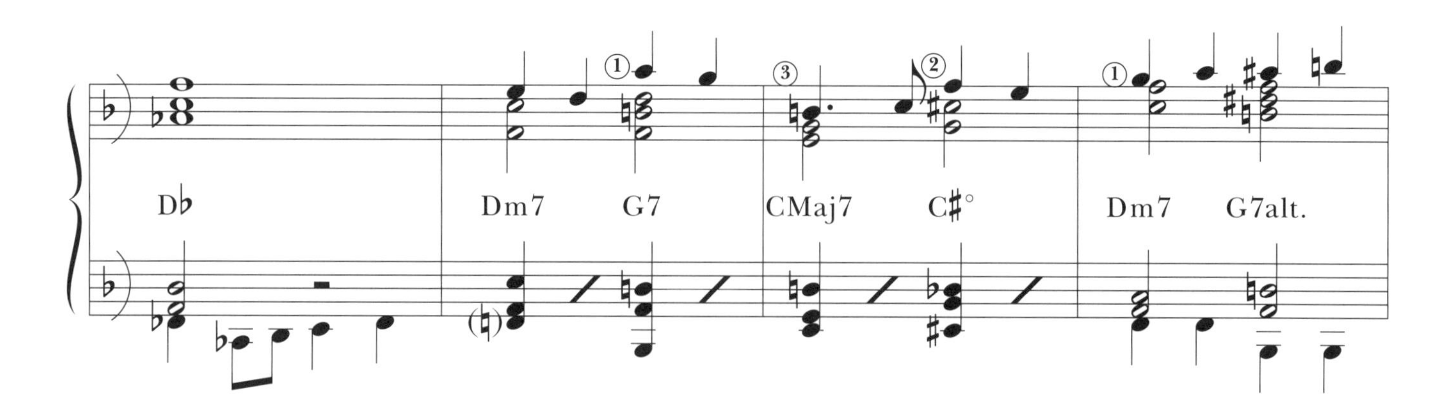

✱ Observe strings indicated for top note of chord voicings

Five-Note Arpeggios

Minor 9 and Diminished 9 chords—Chord Spelling

The diminished 9 chord symbol used below does not indicate the lowering of the 9th chordal degree. Instead, it represents the four-part diminished 7 chord with the major 9th added. This is logical when you compare it with the meaning of minor 9 chord symbols, i.e. minor 7 with 9 added.

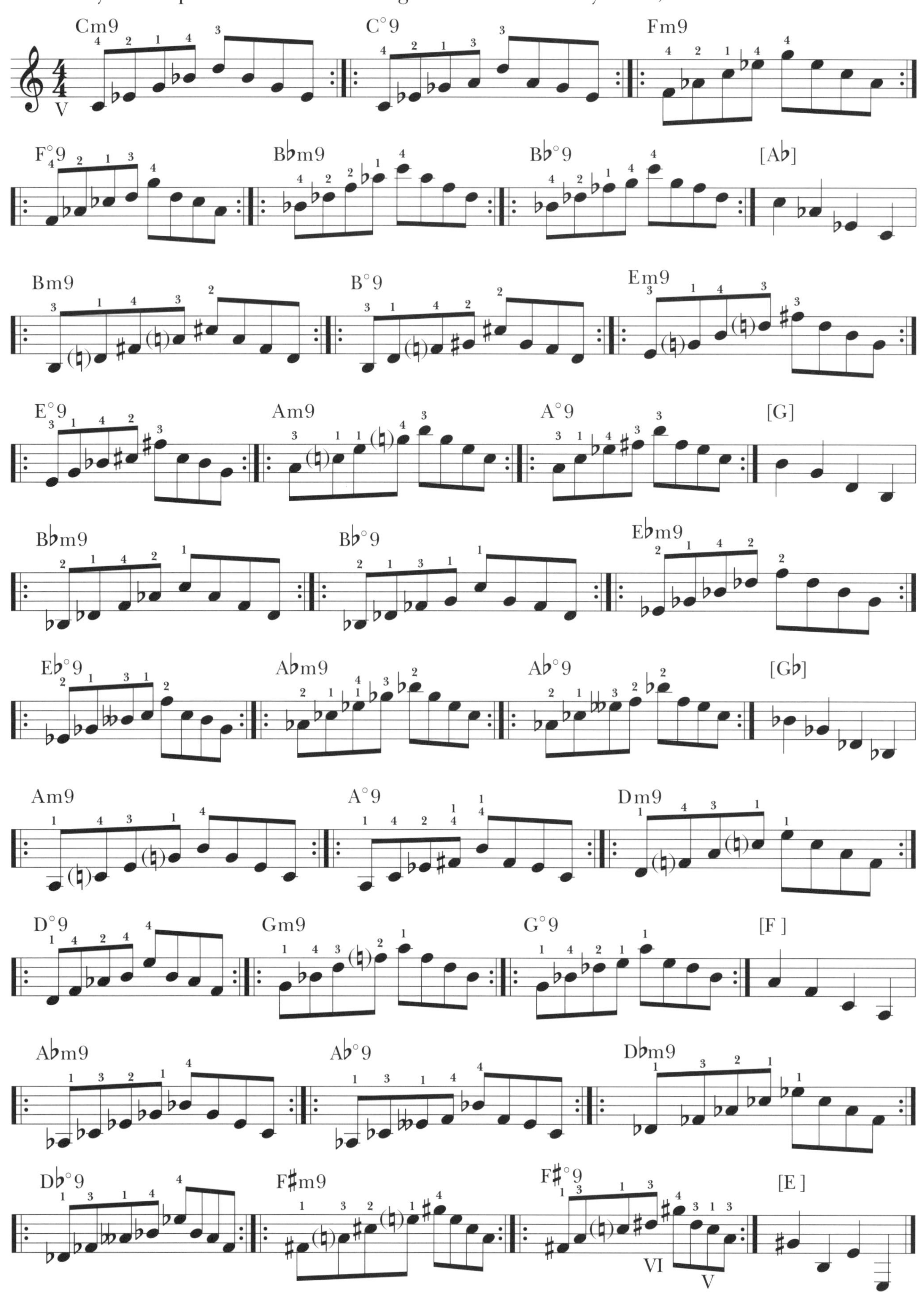

D Major Scale (Twelve Positions)

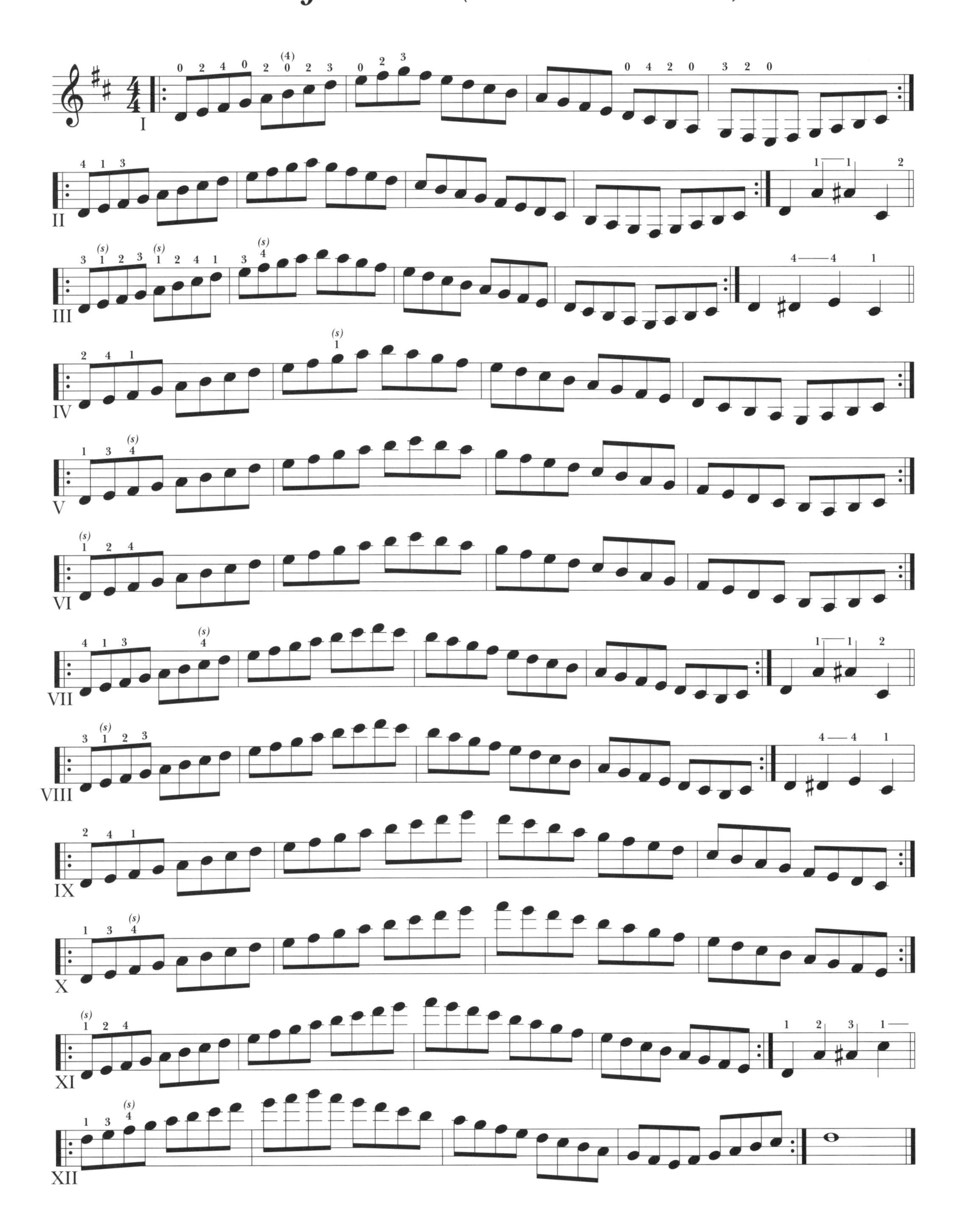

B Harmonic Minor (Nine Positions)

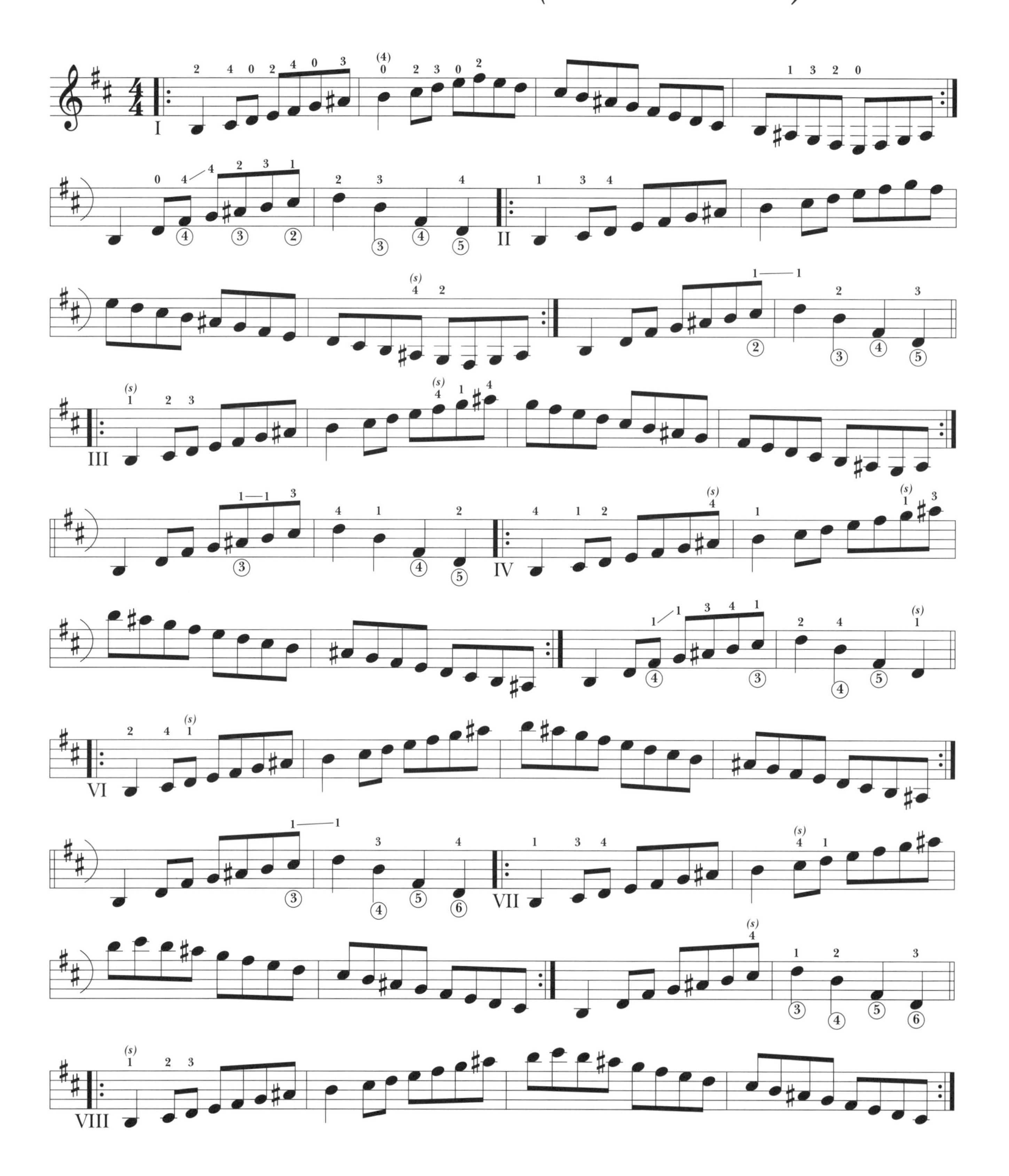

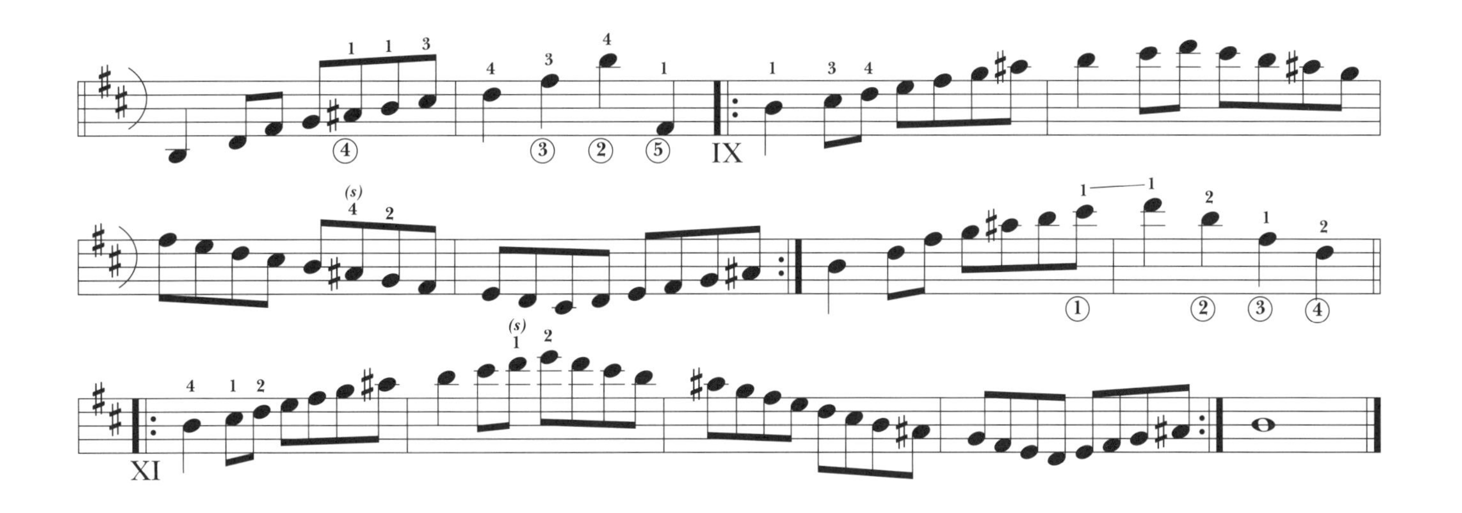

B Minor Etude (solo)

Chords—Three-Note Voicings

Dominant 7 Chord Study with ♭5 (Chromatic Approach) in the Bass

About Chord Progressions (Cycle 5)

To aid in determining the true name of a chord structure, and therefore the related scale and function it represents, be aware that the strongest and most common chord movement is down a 5th (cycle 5). Investigate all possible names for the chord in question, and the one that makes the strongest cadence to the following chord will be the real name.

Examples:

Gm6 to F	= C9 to F	Gm6 to A7	= Em7(♭5) to A7
A° or F♯° to Gm7	= D7(♭9) to Gm7	A7 to F6	= A7 to Dm7
G° or E° to F	= C7(♭9) to F	Gm7(♭5) or B♭m6 to D9	= *A7alt or E♭9 to D9

*When a dominant 7 chord is completely altered (both 9 and 5 chromatically raised and/or lowered), it takes on all the characteristics of the other dominant 7 chords containing the same tritone. This substitute dominant 7 (with tensions 9, +11, 13) is constructed from the ♭5 of the altered V7 chord. The chromatic approach (from above) created by this substitute dominant 7 constitutes a very strong progression, second only to cycle 5. To help in the investigation of multiple names for chord structures, study the information on the next page.

Note: Look ahead to the next chord to analyze a progression. Look back to the preceding chord to determine the related scale.

Theory: Interchangeable Chord Structures

The following chord structures could be referred to as diatonic substitutions, in that they represent (in the proper setting) the exact same scale sound.

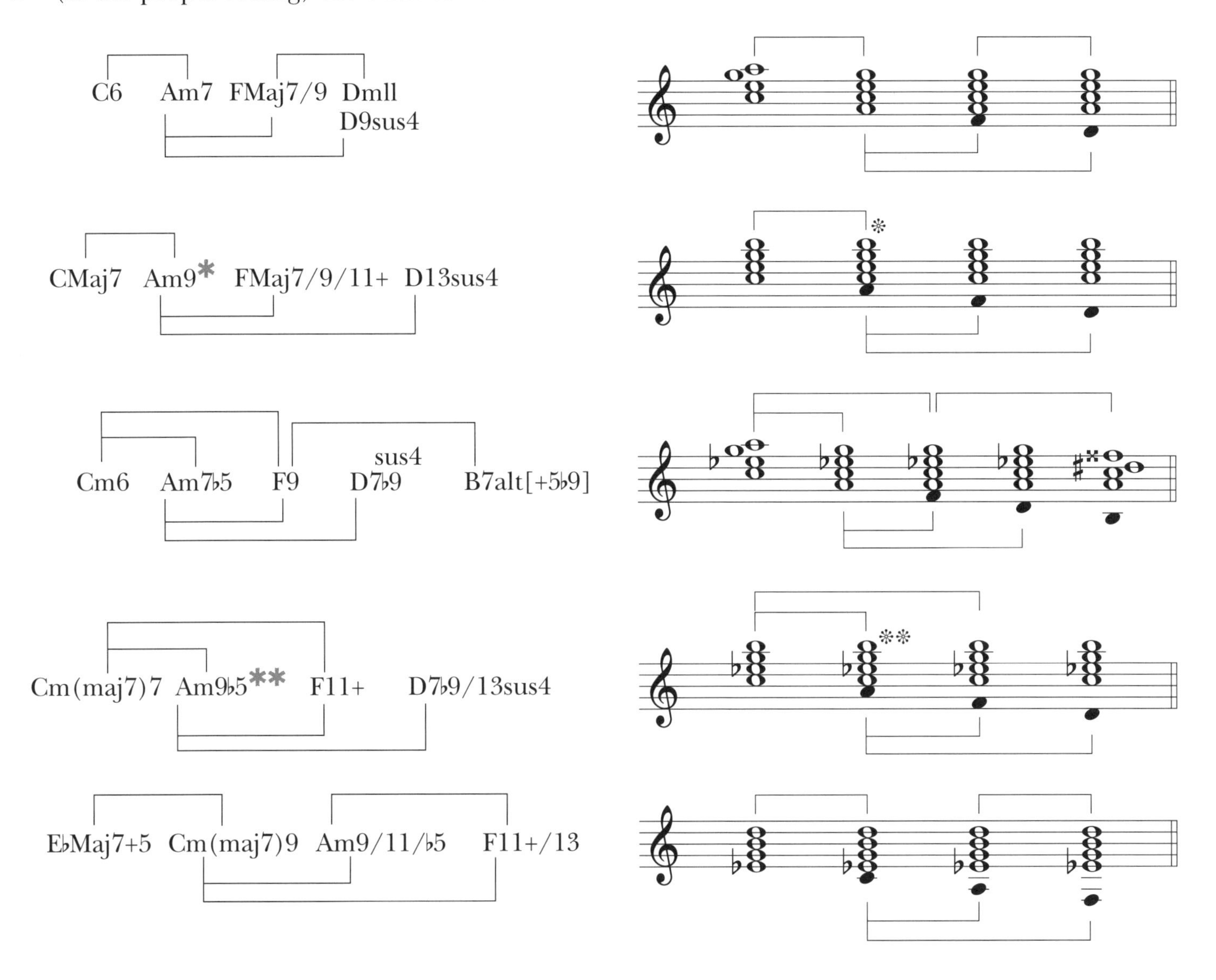

* Am9 can also be considered C6/7
** Am9(♭5) can be considered Cm6/7.

All four names of diminished 7 chords and their related dominant 7(♭9) chords are completely interchangeable.

Rhythm Guitar—The Right Hand

Joropo and Nanigo
Moderately fast to fast

Arpeggio Study—7th Chords

▌ Play from all fingers, but stay in position throughout the entire sequence.

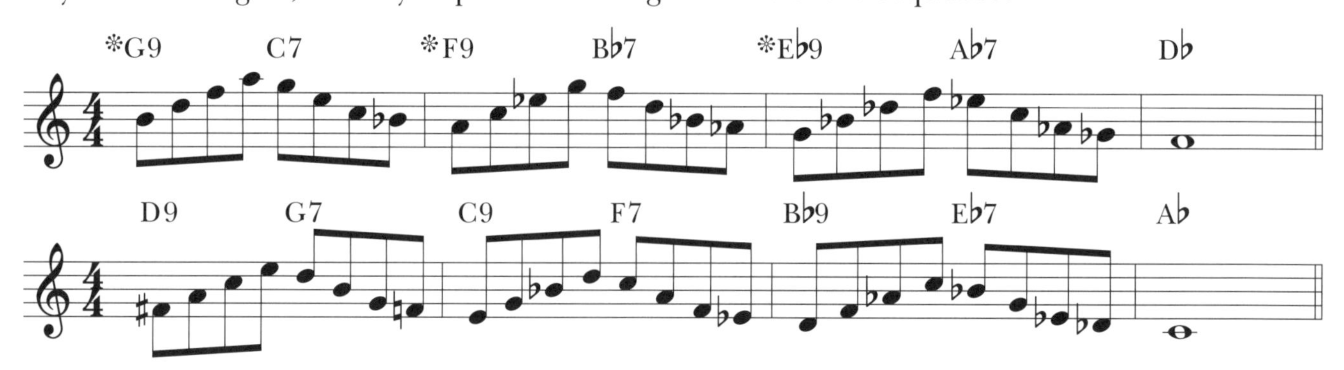

* Also play first chord of each measure as a minor 9 and as a dominant 7(♭9).

Chords—Three-Note Voicings

Melodization of Minor 7 Chords as IIIm7

Melodic degrees: Major scale a 3rd below chord name.

✱ Passing tones only. (Note: ♭9 can be a chord tone of dominant 7 only.)

IIIm7 can be used as a diatonic substitution for I (Am7 = Fmaj7). But stay out of the low register when doing this. The 5th of the IIIm7 chord is the major 7 of the I chord, and the major 7th chord degree should not occur below the note D on the first space below the staff.

Melodization of Minor 7(♭5) Chords as VIIm7(♭5)

Melodic degrees: Major scale a half step above chord name.

VIIm7(♭5) can be used as a diatonic substitution for V7 (Am7(♭5) = F9). But as with IIIm7 for I, this is not good in the low register.

Chromatic Melodization of Dominant 7 Chords

Eleven of the twelve chromatic tones can be considered chord degrees of a dominant 7 structure. The exception is the major 7.

CLOSE VOICINGS

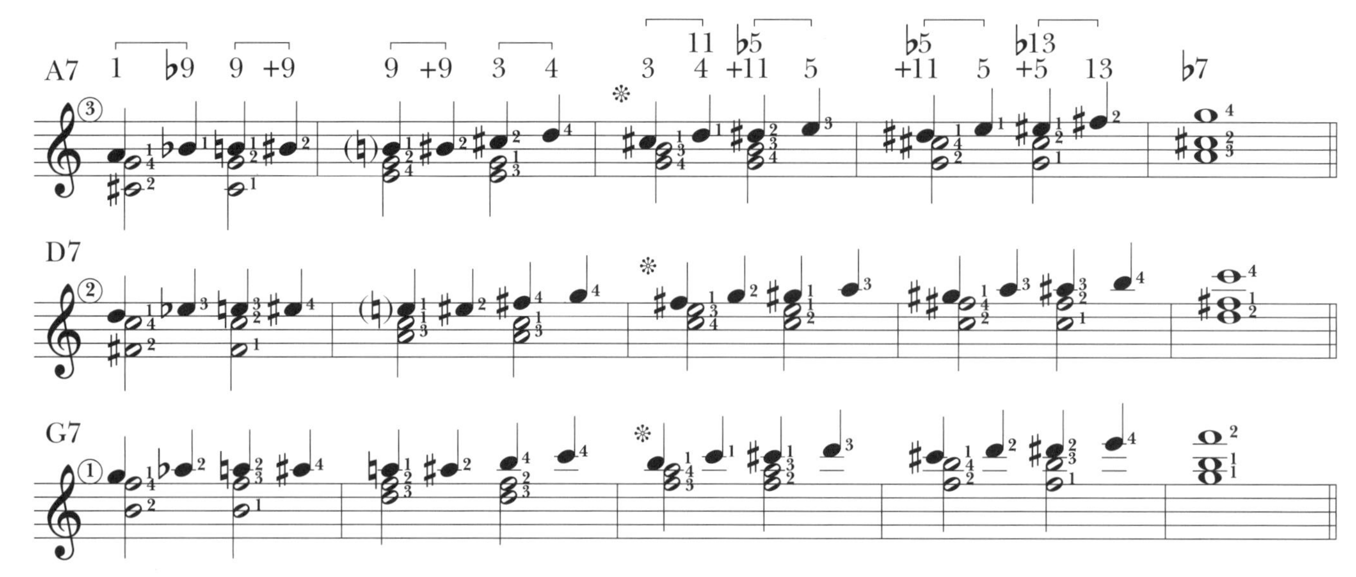

✱ 9 for 1, inside voice.

Also possible with root, but somewhat more difficult physically.

EXAMPLE

OPEN VOICINGS

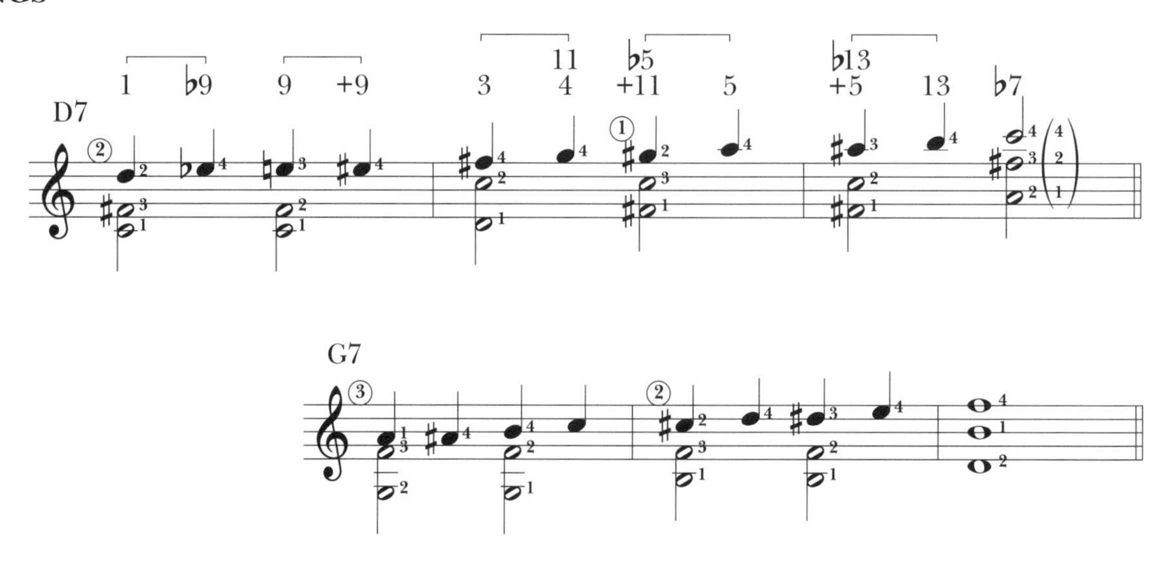

Melodic Rhythm Study No. 11

Five-Note Arpeggios

Minor (6, 9), Major (6, 9), Dominant 9sus4, and Dominant 7(♭9) Chords

Chord Spelling

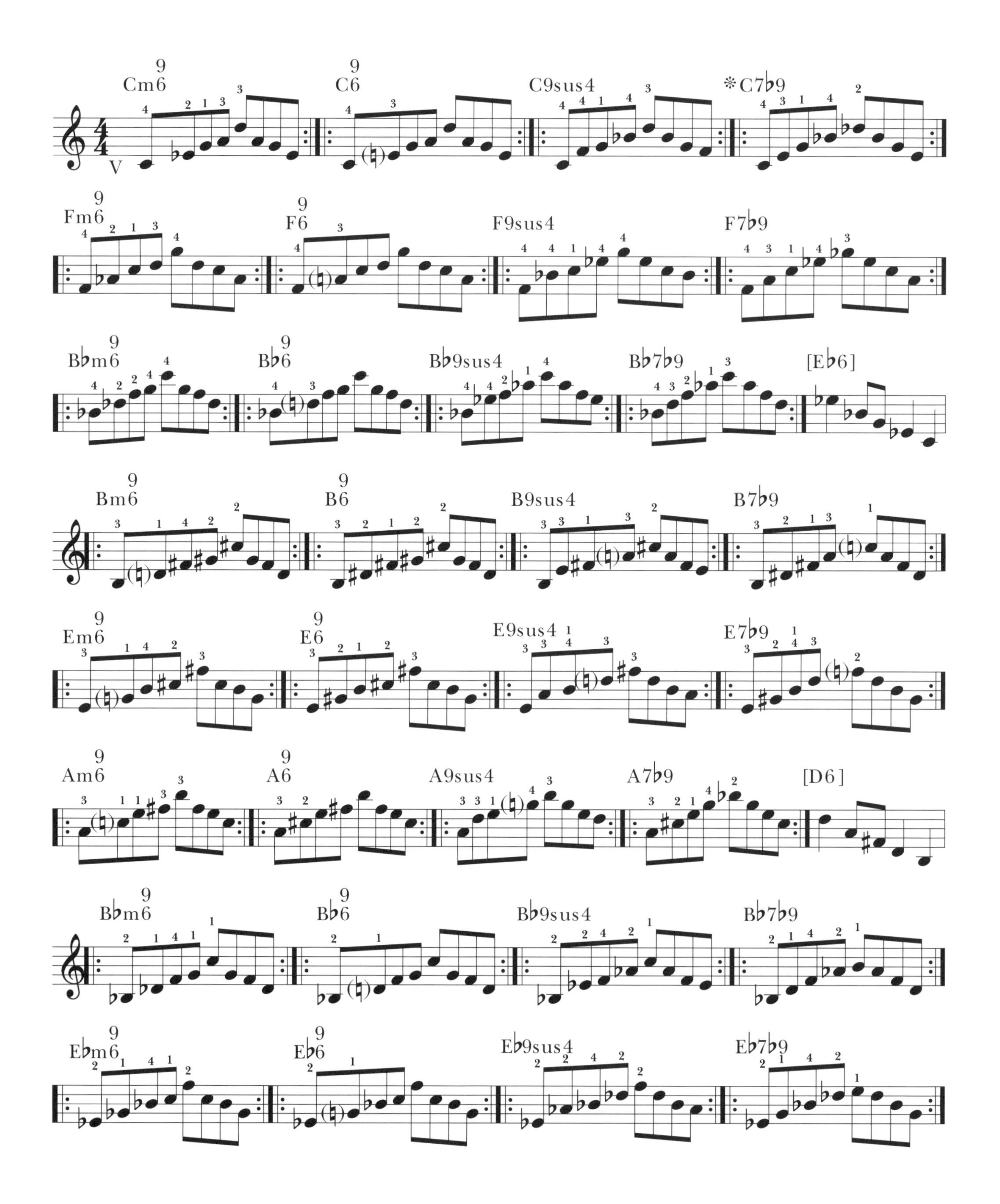

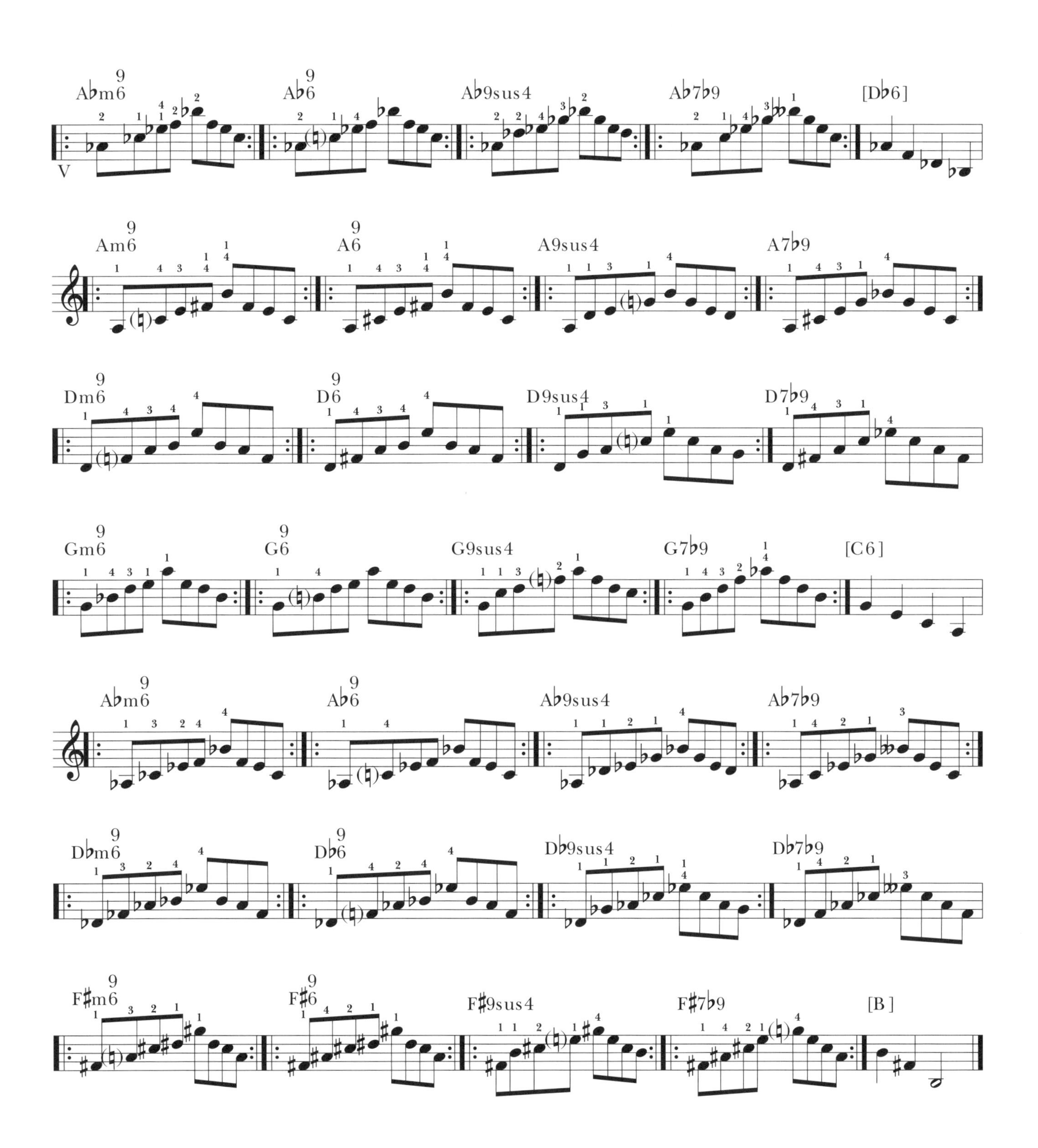

✱ Only dominant 7 and dominant 7sus4 chords will accept an alteration of a half step up or down to this added 9th chord degree.

Chords—Three-Note Voicings

Minor 7 Chords—Close and Open Voicings

♭3RD AND ♭7TH IN THE LEAD

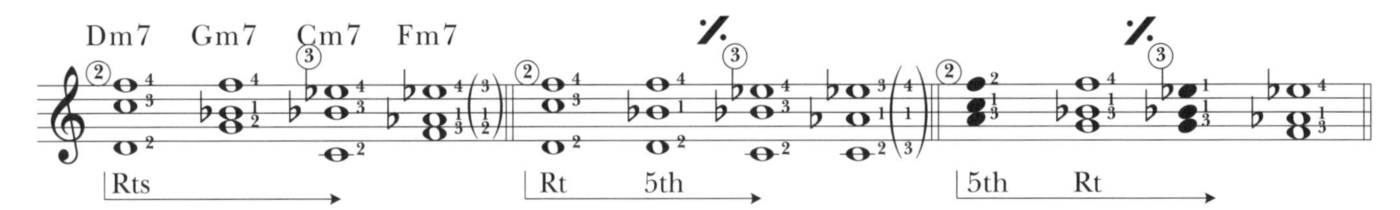

♭3RD AND ♭7TH IN THE LEAD
ROOT AND 5TH, INSIDE VOICE

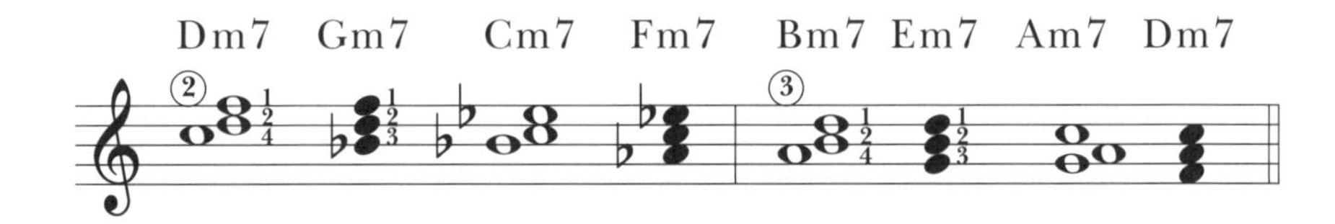

ROOT AND 5TH IN THE LEAD

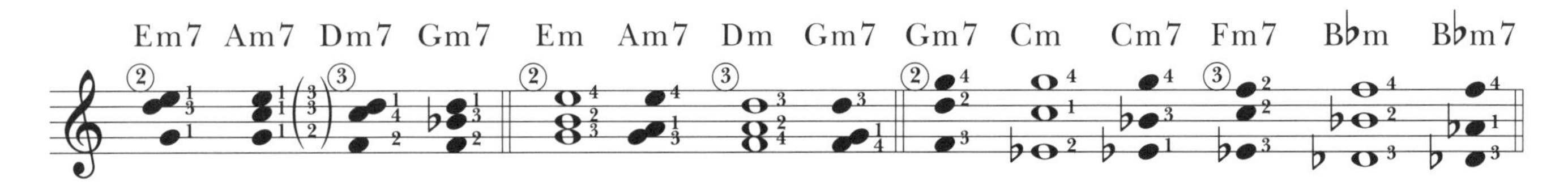

Minor 6 Chords

6TH AND ♭3RD IN THE LEAD

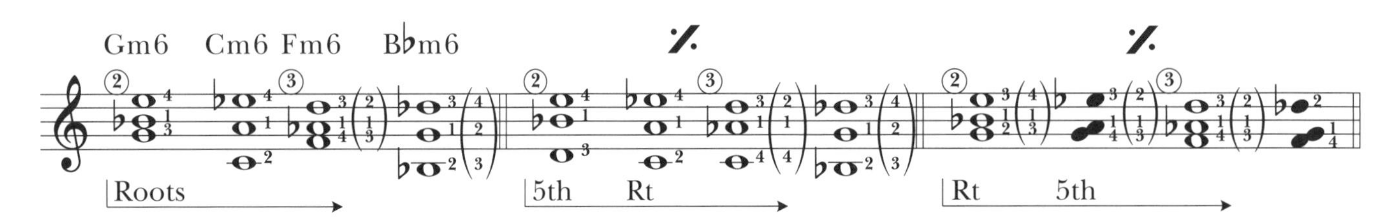

♭3RD AND 6TH IN THE LEAD
ROOT AND 5TH, INSIDE VOICE

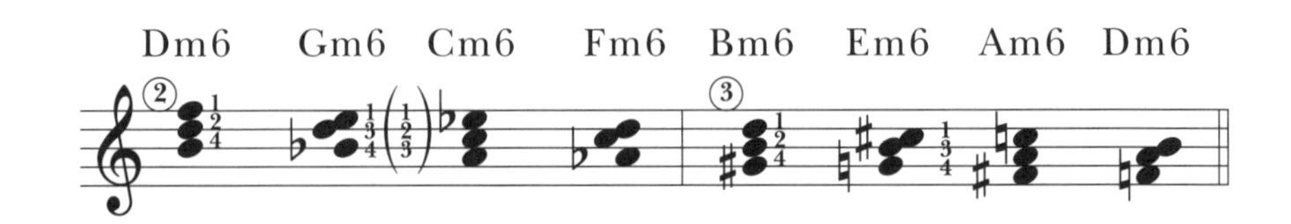

ROOT AND 5TH IN THE LEAD

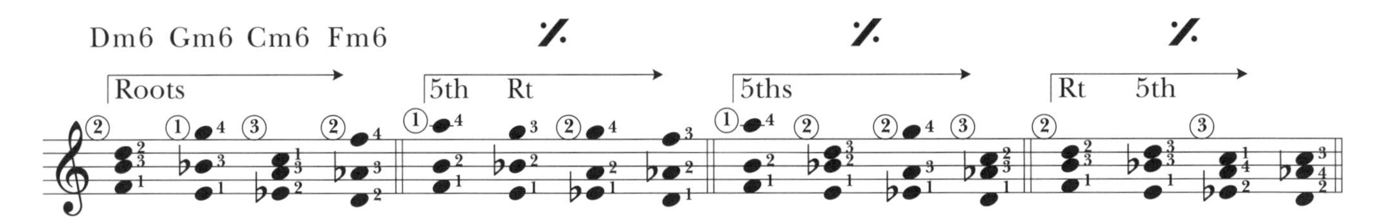

Minor 7 Chords—Open Voicings, All Inversions

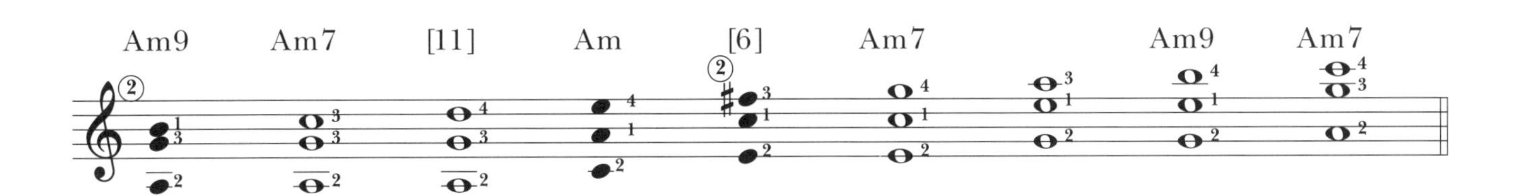

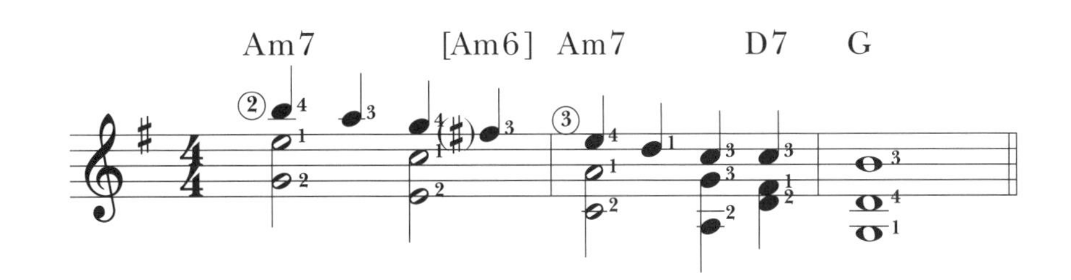

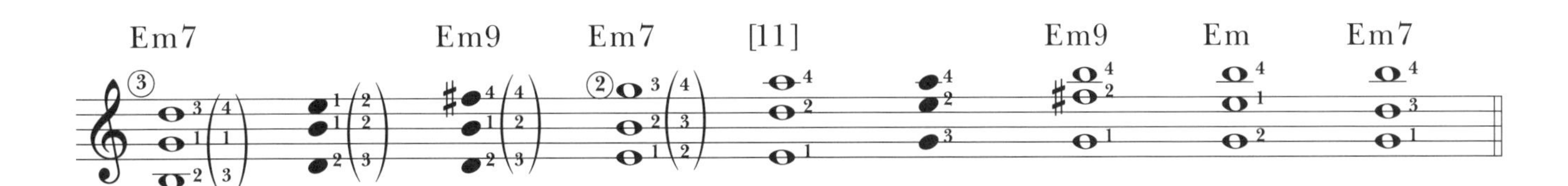

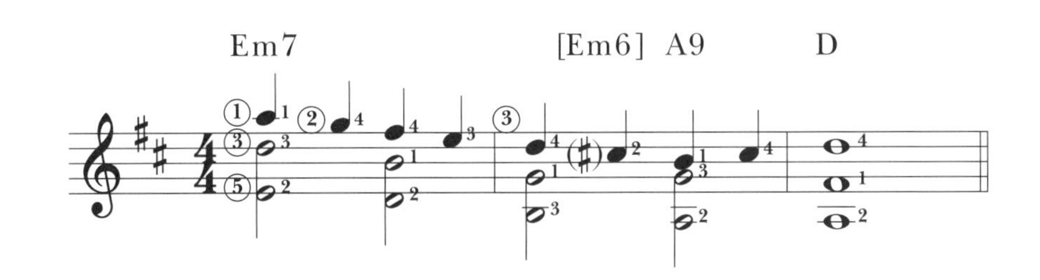

IIm7–V7–I Chord Study

Chord-Scale Relationships

For improvisation.

SPECIAL ALTERATIONS ON DOMINANT 7 CHORDS WITH SCALE TONE ROOTS (EXCEPT IV7)

sus4	The subdominant sound of IIm7 (or IV6); treat accordingly
sus4(alt 9)	Subdominant minor sound of IIm7(♭5) (IV6); treat accordingly
	Note: 3rd degree of sus4 chords must be a melodic passing tone only.
Alt 5	On dominant 7 chords that contain an unaltered 9th, I7, II7, V7, VI7 = Whole tone scale from any chord tone.
	The specified ♯5 can often be treated as ♭13, and specified ♭5 can be treated as +11.
	See below, ♭13 and +11.
Alt 5 and 9	Real melodic minor scale from ♭9 of chord.
	Sometimes the alt 9 is not specified and must be remembered as already being present. Ex: III7 and VII7.
	For optional melodic treatment of ♯5 (alt 9) see below, ♭13(alt 9).
	For optional melodic treatment of ♭5 (alt 9) see below, +11(alt 9).
Alt 9	On V7, II7, I7, use real melodic minor from ♭7 of chord. Or, major scale with ♭6 from intended tonic.
	Also, you may combine both scales, real melodic minor with added ♯4.
Alt 9 on VI7	Harmonic or natural minor from intended tonic.
Unaltered 9 on III7 and VII7	Real melodic minor from intended tonic.
11	Sus4 on dominant 7.
	(See sus4.)
Aug 11 ♯11, +11	On all dominant 7 chords, use real melodic minor from chord 5th.
	The 9th is considered unaltered with +11 unless specified alt.
+11(alt 9)	Diminished scale from chord degrees 3, 5, ♭7, ♭9.
13	On dominant 7 chords with scale tone roots (except IV7), use the major scale from the intended tonic.
	The 9th is considered unaltered and the 11th natural with these 13th chords unless otherwise specified.

13(alt 9)	Same as alt 9 on V7.
13(+11)	Same as augmented 11.
13 (+11, ♭9)	Same as +11(alt 9).
♭13	On dominant 7 chords with unaltered 9ths, I7, II7, V7, (VI7) use real melodic minor from intended tonic.
♭13 (alt 9)	Harmonic (or natural) minor from intended tonic.
	Remember ♭13 and alt 9 are already contained in III7 and VII7 and therefore do not constitute any alteration on them.

SPECIAL ALTERATIONS ON IV7 AND DOMINANT 7 CHORDS WITH NON-SCALE TONE ROOTS

sus4	The sound of IIm7 (or IV6); treat accordingly.
Alt 5	Whole tone scale from any chord tone.
♭5	No alteration; ♭5 is already present as +11.
♯5	Same as alt 5 because ♭5 is already present as +11.
Alt 9	Diminished scale from chord degrees 3, 5, ♭7, ♭9.
Alt 5 and 9	Real melodic minor scale from ♭9 of chord.
11	See sus4.
Aug 11	No alteration (already contained in chord).
+11(alt 9)	Same as alt 9.
13	No alteration.
13(alt 9)	Same as alt 9.
♭13	Same as alt 5 (♭13 must be considered ♯5 here).
♭13 (alt 9)	Same as alt 5 and 9.

Pretty Please (duet)

Em7 A7alt D E♭°
Em7 A9
F♯Maj7 E° E♭7♭9 Dm7 G13♭9 G7+
CMaj7 E♭7
Dm7 G13♭9 F° Em7 E♭°
Dm7 G13♭9
F♯m7♭5 FMaj7 Em7 E♭7
Rit.
Dm7 G13 G7alt. CMaj7

Five-Note Arpeggios

Dominant 7 (aug 9) Chords

Chord Spelling

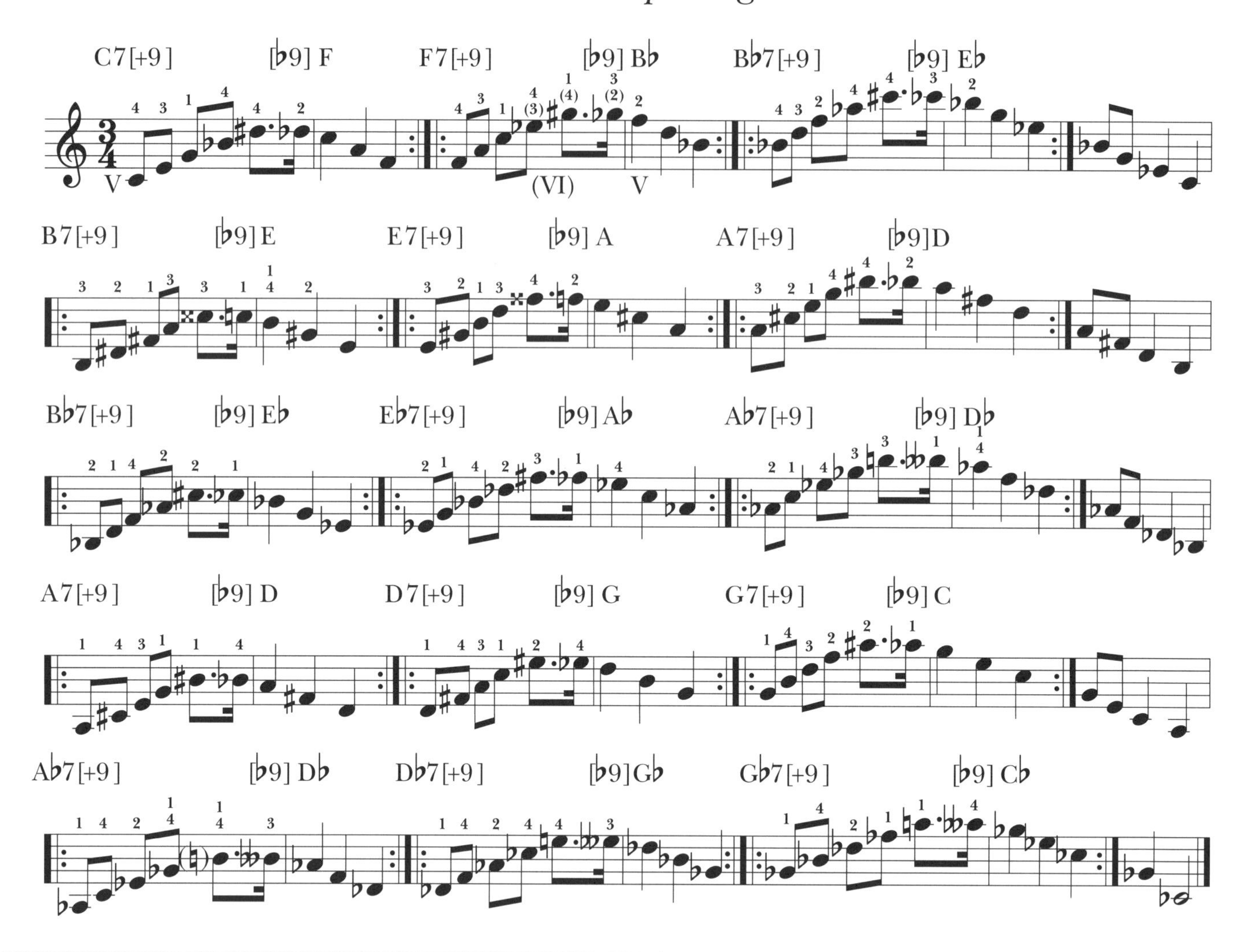

Harmonizing a Melody—From a Lead Sheet with Chords Indicated

Think of the melody as being written an octave higher. Add the most important chord tones under it that are physically available.

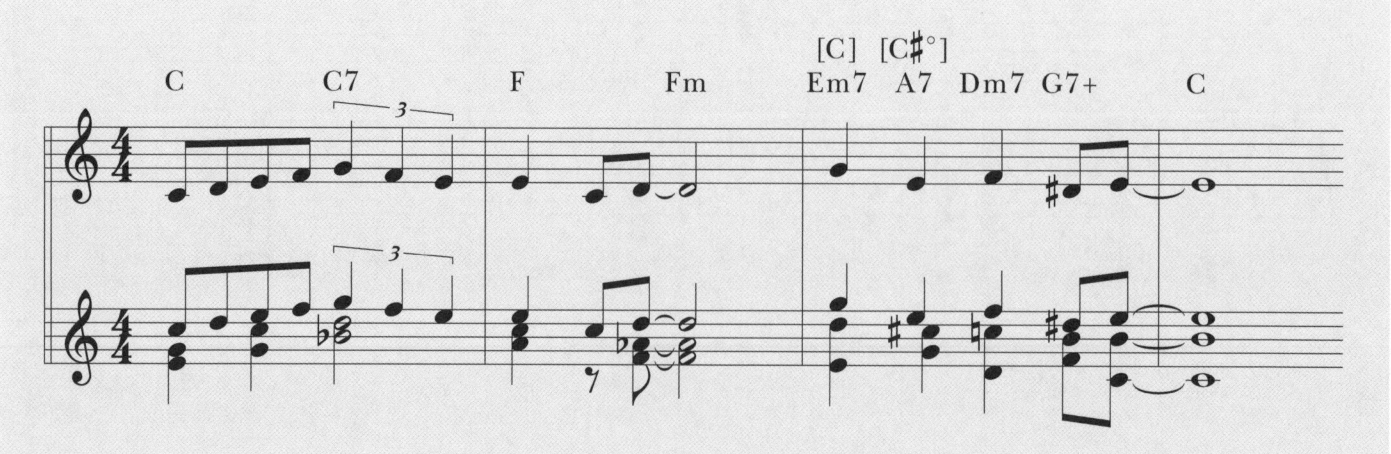

To attempt to play a chord for every melody note is impractical, and it denies you one of the most striking effects of guitar chord-melody playing—that of a moving melody over sustained chord tones.

E♭ Major Scale (Twelve Positions)

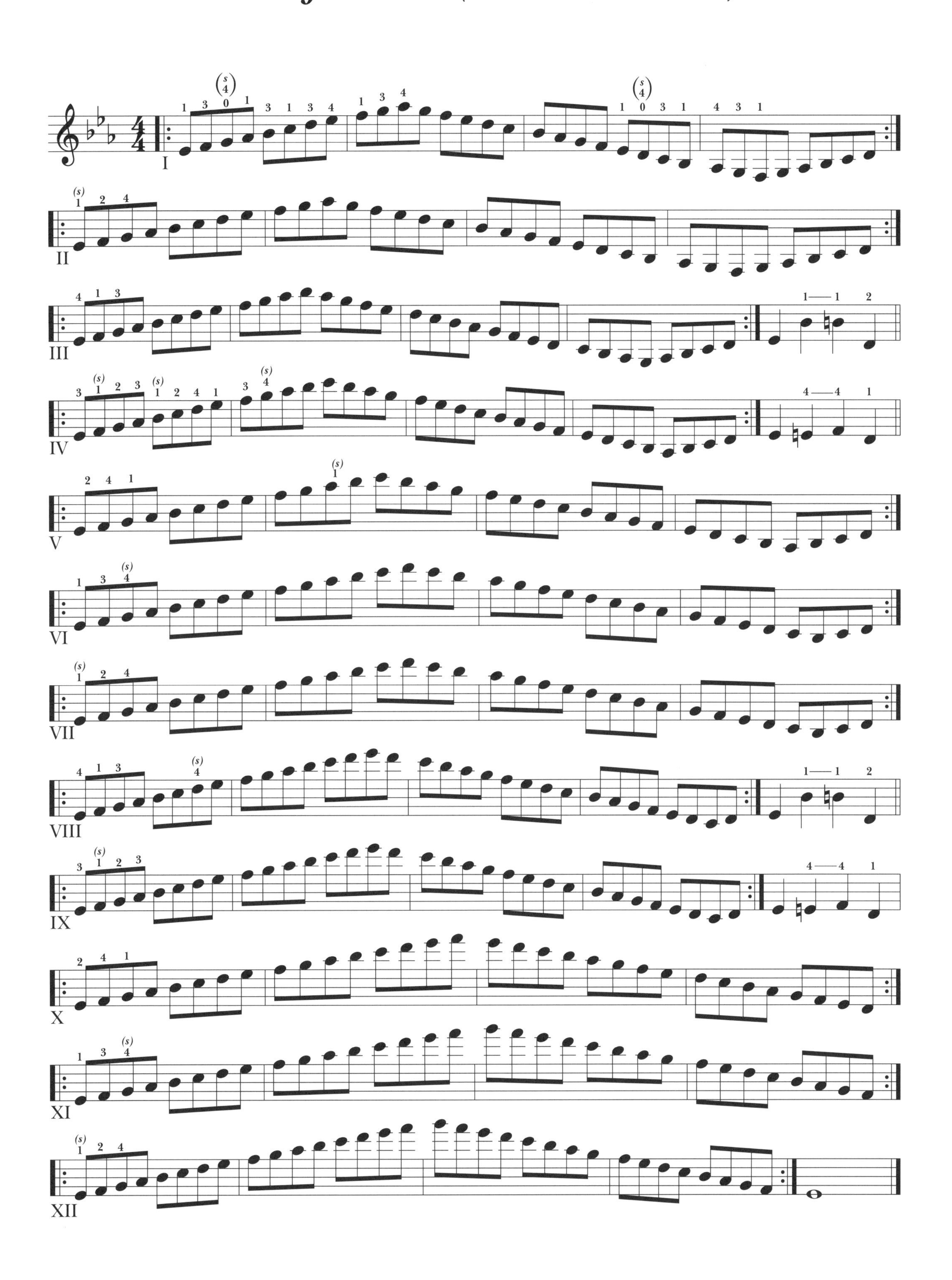

C Harmonic Minor (Nine Positions)

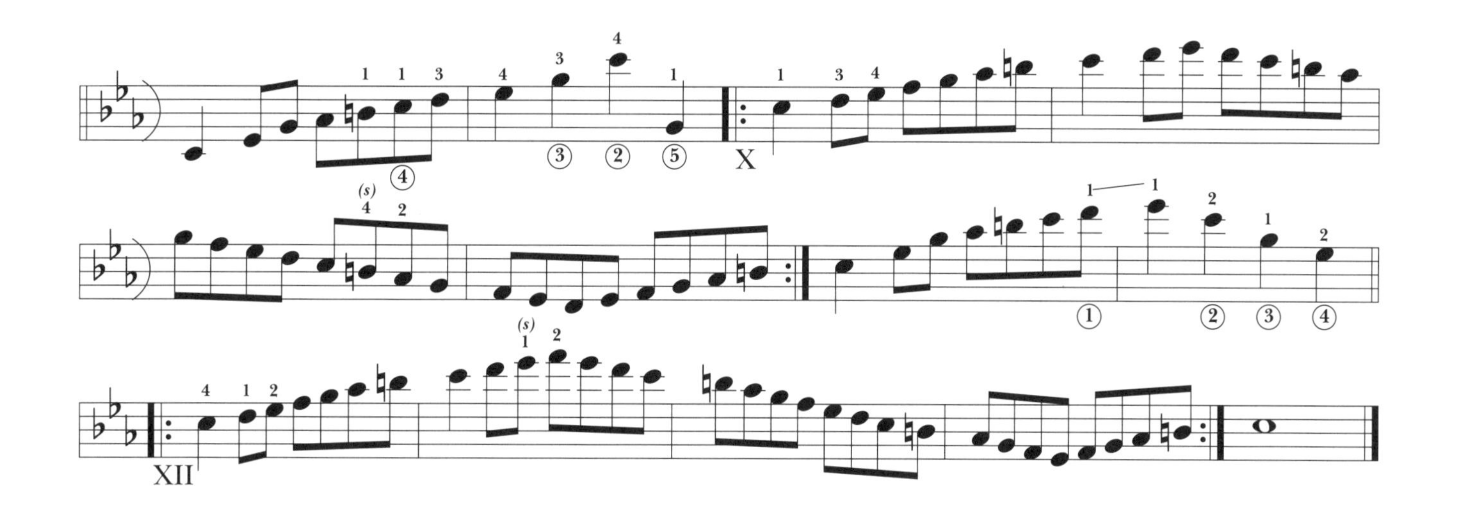

Etude in C Minor (solo)

Chord-Scale Relationships

For improvisation.

Remember: Look ahead to the next chord to analyze a progression. Look back to the preceding chord to determine the related scale.

Major Chords

Major chords with scale tone roots (except IV) represent a tonic sound. Scale = major from chord name.

The IV chord and all major structures with non-scale tone roots represent the subdominant sound. Scale= Major from 5th degree of chord.

All major chords will accept being melodized as IV chords. But realize that the +11 is being forced on those that normally represent the tonic sound.

Also be advised that very occasionally, a nondiatonic major chord with a scale tone root represents a modal sound. That is, the writer wants only the major triad harmonically, but the melodic tones are to be the same as those used with a dominant 7 structure of the same letter name.

Minor 7 Chords

All minor 7 chords represent the subdominant sound of IIm7 (for IV), except IIIm7, VIm7, and VIIm7, which represent tonic sounds. IIIm7 and VIm7 are diatonic substitutions for I. VIIm7 = IIIm7 for I (key of the dominant).

IIm7	Major scale from ♭7 of chord
IIIm7 and VIm7 (for I)	Major scale from name of tonic chord being replaced
VIIm7 (as IIIm7 for I)	Major scale from name of tonic chord being replaced

A comparison of minor 7 chords with their related major 6 chords (containing the same notes) will reveal some second choice VIm7-for-I relationships. Scale = Major from name of related major 6 chord.

Note: All second choice scale relationships must be handled with care.

Chords—Three-Note Voicings

Minor-Major 7 and 6 Chords—Close and Open Voicings

MAJOR 7TH AND 6TH IN THE LEAD

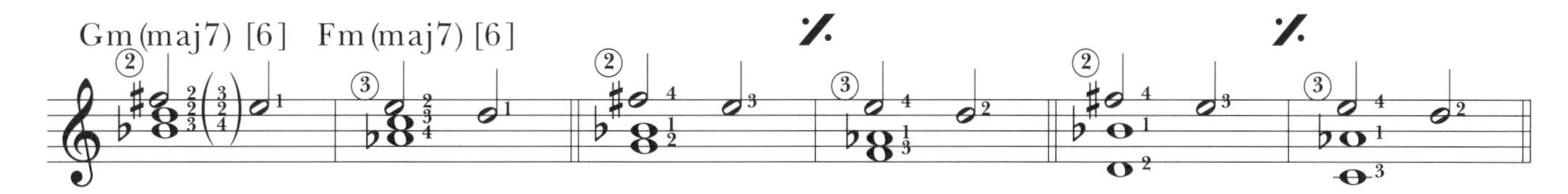

5TH IN THE LEAD

♭3RD IN THE LEAD

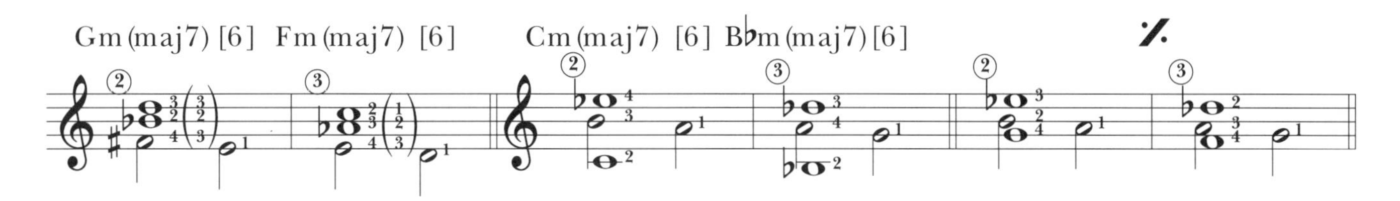

MAJOR 7TH AND 6TH COMBINED IN SAME VOICING

MAJOR 7TH AND 6TH IN LEAD

6TH AND 5TH IN LEAD

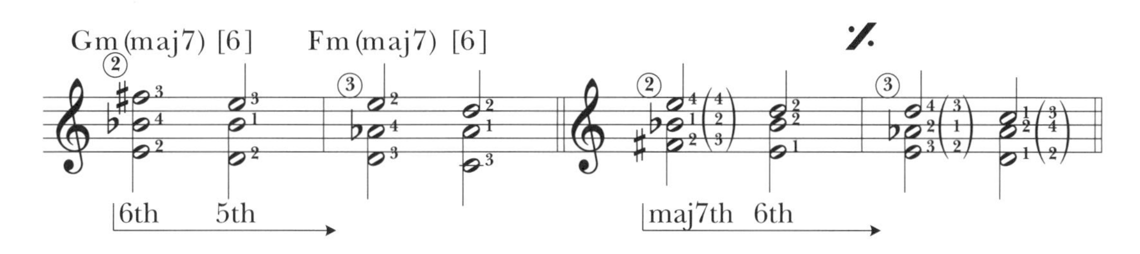

Minor 6, Minor-Major 7 Chords—Open Voicings, All Inversions

Five-Note Arpeggios

Dominant 7 (+5, +9), Dominant 9 (+5), and Dominant 7 (+5, ♭9) Chords

Chord Spelling

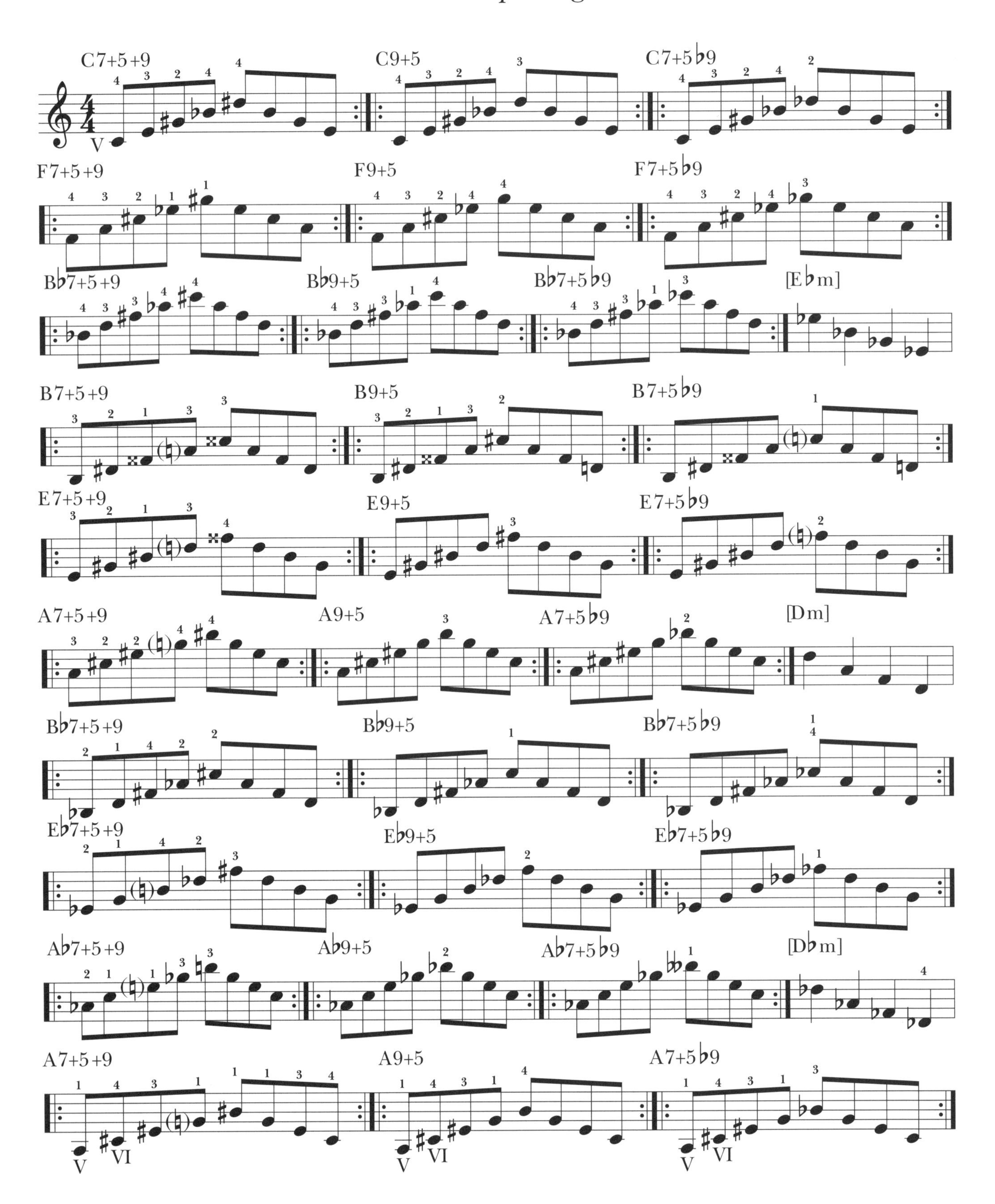

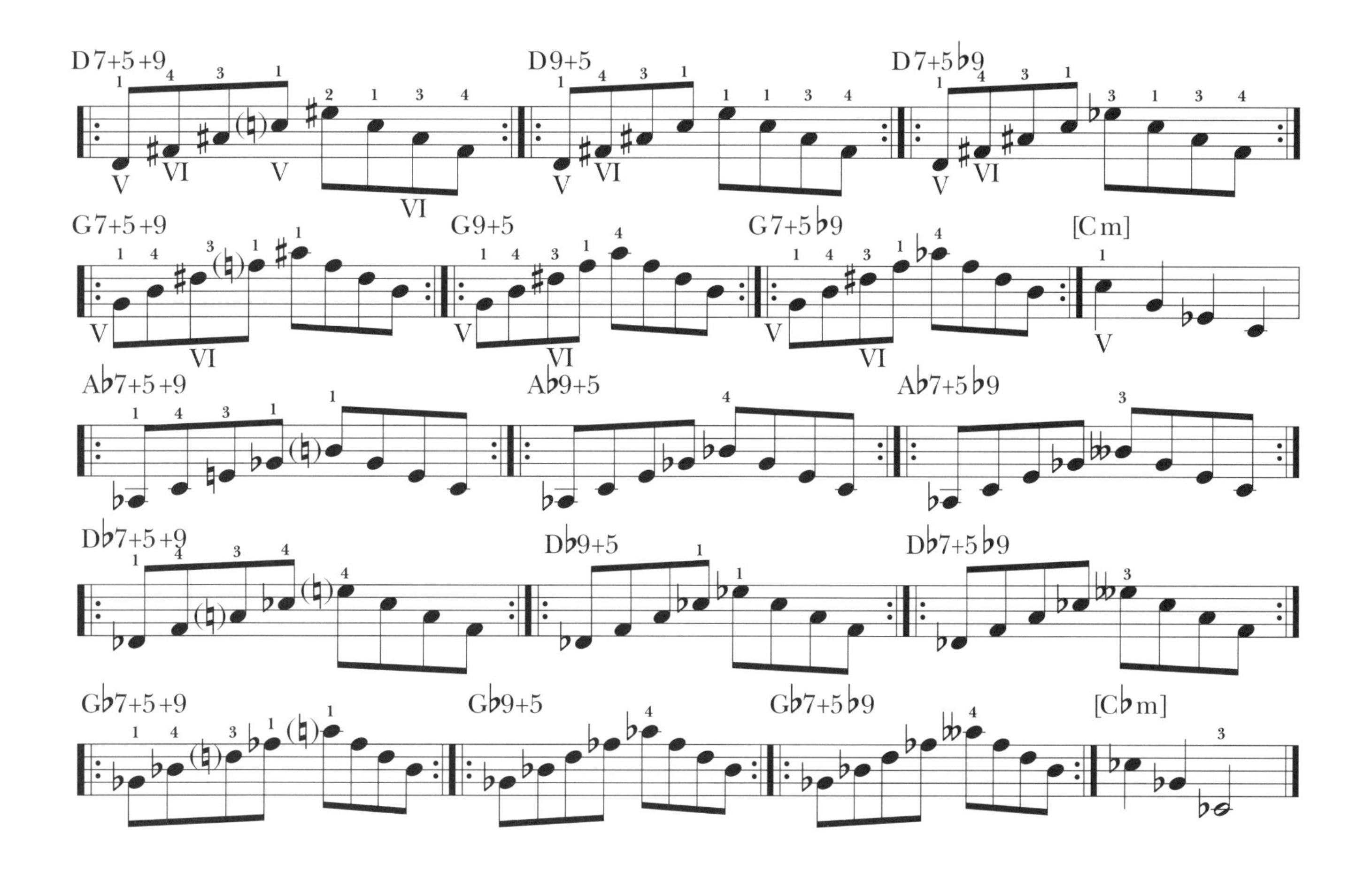

Chords—Three-Note Voicings

Melodization of I Minor Chords with Harmonic Minor Scale

Melodic degrees: Harmonic minor scale from chord name

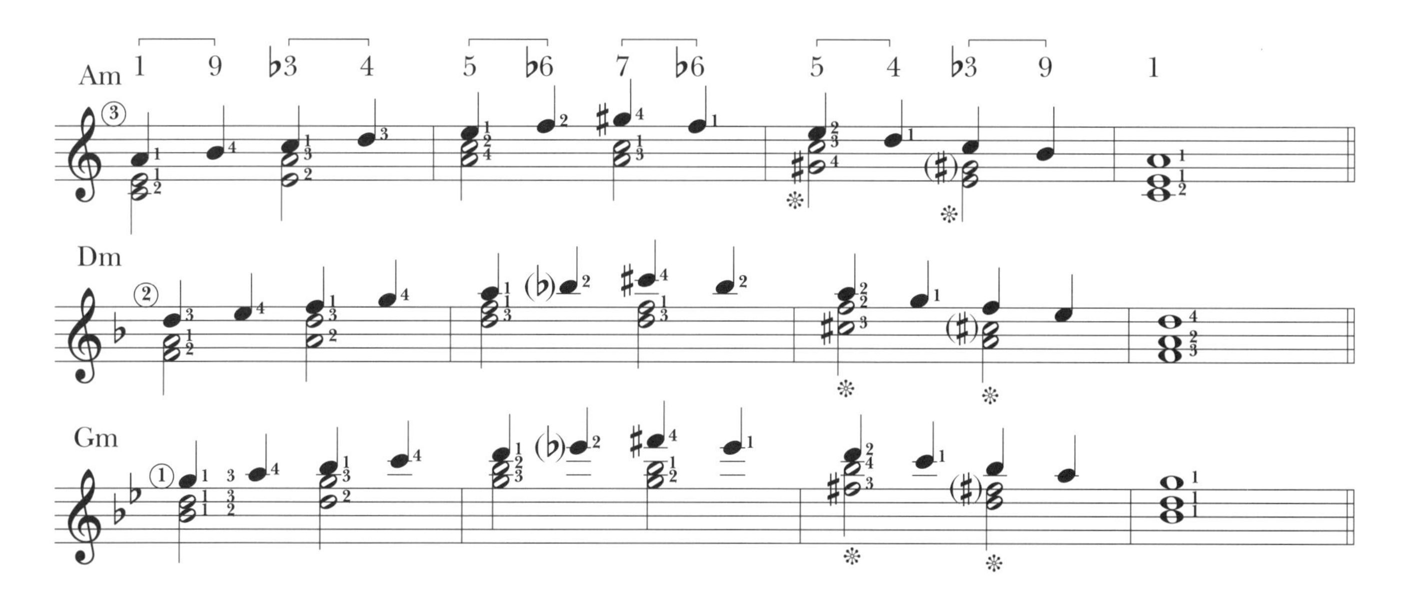

✱ Major 7 necessary as an undervoice

Melodization of IIm7(♭5) Chords with Harmonic Minor Scale

Melodic degrees: Harmonic minor scale from ♭7 of chord

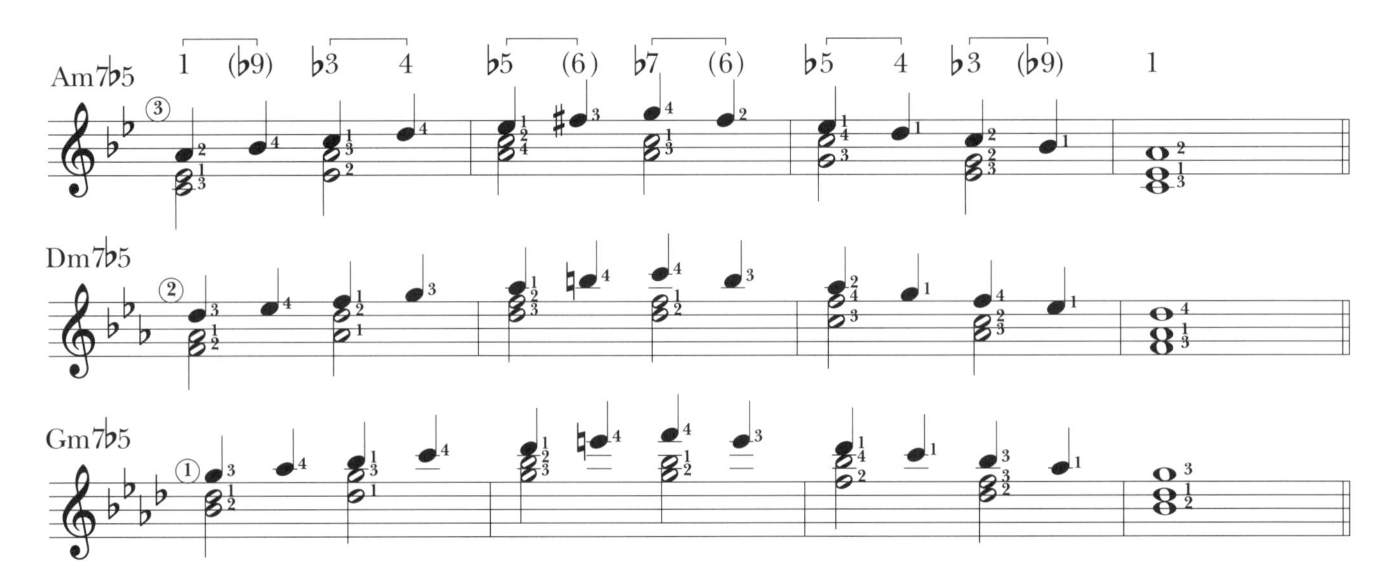

Melodization of Dominant 7 Chords with Harmonic Minor Scale

Melodic degrees: Harmonic minor scale from intended tonic

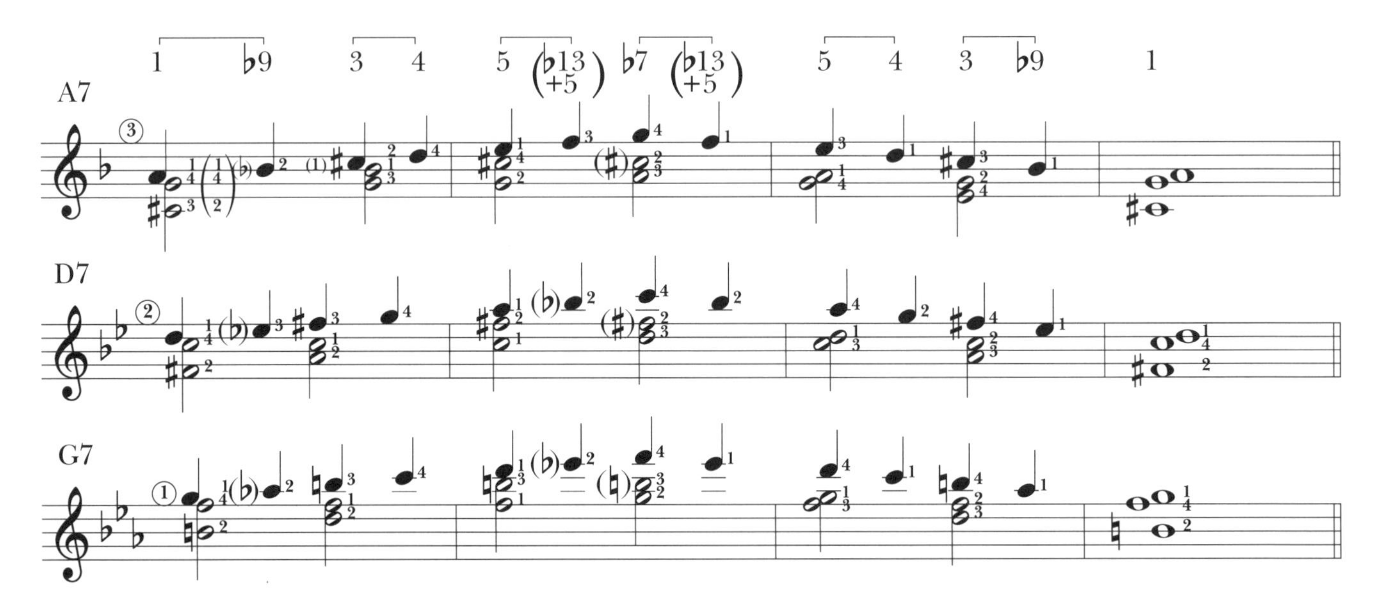

* = ♭9 for undervoice

Teeah-Wanna

Optional Duet with Rhythm Guitar

The notes contained in the bottom staves of the following study represent the chord-scale relationships. They are to be played with the rhythm guitar part (not the melody) to further acquaint the ear with these related sounds.

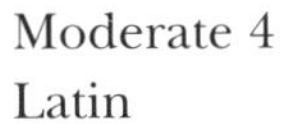

Moderate 4
Latin

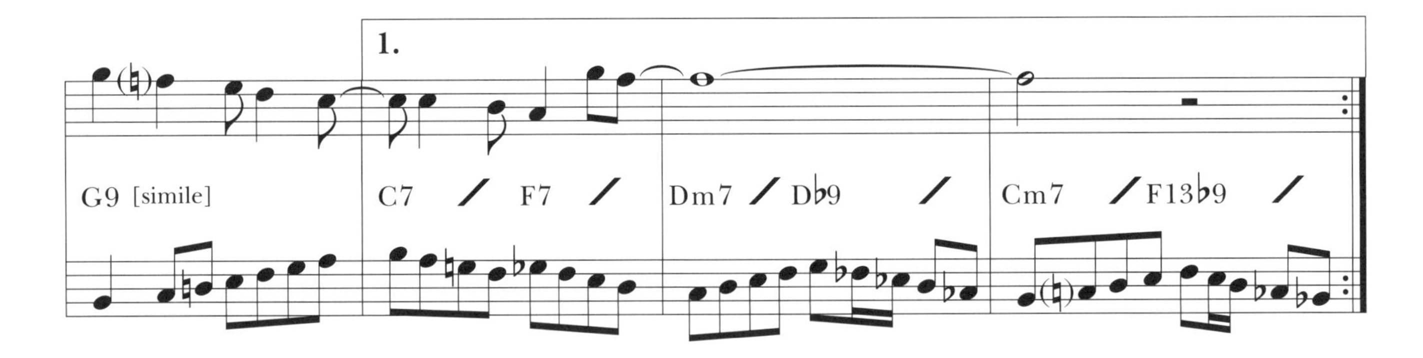

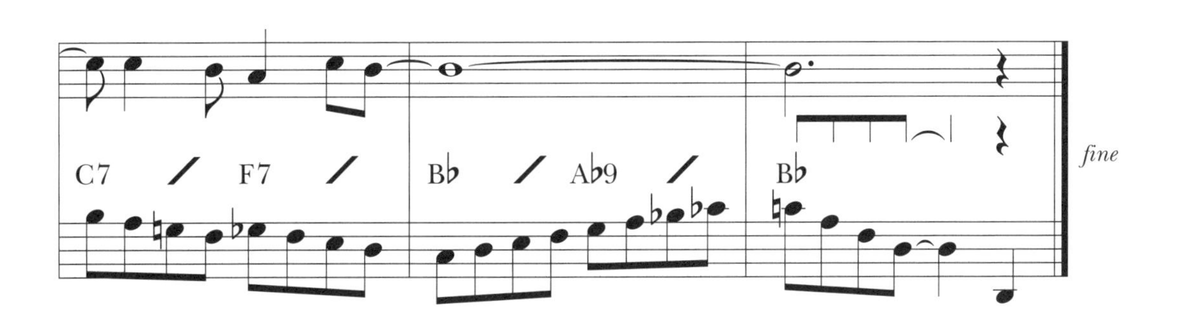

To aid in the analysis of the preceding chord-scale relationships, observe the following numerical breakdown.

I / / / | VII7 / / / | I / / / | III7 / / /

VI9 / / / | 1. II7 / V7 / | IIIm7 / ♭III7 / | IIm7 / V7♭9 / :||

2. II7 / V7 / | I / / / | I7 / / / || IV7 / / /

IV7 / / / | I / IIm7 / | I / IIIm7 ♯I° | II7 / / /

II7 / / / | IIm7 / / / | V9+5 / / / || I / / /

VII7 / / / | I / / / | III7 / / / | VI9 / / /

II7 / V7 / | I / ♭VII7 / | I / / 𝄽 ||

Rhythm Guitar—The Right Hand

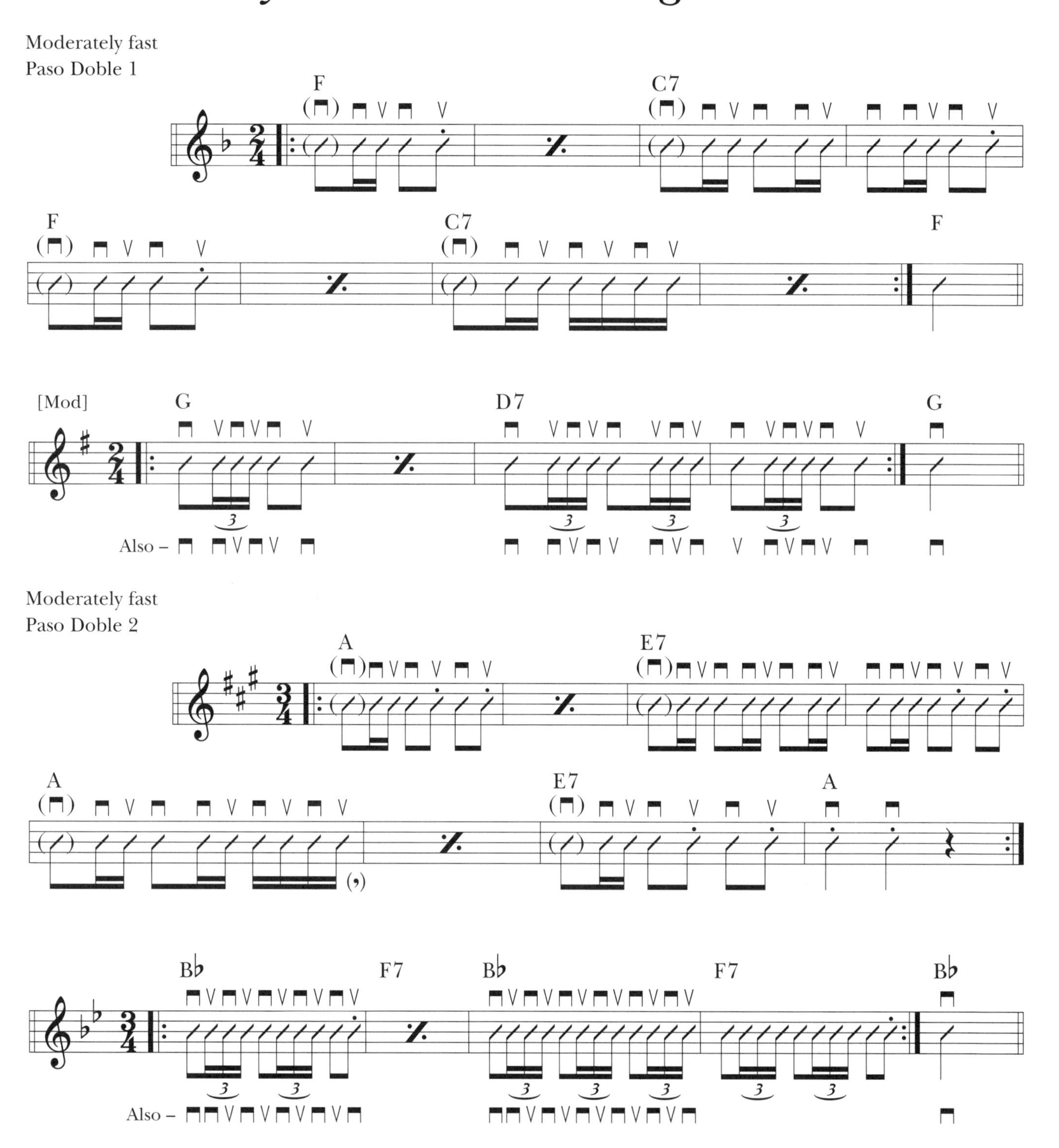

Chord Study—Minor 7 with ♭5 (Chromatic Approach) in the Bass

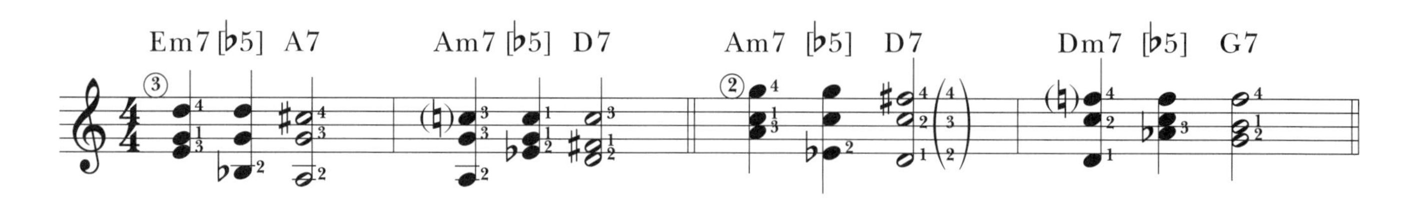

Five-Note Arpeggios

Minor (maj 7, 9) and Dominant (♭5, ♭9) Chords

Chord Spelling

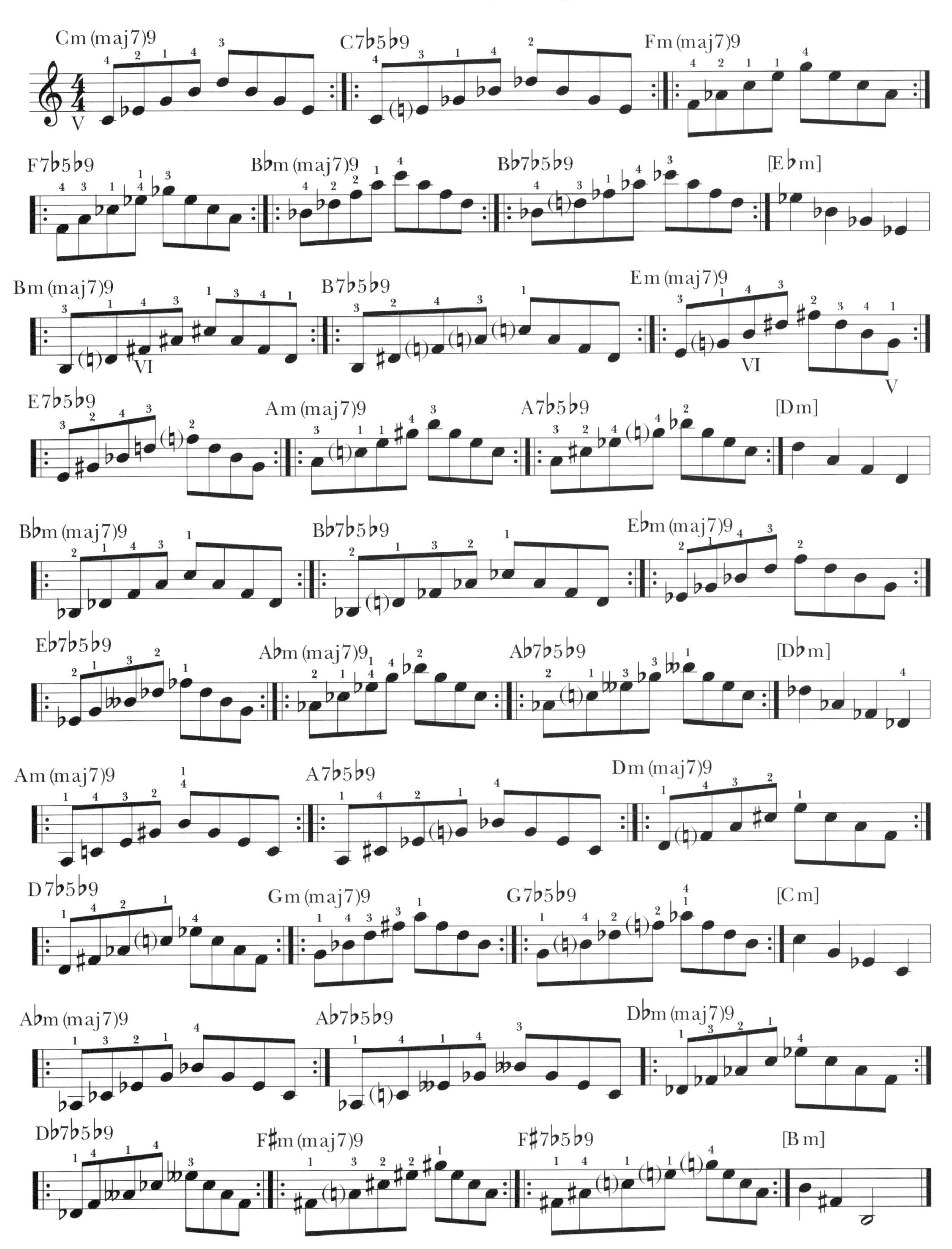

Chord-Scale Relationships

For improvisation.

Minor 6 Chords

All minor 6 chords can be considered as representing the subdominant or tonic minor sound. Scale = Real melodic minor from chord name. (However, IIm6, Vm6, and VIm6 will sound slightly forced. See next relationship.)

IIm6, Vm6, VIm6 are best treated as representing the dominant sound of IIm6 for V9. Scale = major from a whole step below the minor 6 chord.

A comparison of other minor 6 chords with their related dominant 9 chords (containing the same notes) will reveal that IIIm6, ♯IVm6, VIIm6, and ♯Im6 can also be treated as IIm6 for V9. But the scale for this harmonic situation is real melodic minor from a whole step below the minor 6 chord.

Minor 7(♭5) Chords

Minor 7(♭5) chords most frequently represent the dominant sound of VIIm7(♭5) for V7. IIIm7(♭5), ♯IVm7(♭5), VIIm7(♭5) = Major scale from half step above chord.

All other minor 7(♭5) chords represent the subdominant or tonic minor sounds of IIm7(♭5) (for IVm6) or VIm7(♭5) (for Im6) = Real melodic minor from ♭3 of chord.

A comparison of minor 7(♭5) chords with non-scale tone roots (except ♯IV) with their related dominant 9 structures will reveal some second choice chord-scale relationships. Scale = Real melodic minor from half step above min 7(♭5).

(Ex: ♯Im7(♭5) = VI9, ♯IIm7(♭5) = VII9, ♯Vm7(♭5) = III9, ♯VIm7(♭5) = ♯IV9)

Also a minor 7(♭5) chord represents the II chord in a minor key. It is often treated as a "package deal" with the V7 of that minor key when it is the next chord. Example: Bm7(♭5) to E7 = The harmonic (or natural) minor scale for both chords. (It is always the option of the player to treat the chords in this situation as one unit or independently.)

A Major Scale (Twelve Positions)

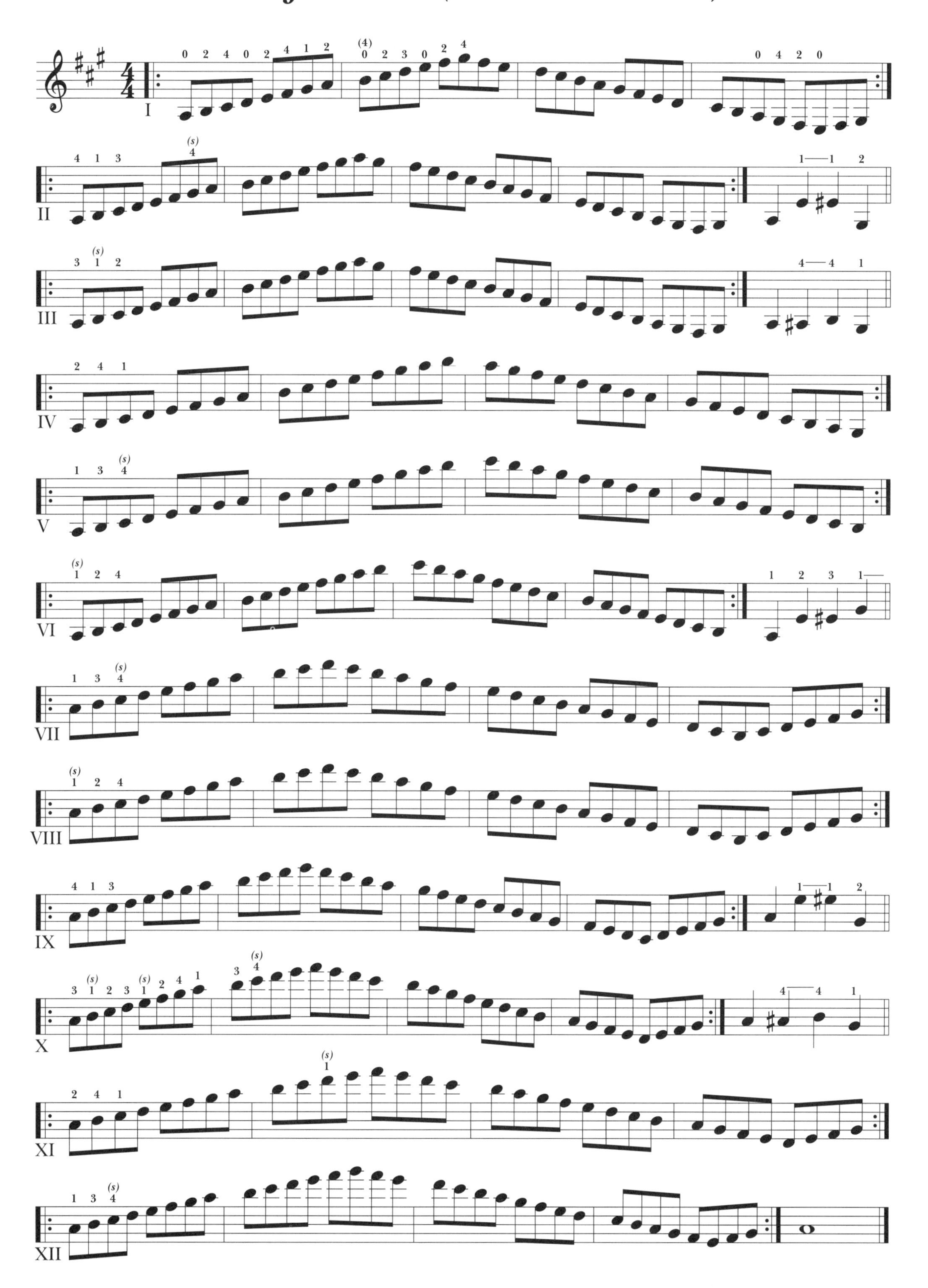

F♯ Harmonic Minor (Nine Positions)

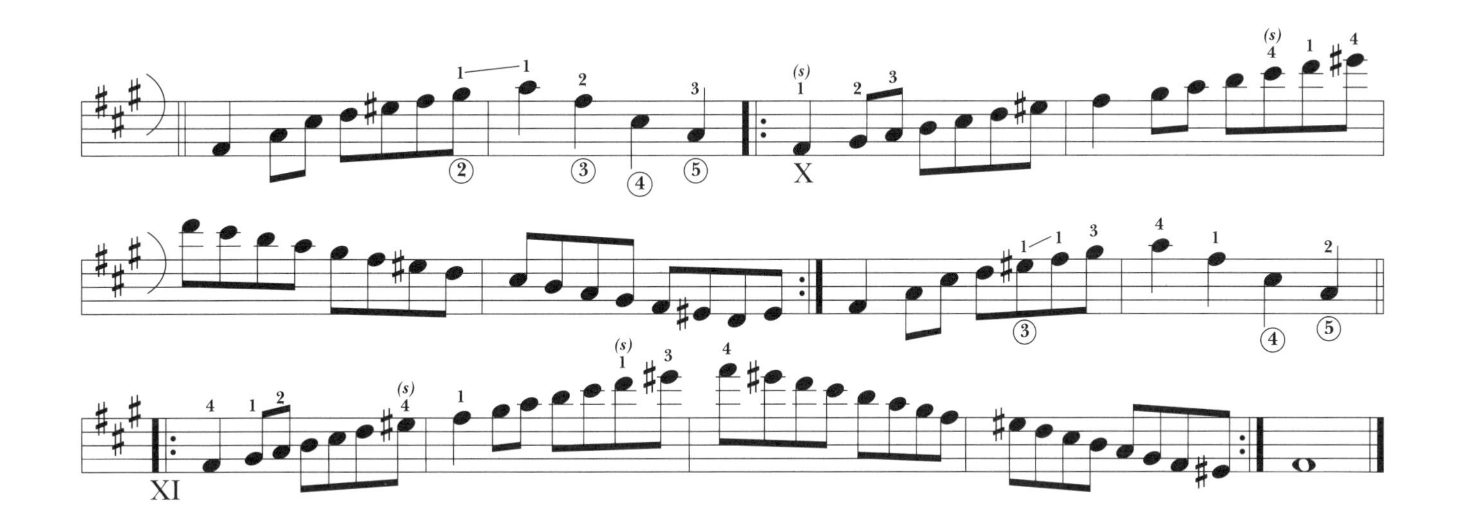

F♯ Minor Etude (solo)

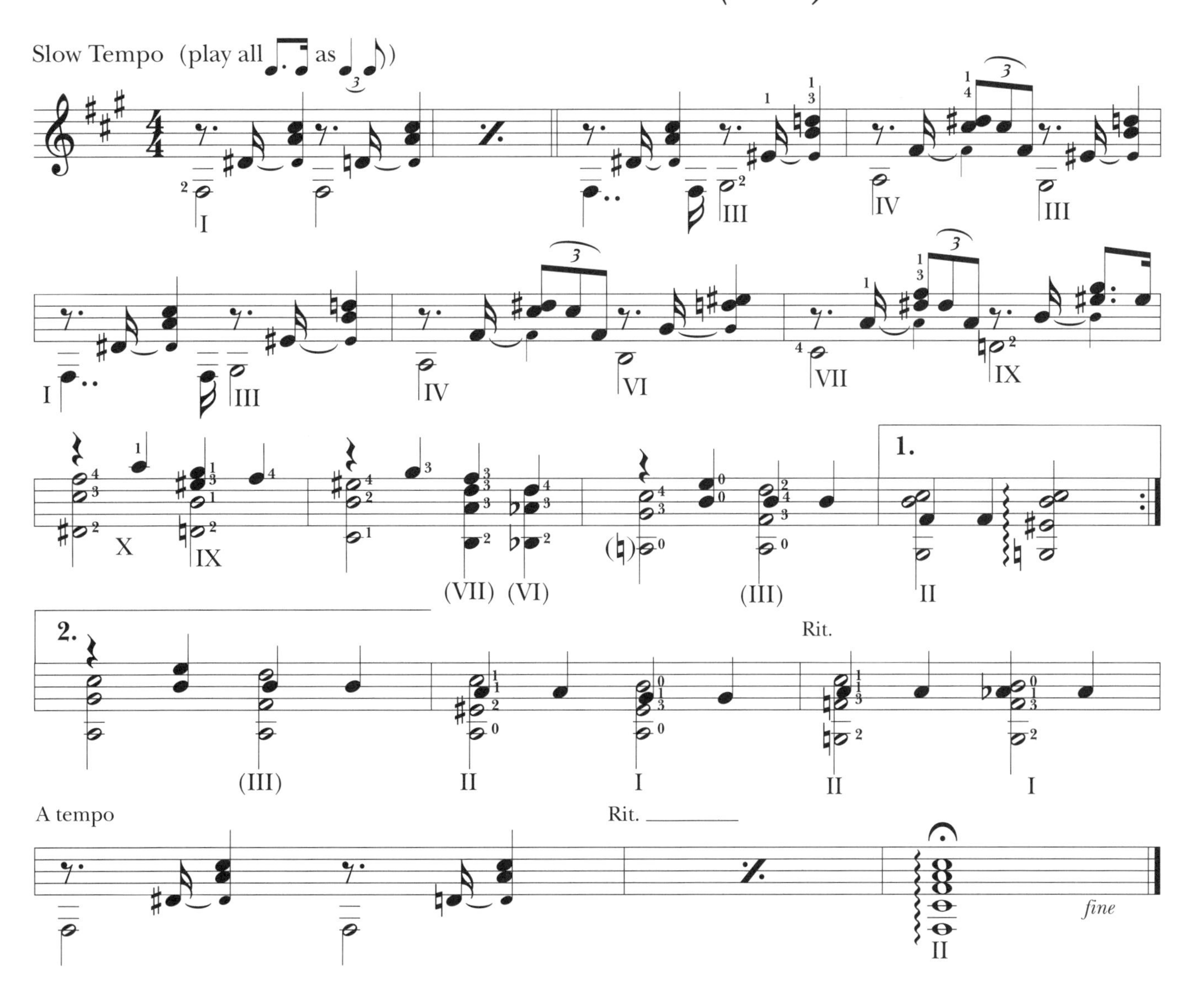

Five-Note Arpeggios

Dominant 7(♭9)sus4 and Dominant 9(♭5)

Chord Spelling

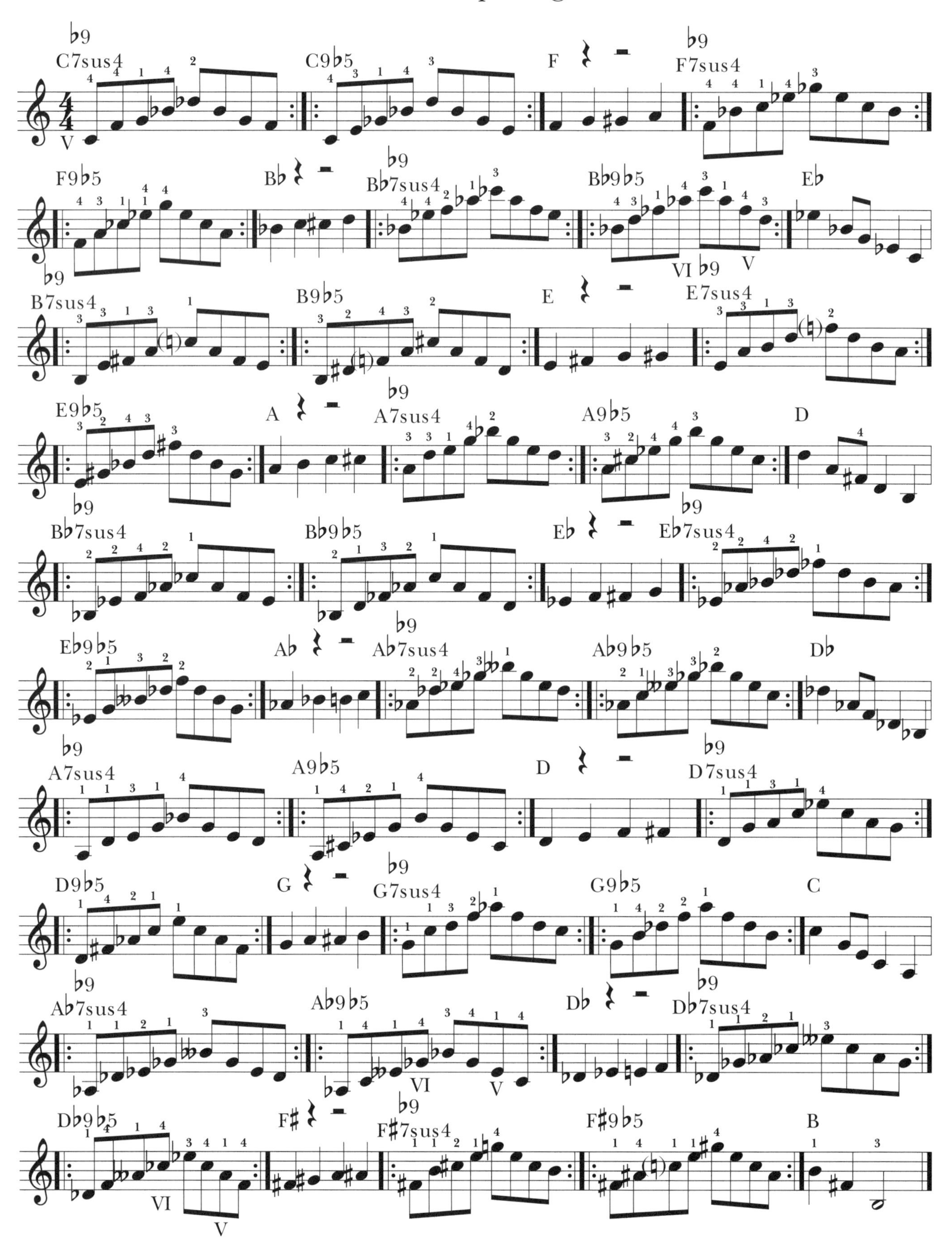

Chords—Three-Note Voicings

Study in F Major

Study in F Harmonic Minor

Five-Note Arpeggios

Dominant 7(+9)sus4 and Dominant 7(♭5, +9) Chords

Chord Spelling

✱ +9 on all sus4 chords enharmonically notated here as ♭3.

Additional Fingerings for Minor Scales

These fingerings are less practical for general use, as they will not accommodate as many interval combinations as those presented earlier.

The principal fingerings shown are a result of the alterations on the major scale fingering type from which the minor scale is derived.

The optional fingerings (shown in parentheses) suggest some of the combinations possible when fingering types are mixed. When all fingerings have been mastered by thorough and precise study, you can and will do this without conscious effort.

Real Melodic Minor

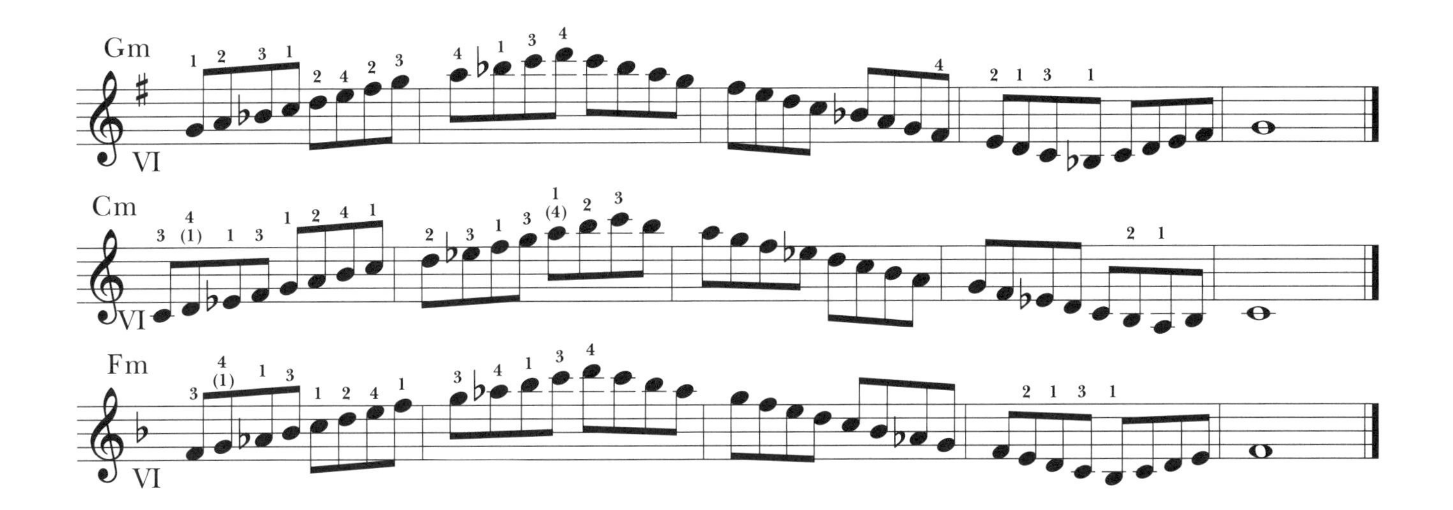

Harmonic Minor

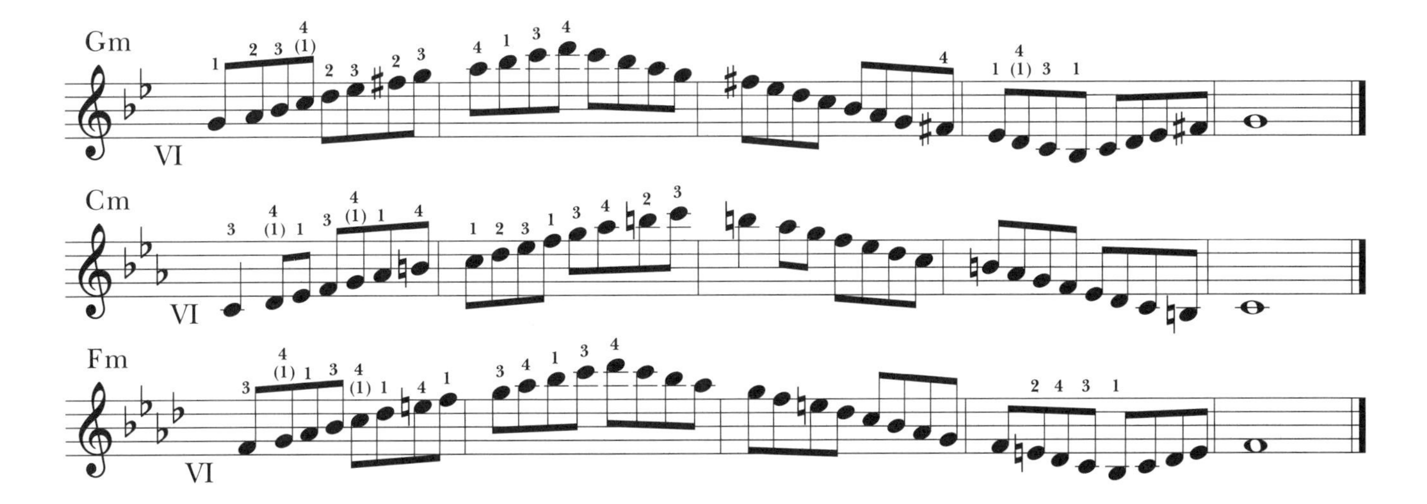

Chord-Scale Relationships

For improvisation.

Diminished 7 Chords

All diminished 7 chords will accept a diminished scale from any chord tone. (In most cases, these are not perfect relationships.)

Be advised that diminished 7 chord names are frequently misleading, in that most of the time they indicate only part of a larger harmonic structure. (The related scale remains hidden until the name of the complete chord is realized.)

The following will help in the proper treatment of diminished 7 chords.

Any diminished 7 chord that can be analyzed as:

♯I° almost always = VI7(♭9)	(Occasionally ♯I° = I7(♭9)
II° almost always = III7(♭9)	(Occasionally II° = V7(♭9)
I° is usually a true diminished 7, but is more musical when melodically treated as VII7(♭9).	(Occasionally I° = II7(♭9)

Also note: As all dominant 7(♭9) chords contain a diminished 7 built on 3, 5, ♭7, and ♭9 of the dominant 7, they will accept melodization with diminished scales from these notes. This chord-scale relationship is imperfect, but the uniformity of sound makes it work.

Augmented Triads

Augmented triads are primarily melodized with the whole tone scale from any chord tone (including 9).

As I and IV are the only scale degrees on which augmented structures could occur as strict triads, note the following relationships:

- I+ can be melodized with a harmonic or real melodic minor scale from a minor 3rd below the chord name. You may also use the real melodic minor from the intended tonic.
- IV+ can be melodized with the real melodic minor from a minor 3rd below.

Be advised that an augmented triad on anything other than I or IV is an incompletely named chord. Include the 7th in your analysis of these structures to determine the related scale.

Preparation of Four-Part Open Voicings

Adding the 5th Degree to Three-Part Open Voicings

Preparation of Four-Part Open Voicings

Adding the Root to Three-Part Open Voicings

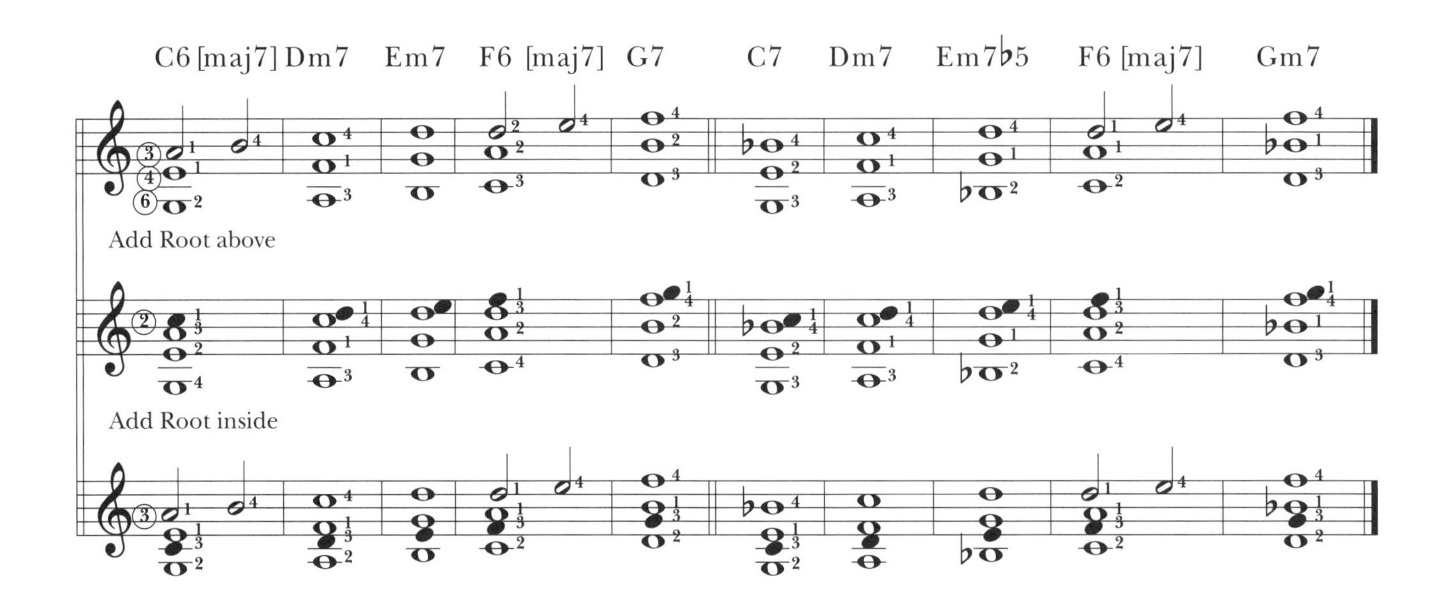

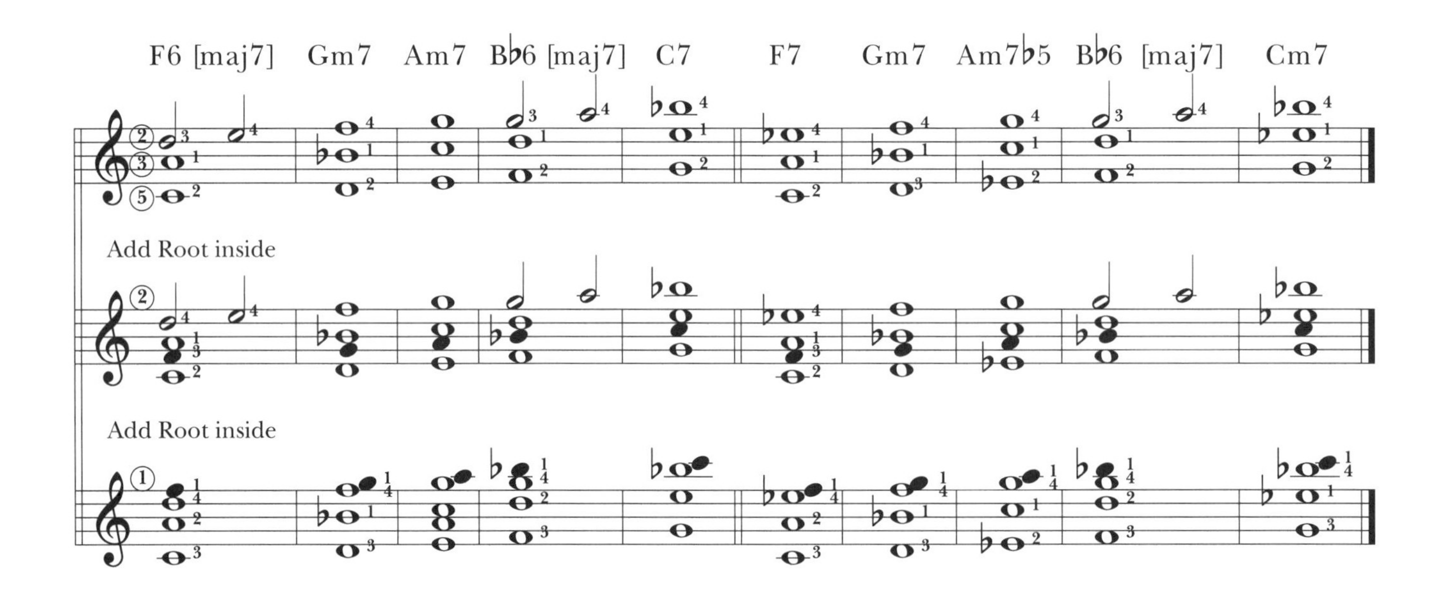

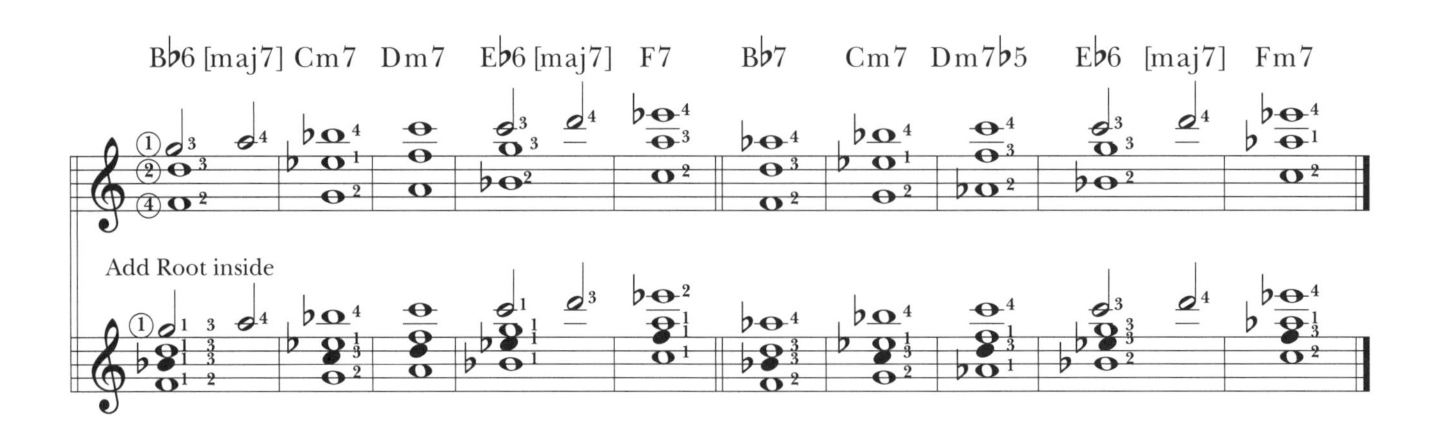

Five-Note Arpeggios

Minor 9(♭5) Chords

Chord Spelling

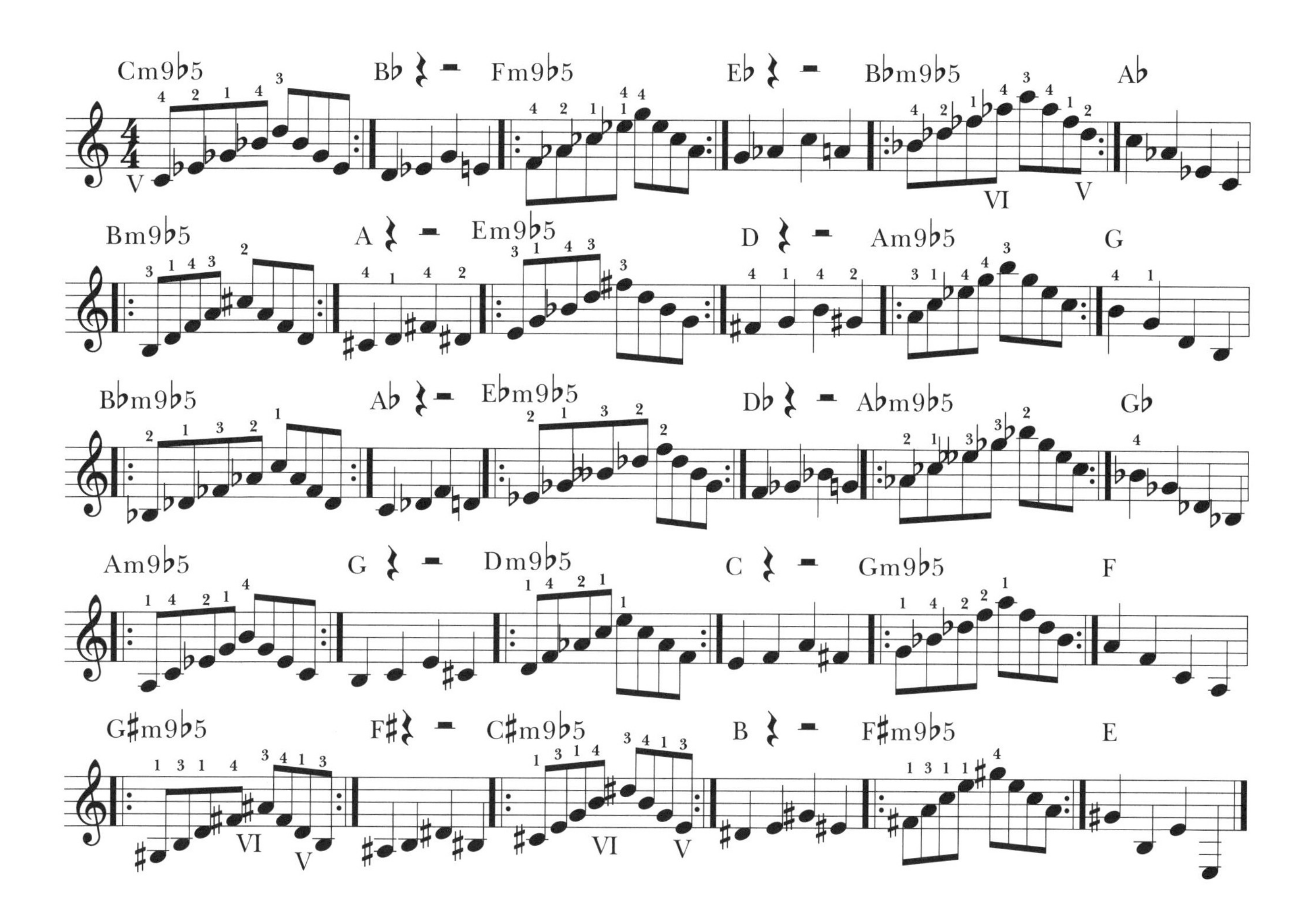

About Improvisation

Chord-scale relationships provide you with all the raw material (both melodic and harmonic) for any chord structure in any situation, but they will not make music for you.

In the final analysis, consideration must be given to each chord, for they contain a variety of sounds, such as the "warm" notes (3 and ♭7), the "bland" ones (1 and 5), and the various tensions and altered degrees that add the "sparkle" and/or the "buzz." Variety is certainly a factor in interesting music.

Also, very important are the "lines" that exist in a chord progression. These lines, resulting from the chromatic and scalewise movement of the inner voices of chords, form a solid basis for the creation of secondary melodies (especially valuable in comping.) Look for the chromatic motion that occurs between chords. Look for the tension and resolve possibilities available on each structure, for these are the pretty notes on which to build melodic ideas.

It's Late

Slow 4
FMaj7
E♭9
Dm7
G7
G7sus4
G7
C9sus4
D♭Maj7
1.
2.
CMaj7
C9
C7♭9
CMaj7
Dm7 Em7
FMaj7
F♯13 [♭9]
Bm7
E7
AMaj7
A6
A♯m7
Bm7
E7alt.

AMaj7
C♯m7
F♯m7
Fm7
B♭7
E♭Maj7
Cm7
C°
Fm7
♭9
B♭13
B♭7+
E♭Maj7
C7♭9
FMaj7
E♭9
Dm7
G7
G7sus4
G7
C9sus4
D♭Maj7
[11+]
CMaj7
B♭9
F
Am7
A♭Maj7
Gm7
B♭m/C
[+11]
G♭Maj7
[+11]
FMaj7

Preparation of Four-Part Open Voicings

Adding the 3rd Degree to (Very Incomplete) Open Voicings

Because these voicings have the 7th (or 6th) degree as the bottom note, tonality must be established before using them.

No 3rd degree present—use with discretion:

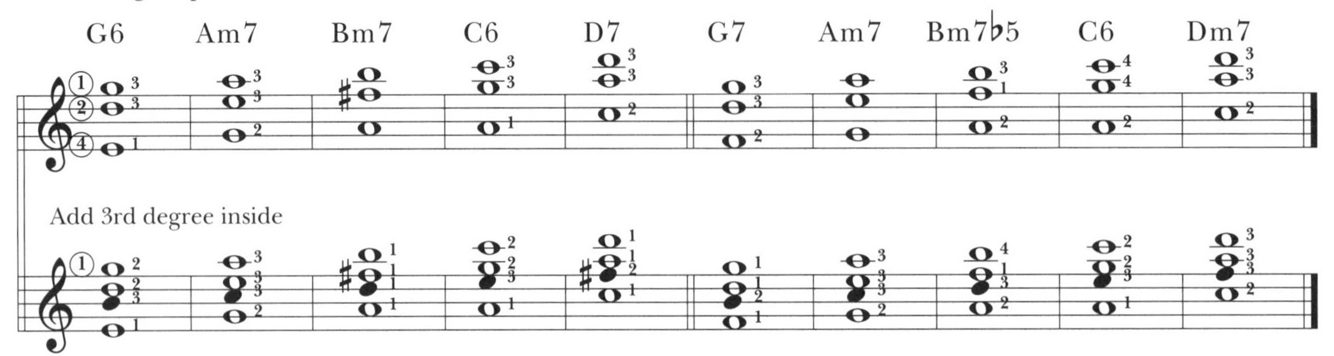

No 3rd degree present—use with discretion:

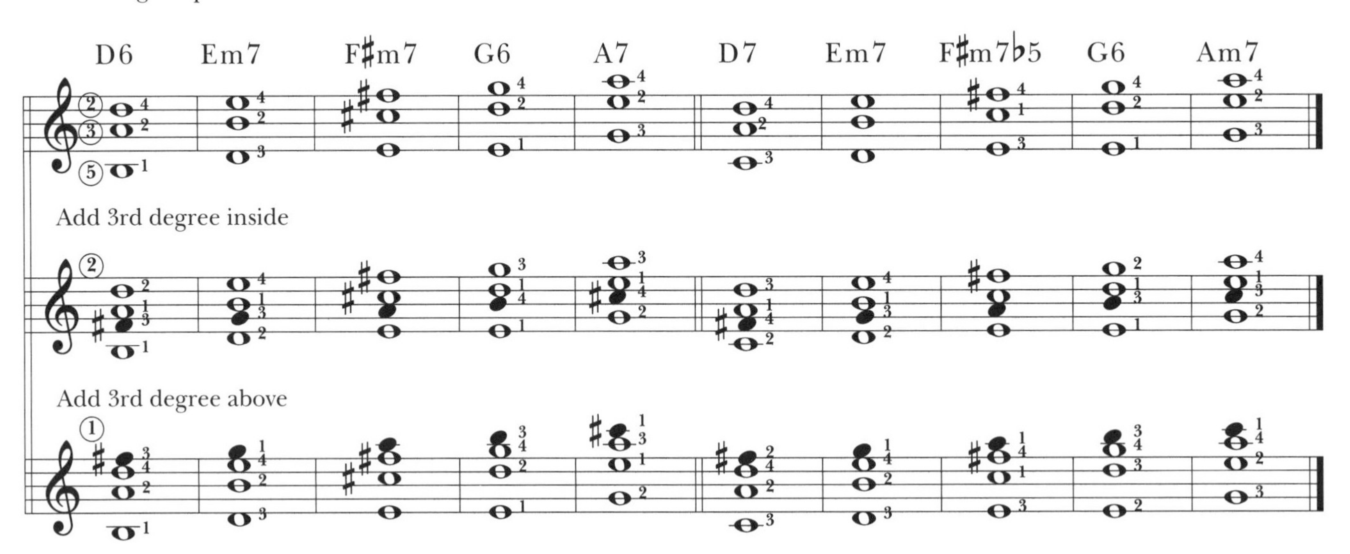

No 3rd degree present—use with discretion:

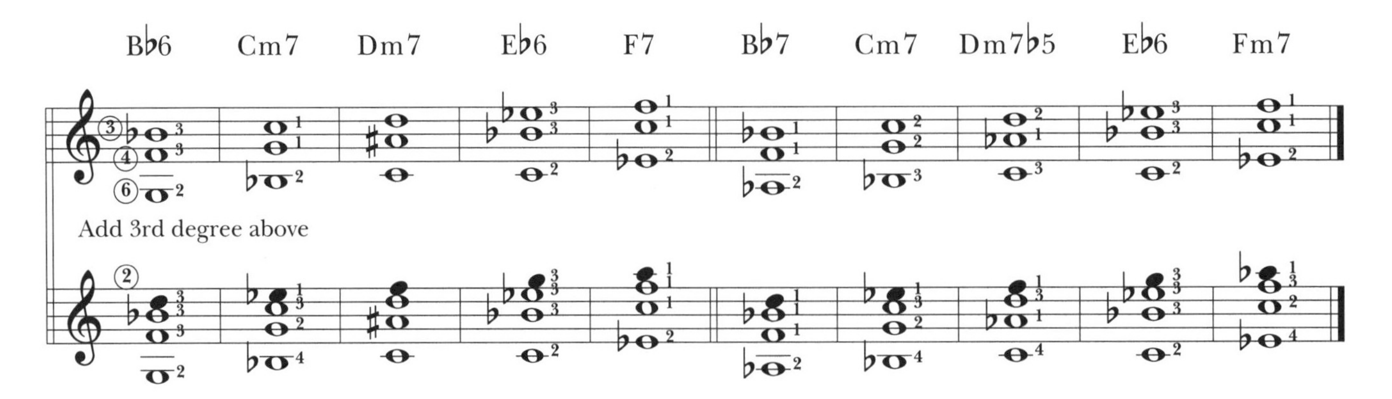

Be especially careful of these 7ths (or 6ths) on the bottom in the low register. Observe rules for use. (See *Vol. II*, pg. 100.)

Preparation of Four-Part Open Voicings

Adding the 7th Degree to Three-Part Open Voicings

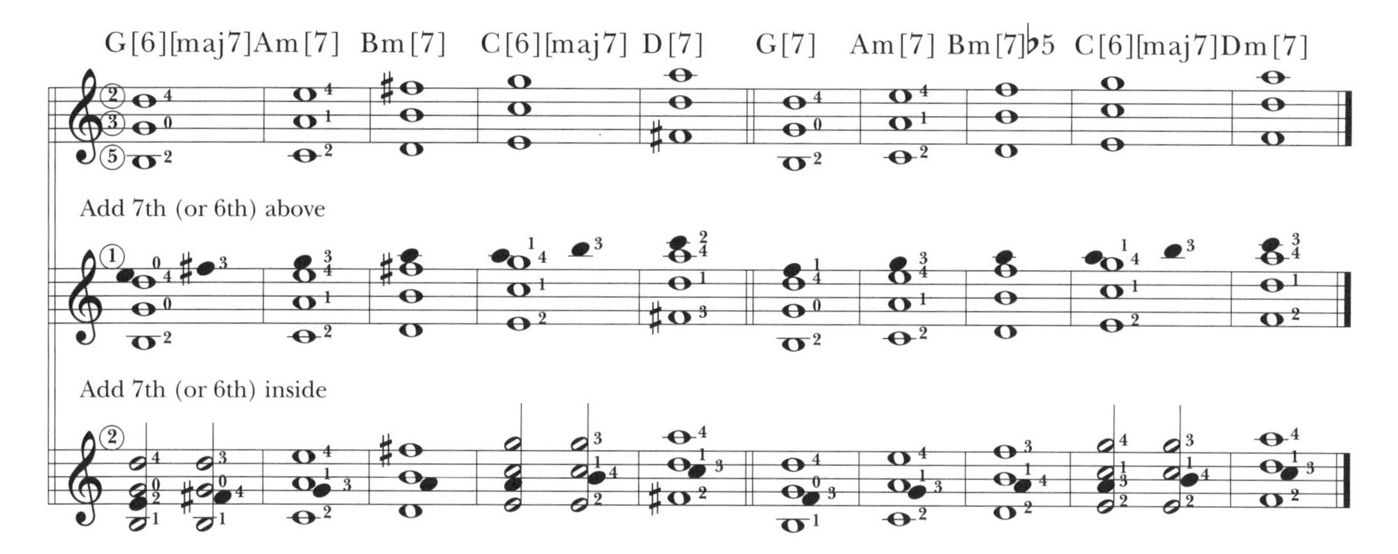

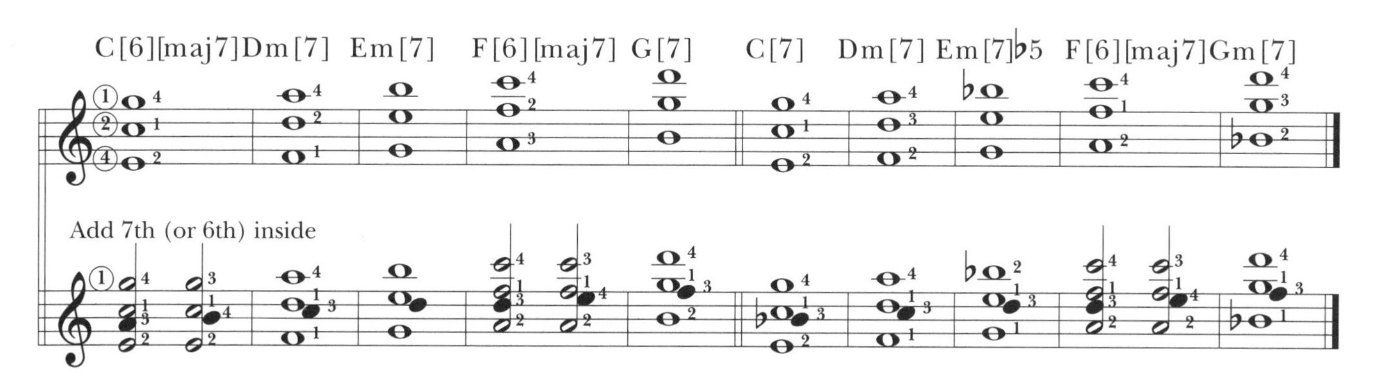

Scale-Chord Relationships

Major Scales

1. All diatonic structures in a major key.

2. All nondiatonic major chords with scale tone roots except IV, use the scale from chord name.

3. IV and all major chords with non-scale tone roots, use the scale from the 5th degree of the chord. (Note: This also includes all major chords with indicated +11 and is a second choice for the above-mentioned major chords with scale tone roots.)

4. All nondiatonic minor 7 chords (except VIIm7) usually function as IIm7. Use the scale from the ♭7 of the chord. (Note: VIIm7 is IIIm7 for I. Also note: A comparison of nondiatonic minor 7 structures with their related major 6 chords will reveal some second choice VIm7-for-I relationships.)

5. I7, II7, and all 13th chords with scale tone roots, except IV7, use the scale from the intended tonic.

6. III7, VI7(♭9), VII7 (second choice), use the scale from a major 3rd below the chord name. This can also be considered a natural minor scale from the intended tonic. (Note: The scale does not include the 3rd degree of the chord, and some melodic patterns may require the addition of this note.)

Harmonic Minor Scales

1. All diatonic structures in a minor key.

2. III7, VII7, VI7(♭9) (in a major key), use the scale from the intended tonic.

3. Diminished 7 chords that can be analyzed as I°, treat as VII7.
   Diminished 7 chords that can be analyzed as ♯I°, treat as VI7(♭9).
   Diminished 7 chords that can be analyzed as II°, treat as III7.

4. All dominant 7 chords with altered 9 and ♭13 (or ♯5 considered as ♭13), use the scale from the intended tonic.

5. I aug (I+) triad (second choice), use the scale from a minor 3rd below.

Real Melodic Minor Scales

1. IVm6 and Im6, use the scale from chord name.

2. IIm7(♭5) (occurring in a major tonality) treat as IVm6.

3. IV7 and all dominant 7 chords with non-scale tone roots, use the scale from the chord 5th. (Note: This is also a second-choice relationship for all dominant 7 chords, except IV7, with scale tone roots.)

4. All dominant 9 chords with specified +11 and 13, also I7(+11), II7(+11), V7(+11) (or ♭5 considered +11), scale from chord 5th.

5. All dominant 9ths with ♭13 (or ♯5 considered as ♭13), use the scale from the intended tonic. (Note: This includes VI7, III9, and VII9, each of which has a built-in ♭13.)

6. All completely altered dominant 7 chords (this means alt 9 and 5), use the scale from the ♭9 of the chord. This includes III7 (alt 5) and VII7 (alt 5), as they have a built-in altered 9. (Note: This can be a second choice of scale relationship for III7, VI7(♭9), and VII7 without the indicated alt 5 because of the built-in alterations of 9 and/or 13, and the fact that ♭13 can sometimes be treated as ♯5, or in this case, alt 5. However, the relationship is imperfect, so handle with care.)

7. I7(♭9), II7(♭9), V7(♭9), and all dominant 13(♭9) (or alt 9) chords with scale tone roots (except IV7), use the scale from the ♭7 of the chord. (Note: Scale does not contain the 3rd degree of the chord. Some melodic patterns may require the addition of this note.)

8. These do not occur very often. Use very cautiously:
   Diminished 7 chords that can be analyzed as I°: treat as II7(♭9).
   Diminished 7 chords that can be analyzed as ♯I°: treat as I7(♭9).
   Diminished 7 chords that can be analyzed as II°: treat as V7(♭9).

9. I+ and IV+: Triads (second choice), use the scale from a minor 3rd below. I+ triad (second choice), use the scale from the intended tonic.

Whole Tone Scales

All major and dominant 7(♯5) (or alt 5), use the scale from any chord tone. (Note: The 9th must be unaltered in these structures. Whole tone scales are especially necessary for augmented dominant 7 chords with non-scale tone roots.

Diminished Scales

1. Diminished chords that can be analyzed as I°, use the scale from chord tones. (Note: This is theoretically more perfect than the previously mentioned treatment as VII7, but less musical.)

2. Diminished 7 chords that can be analyzed as ♯I° and II°, use the scale from chord tones. (Note: These are less perfect than the VI7(♭9) and III7 treatment, and less musical.)

3. IV7(♭9) and all dominant 7(♭9) chords with non-scale tone roots, use the scale from 3, 5, ♭7, ♭9 of chord. (Note: All dominant 7(♭9) chords may be treated in this manner with varying degrees of imperfection, however the consistent intervals of the scale will hold things together.)

4. All augmented 11(♭9) (or alt 9) chords, use the scale from 3, 5, ♭7, ♭9 of chord.

Remember: Look ahead to the next chord to analyze a progression. Look back to the preceding chord to determine the related scale.

Index